Leadership in the Imagination Age

This book reframes leadership for a world transformed by AI, accelerating technologies, and planetary fragility. It argues that leadership is no longer about control or optimisation but about orientation: knowing what matters, sensing direction, and acting with moral courage when certainty collapses. In this new era, inherited formulas fall short. What leaders need instead is disciplined imagination – curiosity expansive enough to explore new possibilities, yet grounded enough to stay accountable to human consequence.

The book invites readers to see leaders as stewards, not owners; organisations as living systems, not machines; and leadership as an act of storytelling. Every story a leader tells shapes the world – connecting or fragmenting, regenerating or extracting, widening horizons or narrowing them. Drawing on leadership theory, systems thinking, ethics, narrative art, futures studies, and spiritual wisdom, the book blends rigorous insight with poetic depth, urging leaders to listen more deeply, imagine more boldly, and act with integrity.

At its core are three navigational frameworks – the Leadership Compass, the Moral Gyroscope, and Cosmic Leadership – guiding leaders at all levels and across disciplines through purpose, people, performance, possibility, and ethics. Ultimately, the book poses a provocative question: when machines can optimise almost everything, what remains unmistakably human about leadership?

S M A Moin is a Reader (Associate Professor) in Storytelling and Brand Communications at Queen Mary University of London, UK, ranked ninth globally and in the top 0.5% in the areas of storytelling research in 2024 by ScholarGPS, California.

Leadership in the Imagination Age

Navigating Unprecedented Possibilities and Moral Challenges

S M A Moin

Routledge
Taylor & Francis Group
LONDON AND NEW YORK

Designed cover image: Getty Images. Credit: merovingian

First published 2027
by Routledge
4 Park Square, Milton Park, Abingdon, Oxon OX14 4RN

and by Routledge
605 Third Avenue, New York, NY 10158

Routledge is an imprint of the Taylor & Francis Group, an informa business

British Library Cataloguing-in-Publication Data
A catalogue record for this book is available from the British Library

ISBN: 978-1-041-28764-3 (hbk)
ISBN: 978-1-041-28763-6 (pbk)
ISBN: 978-1-003-76641-4 (ebk)

DOI: 10.4324/9781003766414

Typeset in Times New Roman
by Newgen Publishing UK

To all leaders guided by ethics, values, and character, and most dearly to my two sons – may you discover your place in the unfolding cosmic theatre and live in devoted service to humanity, the earth, and the greater universe.

Contents

Figures

Tables

About the Author

S M A Moin is a Reader (Associate Professor) in Storytelling and Brand Communications at Queen Mary University of London. His research impact has been internationally recognised: in 2024, he was ranked nineth globally and within the top 0.5% worldwide in the field of storytelling research by ScholarGPS (California), based on citation performance over the previous five years.

An interdisciplinary researcher and author, his work spans brand storytelling, creativity, innovation, leadership, and strategy. Moin's journey is marked by three transformations. He first served for 15 years in the Bangladesh Navy, retiring as a Lieutenant Commander after international training with the US Navy, the US Coast Guard, and the US Defence Institute. He then transitioned to a decade in UK industries – media, publishing, financial services, and consulting – where he advised leading companies, contributed to the world's largest newspaper, and worked within a $4 billion international subsea project.

His third chapter is academia. Before joining Queen Mary, he held senior leadership roles at Coventry University London, including Associate Head of Research and Scholarship and University Ethics Lead. He is a Principal Fellow of Advance HE, a Fellow of the Chartered Management Institute, and an active reviewer for leading journals. Dr Moin holds an MBA from the University of Strathclyde and a PhD in Management from the University of Nottingham, and has completed executive education at Oxford, Cambridge, and Harvard. His career embodies purposeful leadership, bridging the worlds of military discipline, corporate practice, and academic scholarship.

Foreword

I come to this book not only as a scholar or practitioner of leadership, but as a woman shaped by geographies where leadership has never been an abstract theory. It has been survival. It has been care. It has been resistance. It has been the quiet, persistent labour of holding communities together when institutions failed, when histories pressed heavily, and when futures felt uncertain.

Reading this work, I was struck by how clearly it names the threshold we are living through. The so-called Imagination Age driven by artificial intelligence, planetary interdependence, and moral complexity, demands a new language of leadership: one grounded not in control, but in responsibility; not in hierarchy, but in relationship; not in prediction, but in ethical imagination.

Yet from where I stand – as a woman informed by decolonial and Global South traditions, this threshold is not entirely new. Communities across Africa, Asia, Latin America, and Indigenous worlds have long navigated uncertainty, complexity, and systemic inequity. They have practiced leadership without recognition, power without title, and vision without institutional backing. What is often called "future leadership" in dominant discourse is, for many, a continuation of ancestral ways of guiding, caring, and imagining.

This book speaks into that continuity. It recognises that leadership is no longer a matter of authority alone, but of orientation toward humanity, toward possibility, and toward the moral consequences of our choices.

From a decolonial feminist perspective, however, orientation must also include history. We cannot imagine futures responsibly without confronting the colonial architectures that shaped our present: economies built on extraction, institutions rooted in exclusion, and knowledge systems that elevated some voices while silencing others.

Global South thinkers have long insisted on this reckoning. Kenyan scholar Wangari Maathai taught that leadership must be grounded in ecological and communal stewardship. Indian feminist Vandana Shiva reminds us that development without justice reproduces violence. Latin American decolonial scholar María Lugones urged us to see how colonialism reshaped not only land and labour, but gender itself. Their work expands leadership beyond organisational success into the terrain of dignity, land, and life.

Black feminist scholarship offers an equally powerful compass. Audre Lorde's insistence that "the master's tools will never dismantle the master's house" calls leaders to question inherited structures, not merely operate within them. bell hooks frames leadership as an ethic of love; radical, accountable, and collective. Patricia Hill Collins speaks of an "ethic of care" that centres responsibility and relational survival. Angela Davis reminds us that imagination itself is a political act: the first step toward freedom.

Together, these voices shift the ground beneath leadership discourse. They remind us that imagination is not neutral. It can liberate or it can replicate domination.

The Imagination Age intensifies this tension. As artificial intelligence reshapes labour, identity, and governance, leadership faces a profound choice: will technology amplify dignity, or deepen inequality? Will innovation serve markets alone, or communities and ecosystems? The book before you argues that imagination must be disciplined by ethics and anchored in humanity.

From a feminist decolonial standpoint, that discipline emerges through relational accountability. Leadership is not an individual performance; it is a collective practice shaped by memory, responsibility, and care. It asks us to listen to those most affected by decisions, to centre those historically excluded, and to recognise that the margins are often where new futures are first imagined.

This is why the personal matters.

Leadership has too often been narrated through heroic, masculine, and imperial archetypes – the lone visionary, the commanding strategist, the architect of systems. But feminist and Global South traditions teach a different story. Leadership is also the mother organising food distribution in a flood. The community elder mediating conflict. The young activist translating policy into lived experience. The teacher nurturing imagination in a classroom without resources. The worker holding dignity in a system that denies it.

These are not peripheral stories. They are the foundation of a more human leadership.

In this text, the *Leadership Compass* and *Moral Gyroscope* as proposed by S M A Moin offer a powerful framework for navigating complexity, aligning imagination with responsibility and ethics.

Through a decolonial feminist lens, these tools resonate deeply. Purpose becomes not merely strategic clarity, but commitment to collective wellbeing. People are not stakeholders, but kin in an interconnected world. Performance is not efficiency alone, but the measure of whether lives are improved. Possibility becomes the courage to imagine futures where justice is not aspirational but lived.

Storytelling, too, takes on renewed meaning. Who tells the story of leadership and whose stories are told shapes what leadership becomes. Decolonial feminist thought insists that storytelling is not ornamental; it is a form of power. It can erase, or it can restore. It can dominate, or it can liberate.

This book participates in that restoration. It calls for leaders who can integrate vision with humility, innovation with care, and imagination with accountability. It reminds us that leadership in the Imagination Age is not reserved for elites, institutions, or technologists. It is a shared human responsibility.

For me, reading this work was also a personal reckoning. It asked me to consider the futures my own choices are shaping. It reminded me that leadership is not something we step into only when given authority, it is something we practice daily, in how we listen, decide, include, and imagine.

Global South feminist traditions often describe leadership as relational stewardship: the work of sustaining life across generations. This perspective shifts the question from *How do I lead?* to *Who is carried forward by my leadership? Who is left behind?*

The Imagination Age will not be defined solely by technological breakthroughs. It will be defined by whether leadership evolves toward justice, care, and planetary responsibility or retreats into extraction, speed, and control.

Decolonial feminist leadership offers another path. It insists that imagination must be collective, that power must be accountable, and that the future must be shaped with, not for humanity in all its diversity.

This book by S M A Moin is a guide for that journey. It is also a call.

A call to leaders willing to confront history as they design the future. A call to centre humanity in systems increasingly driven by machines. A call to imagine not only what is possible, but what is just.

And above all, a call to remember that leadership is not a position we occupy, but a responsibility we carry toward each other, toward the planet, and toward generations yet to come.

May this text accompany you as you step into that responsibility. May it expand your imagination, deepen your care, and strengthen your courage to lead in ways that honour life, dignity, and collective flourishing.

Dr Yasmin Ibrahim
Professor of Digital Economy & Culture
Deputy Dean for the School of Business and Management
Queen Mary University of London
United Kingdom

Acknowledgements

With a heart full of humility, I offer my deepest gratitude to the Almighty – the Originator of the cosmos – who inspired within me the thought of *Cosmic Leadership* and awakened in me the enduring question that shapes this book: What is our role in this vast universe?

In moments of silence and reflection, I came to realise that leadership is not merely about authority, performance, or position, but about alignment – aligning our purpose with the greater order of existence. The idea of Cosmic Leadership did not arise from ambition, but from contemplation that each of us is entrusted with a role in the unfolding symphony of the cosmos. For the inspiration to glimpse leadership through this wider horizon, I remain profoundly grateful.

I thank my teachers, whose wisdom illuminated my path and nurtured the discipline of thought and reflection. I am deeply grateful to my wife and sons, who remind me daily that love, patience, and presence are the truest expressions of leadership. I am equally grateful to my siblings, whose encouragement strengthened my resolve and especially to my eldest brother, whose unwavering love, support, and belief in me became the catalyst for the risks I dared to take and the confidence I gradually developed.

I honour the memory of my mother, whose early departure left in me a lifelong yearning to understand the depth of unconditional love. I remain indebted to my father, my first teacher and moral compass, whose quiet strength shaped my understanding of responsibility and character.

Finally, I am thankful to my students, whose questions, debates, and intellectual courage continue to refine my thinking and remind me that to lead is first to learn.

In acknowledging all of them, I recognise that none of us journeys alone. We strive, stumble, and grow within a larger design – each seeking, in our own way, to discover our place in the cosmic order.

Before the Voyage Begins: A Letter from the Author to the Readers

Dear Reader,

Thank you for opening this book. Perhaps you arrived here out of curiosity, or perhaps you are carrying a question that has become impossible to ignore: *How do we lead well when the world is changing faster than our certainty?*

My own journey into leadership had begun long before I understood what leadership was. As a Year VII student, I encountered a Bengali poem about a sailor in a storm – battered by cyclonic winds, struggling at the helm, yet refusing to surrender his mission. Even when he lost one of his hands, he held the course and the future steady with his other hand. That image stayed with me. It taught me early on that leadership is not about comfort. It is a responsibility. It is courage under pressure. It is faith – not merely in outcomes, but in purpose.

Years later, my own voyage unfolded across very different horizons. I began my career in the Navy, where discipline, duty, and responsibility were not abstractions but daily realities. After fifteen years of service, I chose to retire voluntarily and step into new waters, spending more than a decade working across diverse industries in the United Kingdom, navigating strategy, markets, organisations, and the practical demands of performance. Eventually, I found my way into academia, driven by a desire to contribute to the development of future leaders. Across these worlds ranging from the command decks to corporate corridors to university lecture theatres and classrooms, one truth became unmistakably clear: in the Imagination Age, leadership cannot be reduced to performance alone. Our systems are too interconnected. Our tools are too powerful. And the consequences of our decisions now travel farther and faster than ever before.

This book is an invitation to lead with a different kind of strength: disciplined imagination anchored in purpose and moral clarity. You will meet the Leadership Compass: Purpose, People, Performance, and Possibility – a way of staying oriented when everything is moving. You will explore Storytelling as the Needle, because direction only becomes real when it becomes *shared meaning*. You will encounter the Moral Gyroscope, the inner stability of ethics, values, and character – the quiet force that prevents drift when incentives distort judgement. You will be guided through a Leadership Manifesto that turns ideas into practice, so leadership becomes a daily discipline rather than a distant ideal. And you will step into Cosmic Leadership, a widening of perspective that asks not only *what we can do*, but *what our rightful role is* within the greater rhythm of life and in the cosmic theatre.

Finally, the journey returns to where it must: humanity at the helm. This is because the future will not be shaped by intelligence alone, but by conscience as well.

By the stories we tell.

By the dignity we protect.

By the kind of leaders, we choose to become.

If you read this book with intent, reflectively, and with honesty, I hope it will not simply give you frameworks – I trust it will give you *orientation*. The storm will not always pass. But we can learn to hold the helm with steadiness, integrity, and care.

Welcome to the journey.

With warmth and respect,

S M A Moin, Author

Chapter 1

Entering the Imagination Age

Reimagining Possibility and Responsibility

Introduction

Richard Branson's message to the next generations of dreamers from his spaceship reminds us not just of ambition, but of responsibility.

> I was once a child with a dream looking up to the stars. Now I'm an adult in a spaceship looking down to our beautiful Earth. To the next generation of dreamers: if we can do this, just imagine what you can do.
>
> (Branson, 2021)

We are standing at the threshold between two worlds.

One world shimmers with possibility: technologies that could heal diseases, connect continents, and elevate the human spirit; innovations that could bring abundance, sustainability, and dignity within reach for all. The other world bodes with the fear of challenges that can overtake the superiority of humanity and the machines being created may no longer be under their control.

There is, however, another world where millions still live without safety, food, or shelter – where conflict and fear undermine progress, where algorithms sometimes deepen inequality as fast as innovation attempts to solve it. The Imagination Age is not simply an era of creativity. It is an era of moral consequence. A time when humanity is playing the game of life with the highest stakes we have ever known.

We stand at such a crossroads now. The Fourth Industrial Revolution – powered by artificial intelligence, biotechnology, automation, and planetary-scale systems – has brought us to the edge of unprecedented transformation. Some call it an age of miracles; others warn of dystopia. In truth, it is both. It is a spectrum of possibility stretching from abundance to scarcity, compassion to cruelty, flourishing to fracture. Life has become more like a dreamscape: extraordinary and surreal, filled with breathtaking potential and looming peril.

The aspiration to build a better world marks the point at which leadership becomes not merely functional, but existential. In the Imagination Age, leaders are no longer defined by authority or control, but by their capacity to steer humanity toward futures in which technology amplifies dignity rather than division; where

DOI: 10.4324/9781003766414-1

innovation serves people rather than replaces them; and where imagination is used not for escape, but for creation.

This book begins with the premise that we must not only harness emerging technologies – we must also reimagine what it means to be human. To write the next chapter of human history, we need leaders who can hold both wonder and responsibility; who can look at the world as astronauts do – without borders, without illusions, without apathy; and act with courage, creativity, and moral clarity.

The purpose of this chapter is to set the ground beneath your feet before we journey deeper. It invites you to understand how we arrived at this moment: from the mechanised gears of the Industrial Age, through the circuitry of the Information Age, and now into the shimmering, unpredictable landscape of the Imagination Age. It invites you to look both upward and inward to expand your sense of what is possible while grounding yourself in what is right.

This is not a book about leadership in the traditional sense. It is a book about orientation – how to guide yourself and others through an age where the old maps no longer work. It is about the kind of leadership that places humanity at the helm, using science and technology not simply to drive efficiency, but to safeguard the planet, elevate human dignity, and rewrite the narrative of our collective future.

In the Imagination Age, we are all dreamers – but more importantly, we are all accountable for how those dreams shape the world (Moin, 2022). What is now required is a quieter and deeper capacity: disciplined imagination – an imagination curious enough to explore new possibilities yet grounded enough to remain accountable to human consequence. Disciplined imagination does not rush toward novelty for its own sake, nor does it retreat into caution or control. It pauses, listens, and asks what kind of future our ideas are quietly authoring. It invites leaders to imagine boldly, while holding responsibility for the lives, relationships, and systems their imaginations touch. And so, with curiosity guided by conscience, we begin.

Setting the Context: From Industrial to Imagination Age

Thank you for opening these pages. Before we go any further, may I invite you to pause for a moment, close your eyes if you wish, and imagine how humanity arrived at this remarkable moment in history. The Imagination Age did not emerge suddenly; it rose through centuries of technological, cultural, and economic transformation. To understand its significance, we must retrace our steps through the epochs that shaped our systems, societies, and ways of thinking. Each age expanded the boundaries of what humanity could create, while also revealing the limitations that eventually sparked the next wave of innovation (Perez, 2002).

Humanity's story can be read as a series of expanding horizons. Every age stretched our capacity for invention and challenged our assumptions about what it means to lead. The leadership models that served one era often proved insufficient for the next (Kellerman, 2012). The Imagination Age, too, requires a new kind of navigation.

The Industrial Age: Systems and Scale

The Industrial Age, beginning in the late 18th century, reshaped society through mechanised production, steam power, and the reorganisation of labour (Mokyr, 1990). Leadership in this era was rooted in hierarchy, control, and efficiency – principles epitomised by Frederick Taylor's scientific management (Taylor, 1911) and Max Weber's theory of bureaucracy (Weber, 1947). Factories required predictability; machines demanded discipline.

This era taught humanity how to scale operations and build durable systems, but its models of leadership often undervalued creativity, humanity, and imagination (Burns, 1978). Yet the Industrial Age, for all its rigidity, laid the foundation for everything that was to follow.

The Information Age: Knowledge as Power

By the late 20th century, computing and global networks ushered in the Information Age, where data became a central resource and communication accelerated exponentially (Castells, 1996). The rise of "knowledge workers," described by Peter Drucker, signalled a shift from manual labour to cognitive labour (Drucker, 1999). Leadership increasingly depended on communication, collaboration, and the ability to synthesise information in an environment of constant change (Senge, 1990).

However, the promise of information came with paradoxes: abundance without meaning, speed without wisdom. As Simon (1971) observed early on, information consumes attention, and the overproduction of data can overwhelm rather than enlighten. In this new landscape, the leadership challenge was no longer access to information, but the capacity to convert information into insight and action.

The Imagination Age: Where Possibility Meets Responsibility

The Imagination Age, an era emerging from the convergence of artificial intelligence, biotechnology, robotics, and quantum systems (Schwab, 2016). Human creativity, ethical judgment, and imaginative problem-solving have become the most essential leadership capacities, surpassing mere knowledge accumulation.

As Harari (2018) warns, humanity now possesses tools powerful enough to alter life, reshape consciousness, and destabilise political and economic systems. The question is no longer: *Can we build it,* but s*hould we and how?*

The Imagination Age is characterised by:

- *Unprecedented complexity*: climate change, algorithmic governance, cyber insecurity, and widening inequality (UNDP, 2019).
- *Technological acceleration* that outpaces regulation (Brynjolfsson & McAfee, 2014).

- *Moral crossroads*, where every innovation carries both promise and peril.
- *A return to human fundamentals*: empathy, storytelling, purpose, and moral reasoning as essential guides in uncertainty (Gardner, 2006).

To lead in this age is to hold possibility in one hand and responsibility in the other.

Yesterday's Leadership in the Contemporary Mind

Before we look forward, it is worth pausing to look back. Imagine standing by a window in a quiet café, late afternoon light stretching across the table like a soft, golden thread. A warm cup rests in your hands. Outside, the world moves faster than it can be fully grasped. Inside, your thoughts drift backward through time, searching for clues in the leaders who shaped the systems we still inhabit.

Slowly, the figures of yesterday come into view. First appear the shadows of the Industrial Age: James Watt with soot-stained hands harnessing steam; Henry Ford pacing factory floors with relentless precision; Andrew Carnegie forging steel into the backbone of continents.

Leadership in that era was defined by mastery over machines, control of processes, and the disciplined organisation of labour at scale. Progress was measured in output, efficiency, and expansion, as societies learned to industrialise civilisation itself (Weber, 1947; Taylor, 1911).

These models of leadership were not wrong; they were necessary for their time. Yet they were shaped by the assumptions of an age in which stability was prized, systems moved slowly, and human roles were largely defined by production rather than imagination. The traces of these assumptions still linger in how we think about authority, performance, and control – often without our noticing.

The scene shifts. You glimpse the early architects of the Information Age. Bill Gates bent over lines of code; Steve Jobs holding a device as if it were a fragment of the future; Jeff Bezos imagining commerce as a vast digital marketplace before the rest of the world could see it. Leadership became about speed, information, and networks.

Then the images grow more complex. Larry Page and Sergey Brin appear, surrounded by algorithms crawling across humanity's accumulated knowledge. They built empires fuelled not by steel or oil, but by curiosity itself – turning search into currency and attention into power. Mark Zuckerberg follows, standing atop a digital colosseum shaped by humanity's longing for connection, where intimacy and illusion, belonging and conflict, coexisted. What emerged was data capitalism – an era in which human emotion itself became extractable. Some celebrate these figures as the great innovators of the 21st century. Others see digital emperors reshaping privacy, democracy, and public life. Both interpretations feel uncomfortably true.

Yet the story does not end in Silicon Valley. Your thoughts drift eastward. You see Jack Ma, once an English teacher, building Alibaba into a force that redefined commerce across Asia. You see Ratan Tata, blending business with humility and national service. Dr A. P. J. Abdul Kalam, India's "People's President," appears – his scientific brilliance matched by moral gentleness. And Sheikh Rashid bin Saeed Al Maktoum, whose imagination transformed desert sands into a global crossroads. These leaders represent a different pulse – integrative, future-facing, and human-centred.

Hovering between eras like a comet streaking across the sky is Elon Musk: engineer, provocateur, mythmaker. Whether admired or criticised, he embodies the audacity of the age – rockets to Mars, cities underground, industries rewritten through a volatile blend of genius and risk. As these figures pass through your mind, one truth becomes clear: they shaped the world you now inhabit – its possibilities and its fractures.

Still, something feels incomplete. You open *A Whole New Mind* by Daniel Pink and pause on a familiar line:

> The last few decades have belonged to a certain kind of person with a certain kind of mind – computer programmers who could crank the code, lawyers who could craft contracts, MBAs who could crunch numbers. But the keys to the kingdom are changing hands. The future belongs to a very different kind of person with a very different kind of mind – creators and empathizers, pattern recognizers, and meaning makers. These people – artists, inventors, designers, storytellers, caregivers, consolers, big picture thinkers – will now reap society's richest rewards and share its greatest joy.
>
> (Pink, 2008, p. 1)

Suddenly, the story falls into place.
The Industrial Age rewarded those who could build.
The Information Age rewarded those who could process.
The Imagination Age will reward those who can reimagine.
Not only innovators, but integrators.
Not only analysts, but artists.
Not only technologists, but storytellers.

Those who shaped the last century mastered systems, structures, and scale. Those who will shape the next must master something far more elusive: meaning. The future will not yield to faster computation or tighter control. It calls instead for a new quality of thinking – one that recognises, as Albert Einstein warned, "We cannot solve our problems with the same thinking we used when we created them" (cited in Calaprice, 2011).

As the café door opens and a soft breeze moves through the room, a quiet realisation settles in. The future will not be led by those who merely command machines or optimise data, but by those who can illuminate what it means to be human in an age of extraordinary power. And with that recognition, something shifts – not in the world outside, but within the reader. The journey into the Imagination Age begins here.

Alvin Toffler's words echo with renewed urgency: "The illiterate of the 21st century will not be those who cannot read and write, but those who cannot learn, unlearn, and relearn" (Toffler, 1970). In an era defined by transformation, leadership belongs to those willing to let go of certainty, relearn their assumptions, and imagine futures worthy of the humans who must inhabit them.

The New Landscape of Possibility and Uncertainty

Stepping beyond reflection and into the world as it now unfolds, one encounters a landscape that feels sharper, faster, and more fluid than any before it. The Industrial Age reshaped physical environments, the Information Age rewired cognition and communication. The Imagination Age, however, is reshaping reality itself – how meaning is created, how identity is formed, and how futures are imagined. Humanity has arrived at a historical hinge point. The familiar maps – economic, political, social, and moral – are no longer reliable guides. What lies ahead is exhilarating yet disorienting: a world in which old paradigms dissolve faster than new ones can stabilise. Leadership today is exercised not on solid ground, but in shifting terrain where certainty is scarce and possibility abundant.

The Collapse of Old Maps

For much of the past two centuries, industrial-era systems provided a sense of order. Change was relatively linear, problems were bounded, and institutions – though slow – were dependable. Modernity promised predictability and control (Bauman, 2000). Those assumptions no longer hold. The speed, scale, and interconnectedness of contemporary change have rendered many inherited frameworks obsolete (Giddens, 1991; Castells, 1996). Economic models designed for national markets struggle to account for global digital ecosystems. Governance structures built for the twentieth century buckle under the pressures of algorithmic power, climate instability, and transnational crises. As Harari (2018) observes, humanity's political and moral institutions evolved for a world that was slower, simpler, and smaller. Tradition still matters but it can no longer function as a compass on its own.

Complexity as the New Normal

The present moment is best understood through the lens of complex adaptive systems: networks of interdependence where small actions can generate disproportionate, nonlinear effects (Holland, 1995). Leaders now confront:

- Wicked problems with no definitive solutions (Rittel & Webber, 1973).
- Global interdependencies where local decisions carry planetary consequences.

- Fragile systems vulnerable to cascading failure (Taleb, 2012).
- Levels of uncertainty that make prediction increasingly unreliable.

Pandemics, climate shocks, sudden industry collapses, and geopolitical turbulence have revealed a stark truth: we no longer inhabit a world governed by logic alone, but by complexity. Leadership models built on efficiency, standardisation, and command-and-control were designed for a different universe.

Exponential Technologies and Human Identity

Technology in the Imagination Age does not merely change what humans do – it reshapes who they are. Artificial intelligence, quantum computing, biotechnology, robotics, and synthetic biology are not incremental advances; they are ontological innovations that redefine the boundaries of perception, agency, and responsibility (Floridi, 2014).

As Schwab (2016) notes, the Fourth Industrial Revolution is fusing the physical, digital, and biological worlds. At the same time, scholars warn that such transformations challenge the moral foundations of humanness itself (Fukuyama, 2002; Sandel, 2007). Machines now create art, diagnose disease, predict behaviour, and generate knowledge. Some researchers describe this as the beginning of a co-evolution between human and machine intelligence (Russell, 2019). The central question is no longer *What can we build?* It is *What should we allow ourselves to become?*

Possibility and Its Shadow

The tools of this age carry extraordinary promise. Used wisely, they could eradicate extreme poverty, restore ecosystems, expand education, and unlock unprecedented creativity (UNDP, 2019). Perez (2002) describes this potential as the "synergy phase" that follows major technological revolutions – a period of widespread human flourishing.

Yet possibility is inseparable from peril. Every breakthrough casts a shadow: technologies that connect can polarise; systems that optimise can dehumanise; data capitalism can extract not only behaviour, but identity itself (Zuboff, 2019). Harari (2018) warns of new forms of inequality between the technologically enhanced and those left behind.

This is the defining paradox of the Imagination Age: humanity now holds the tools to heal itself – or to fracture irreversibly.

The Leadership Gap

Against this backdrop, one conclusion becomes unavoidable: the deepest crisis of our time is not technological, but leadership.

- Industrial-era leadership prioritised efficiency.
- Information-era leadership prioritised expertise.
- The Imagination Age demands leadership grounded in meaning, ethics, creativity, empathy, and holistic vision.

Heifetz (1994) describes this as adaptive leadership – not the provision of answers, but the courage to reframe questions. Gardner (2006) emphasises the need for minds capable of synthesis and ethical navigation. Pink (2008) argues that the future belongs to meaning-makers. The gap between the world we inhabit and the leadership it requires is widening. How that gap is addressed will determine whether the Imagination Age becomes an era of collective flourishing or profound fragmentation.

Why This Book, and Why Now

This book is written at a moment when leadership itself is undergoing a profound redefinition. Not incrementally, but fundamentally. The Imagination Age is no longer emerging; it is already shaping how organisations operate, how societies organise, and how futures are imagined. Yet many leaders continue to rely on maps designed for earlier worlds – worlds that privileged efficiency over meaning, control over coherence, and prediction over imagination.

The defining challenge of our time is not a shortage of information, capability, or innovation. It is a widening gap between technological power and moral wisdom, between speed and sense-making, and between what can be done and what ought to be done. As systems accelerate and interdependencies deepen, leadership can no longer be reduced to technique, authority, or optimisation alone. It must become an act of orientation – helping people find direction, meaning, and responsibility amid volatility.

This book begins from a simple but urgent premise: when certainty collapses, leaders need a compass rather than a script; and when volatility intensifies, they need a gyroscope rather than a single goal. To meet this need, the book introduces two interdependent leadership instruments.

The Leadership Compass orients leadership attention across five irreducible dimensions: purpose, people, performance, possibility, and storytelling. These are not soft alternatives to strategy; they are the human coordinates without which strategy loses direction. Together, they help leaders sense where they are, clarify what matters, and choose pathways that align ambition with meaning.

Alongside this, the Moral Gyroscope provides stabilisation. In an age where innovation routinely outpaces regulation and algorithms increasingly shape human lives, leadership requires an internal mechanism that maintains ethical balance. Ethics, values, and character are not constraints on imagination; they are what make imagination responsible.

This book is written now because imagination has become the decisive human capability – and leadership is how imagination is either elevated or misdirected.

The future will not be shaped by those who merely control systems, but by those who can integrate creativity with conscience, vision with humility, and possibility with responsibility. What follows is a navigational guide.

Standing at the Threshold

Every historical era has demanded a different form of leadership.

- The Industrial Age required system-builders.
- The Information Age required knowledge-navigators.
- The Imagination Age, however, calls for something more demanding and more human: visionaries grounded in ethics, innovators guided by conscience, and leaders committed to humanity's long-term flourishing.

This book is a response to that call. It offers leaders not abstract ideals, but practical frameworks for navigating possibility and uncertainty with clarity and responsibility. At the centre of this approach are the Leadership Compass and the Moral Gyroscope – two instruments designed to help leaders orient themselves and remain grounded as contexts shift.

The Leadership Compass: A Navigational Framework for the Imagination Age

Every era generates its own leadership metaphors. The Industrial Age borrowed from machines, the Information Age from networks, and the digital age from algorithms. The Imagination Age – defined by fluid possibility, collective creativity, and deep uncertainty – demands a metaphor that is more human, adaptive, and meaning-centred (Uhl-Bien & Arena, 2018).

The Leadership Compass (Figure 1.1) serves this purpose. It provides four orienting directions:

- Purpose (Chapter 2)
- People (Chapter 3)
- Performance (Chapter 4)
- Possibility (Chapter 5)

These are connected by a Storytelling Needle (Chapter 6). These are not competencies to be mastered in isolation, but relational vectors of sensemaking (Weick, 1995). In environments where conditions shift rapidly, leaders cannot rely solely on static plans; they require an internal navigation system capable of continual recalibration.

Each direction reveals a distinct aspect of leadership identity (see Table 1.1). As the Compass turns, leaders encounter different demands; as the Needle moves, meaning is continuously shaped, revised, and shared.

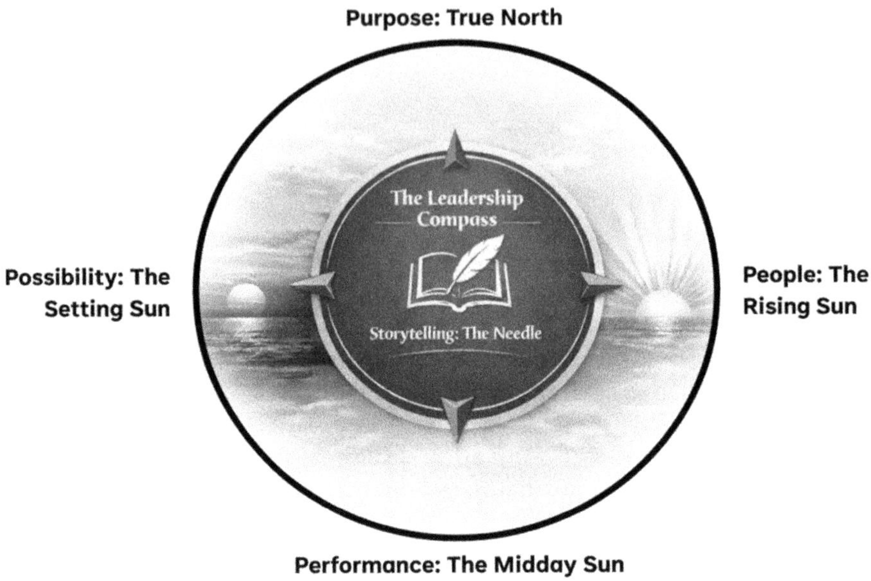

Figure 1.1 The Leadership Compass.

Source: Conceptualised and developed by the author.

The Moral Gyroscope: Stabilising Leadership from Within

If the Leadership Compass provides direction, the Moral Gyroscope provides stability. In the Imagination Age – where velocity, ambiguity, and technological power can pull leaders off-course – orientation alone is not enough. Leaders need an internal stabiliser that keeps judgement, behaviour, and relationships balanced under pressure. The Moral Gyroscope (Chapter 7) is built on three interdependent axes:

X-axis: Ethics
Y-axis: Values
Z-axis: Character

Ethics guides moral judgement and helps leaders navigate dilemmas where legitimate goods collide. Values align priorities, clarifying what matters most when incentives, stakeholder demands, and cultural pressures compete. Character anchors behaviour over time, shaping how leaders respond to temptation, fear, success, and scrutiny (Brown & Treviño, 2006; Schwartz, 2012; Peterson & Seligman, 2004). When these axes are integrated, leaders develop moral agility – the capacity to adapt without drifting into moral compromise.

Table 1.1 The Leadership Compass – Directions, Metaphor, Leadership Focus

Direction	*Metaphor*	*Meaning and guiding question*	*Leadership focus*
North: Purpose	True North	The unwavering guide that defines the leader's 'why', anchoring direction and giving meaning to every journey What anchors me? Why should I lead?	Meaning, mission, intentionality
East: People	The Rising Sun	The true source of energy, igniting connection, collaboration, and the beginning of every great endeavour. Who am I responsible for?	Relationships, empathy, inclusion
South: Performance	The Midday Sun	The peak of effort, where clarity and discipline shine brightest, creating a culture of efficiency and mobilising resources to turn intention into achievement. What am I accountable for?	Execution, discipline, impact
West: Possibility	The Setting Sun	The close of the day that illuminates tomorrow, where every ending carries the seed of a new dawn What future am I imagining and committing to create?	Vision, imagination, foresight
Needle: Storytelling	Narrative Orientation	Leader's Language. Great leaders use stories to: • convey purpose with clarity and impact • connects authentically with people to inspire trust and action • foster a culture of efficiency and high performance by reinforcing shared values and expectations • communicates vision and possibilities that mobilise imagination, collective commitment, motivate and engage How do we make meaning together?	Shared identity and direction

Leadership Manifesto

The journey then turns inward again, toward practice and personal commitment. Leadership Manifesto (Chapter 8) – a call to reclaim freedom, presence, and power in an age that too often fragments attention, accelerates without reflection, and confuses influence with control.

Readers are invited to translate imagination into discipline and ethics into daily action through clear declarations and a practical recalibration pathway. Leadership here is understood not as a title or a technique, but as a lived stance: a courageous willingness to act with clarity amid uncertainty, to balance performance with conscience, and to remain fully human while shaping systems that will outlast us. What begins as a compass and a gyroscope ultimately becomes a way of being that prepares leaders not only to navigate the Imagination Age, but to shape it wisely, inclusively, and with care.

Cosmic Leadership

Direction without grounding leads to drift; grounding without direction leads to stagnation. Together, the Leadership Compass and Moral Gyroscope form a coherent navigational system – linking imagination with integrity, vision with virtue, and aspiration with responsibility. But the Cosmic Leadership (Chapter 9) expands the horizon. If the Compass orients leaders across purpose, people, performance, possibility, and storytelling, and the Gyroscope stabilises leaders morally, Cosmic Leadership expands the frame further: it situates leadership within the wider rhythm of interdependence – across ecosystems, generations, and the living cosmos. In the cosmic theatre, leaders are not masters of the stage, but stewards entrusted with influence for a finite time, called to align their inner world – consciousness, ethics, and intent – with the moral and relational rhythms of the outer world.

Humanity at the Helm

In the Imagination Age, leadership is no longer mechanical. It becomes a profoundly human practice of orientation (Compass), stability (Gyroscope), and stewardship (Cosmic Leadership) – guiding action not only toward organisational success, but toward coherence, care, and flourishing within the larger order to which we belong.

Looking ahead, the question that inevitably emerges is who, ultimately, leadership is for. Therefore, the next step is to place Humanity at the Helm (Chapter 10), moving from orientation to obligation – asking how leadership can become a *symphony rather than a solo*, where imagination, power, and technology are exercised in ways that expand dignity, voice, and opportunity for all. This shift reframes inclusion not as a managerial agenda or institutional policy, but as a moral and existential calling: to design systems, cultures, and futures in which no human being is reduced to a margin, a metric, or a means. Leadership, in this light, becomes an act of listening, enabling, and harmonising – aligning inner purpose with collective flourishing across societies, generations, and the living planet.

Conclusion

This chapter has set the foundation for understanding leadership in the Imagination Age not as a position or a technique, but as a way of being in the world. In an era marked by accelerating complexity, technological power, and moral uncertainty, leadership becomes an act of orientation and responsibility – of discerning direction, sustaining balance, and acting with imagination anchored in integrity. The Leadership Compass offers a means of orientation across purpose, people, performance, possibility, and storytelling, while the Moral Gyroscope provides the inner stabilisation required to remain grounded amid volatility. Together, they frame leadership as a profoundly human practice: creative yet disciplined, visionary yet ethical.

This book now invites you, the reader, to step into this emerging landscape. The Imagination Age is not a distant future; it is the context in which leadership is already unfolding. Its opportunities are immense – unprecedented creativity, collective intelligence, and the possibility of building more inclusive and humane systems. Its challenges are equally real – fragmentation, ethical dilemmas, ecological precarity, and the risk of imagination untethered from responsibility. Preparing to lead in this age requires more than new skills; it calls for a reorientation of mindset, values, and presence.

The chapters that follow are an invitation to begin – or deepen – your own leadership journey: to explore imagination as a force for inclusion rather than extraction, to navigate uncertainty with courage and care, and to cultivate the moral and relational capacities needed to serve a world in transition. Leadership in the Imagination Age is not reserved for a select few; it is a shared human responsibility. What begins here is a call to become the kind of leader capable of shaping a future that is not only innovative, but also just in which possibility is expanded, dignity is protected, and the flourishing of all remains at the helm.

Reflective Questions

1. In a world where artificial intelligence increasingly performs analytical and technical tasks, what uniquely human qualities should leaders cultivate to guide organisations and societies responsibly?
2. How can leaders balance the power of imagination, exploring bold possibilities for the future with moral responsibility for the social, ethical, and environmental consequences of their decisions?
3. When facing uncertainty and disruption, do leaders tend to narrow possibilities through fear and short-term thinking, or expand them through inclusive vision and systems awareness, and where do you see yourself on this spectrum?

References

Bauman, Z. (2000). *Liquid modernity*. Polity Press.

Branson, R. (2021, July 11). *Flying to space onboard Virgin Galactic*. Virgin.com. www.virgin.com/branson-family/richard-branson-blog/flying-to-space-onboard-virgin-galactic

Brown, M. E., & Treviño, L. K. (2006). Ethical leadership: A review and future directions. *The Leadership Quarterly, 17*(6), 595–616.

Brynjolfsson, E., & McAfee, A. (2014). *The second machine age: Work, progress, and prosperity in a time of brilliant technologies*. W. W. Norton & Company.

Burns, J. M. (1978). *Leadership*. Harper & Row.

Calaprice, A. (2011). *The ultimate quotable Einstein*. Princeton University Press.

Castells, M. (1996). *The rise of the network society*. Blackwell.

Drucker, P. F. (1999). *Management challenges for the 21st century*. HarperBusiness.

Floridi, L. (2014). *The fourth revolution: How the infosphere is reshaping human reality*. Oxford University Press.

Fukuyama, F. (2002). *Our posthuman future: Consequences of the biotechnology revolution*. Farrar, Straus and Giroux.

Gardner, H. (2006). *Five minds for the future*. Harvard Business School Press.

Giddens, A. (1991). *Modernity and self-identity: Self and society in the late modern age*. Stanford University Press.

Harari, Y. N. (2018). *21 lessons for the 21st century*. Spiegel & Grau.

Heifetz, R. A. (1994). *Leadership without easy answers*. Harvard University Press.

Holland, J. H. (1995). *Hidden order: How adaptation builds complexity*. Addison-Wesley Publishing Company.

Kellerman, B. (2012). *The end of leadership*. HarperBusiness.

Moin, S. M. A. (2022). *Creativity in the imagination age: Theories, practice and application*. Palgrave Macmillan.

Mokyr, J. (1990). *The lever of riches: Technological creativity and economic progress*. Oxford University Press.

Pérez, C. (2002). *Technological revolutions and financial capital: The dynamics of bubbles and golden ages*. Edward Elgar.

Peterson, C., & Seligman, M. E. P. (2004). *Character strengths and virtues: A handbook and classification*. Oxford University Press.

Pink, D. H. (2008). *A whole new mind: Why right-brainers will rule the future*. Marshall Cavendish Business.

Rittel, H. W. J., & Webber, M. M. (1973). Dilemmas in a general theory of planning. *Policy Sciences, 4*(2), 155–169. https://doi.org/10.1007/BF01405730

Russell, S. (2019). *Human compatible: Artificial intelligence and the problem of control*. Viking.

Sandel, M. J. (2007). *The case against perfection: Ethics in the age of genetic engineering*. Belknap Press.

Schwab, K. (2016). *The fourth industrial revolution*. World Economic Forum.

Schwartz, S. H. (2012). An overview of the Schwartz theory of basic values. *Online Readings in Psychology and Culture, 2*(1), 11.

Senge, P. M. (1990). *The fifth discipline: The art and practice of the learning organization*. Doubleday.

Simon, H. A. (1971). Designing organizations for an information-rich world. In M. Greenberger (Ed.), *Computers, communication, and the public interest* (pp. 37–72). Johns Hopkins University Press.

Taleb, N. N. (2012). *Antifragile: Things that gain from disorder*. Random House.
Taylor, F. W. (1911). *The principles of scientific management*. Harper & Brothers.
Toffler, A. (1970). *Future shock*. Random House.
Uhl-Bien, M., & Arena, M. (2018). Leadership for organizational adaptability. *The Leadership Quarterly, 29*(1), 89–104. https://doi.org/10.1016/j.leaqua.2017.12.009
United Nations Development Programme. (2019). *Human development report 2019: Beyond income, beyond averages, beyond today*. United Nations.
Weber, M. (1947). *The theory of social and economic organization* (A. M. Henderson & T. Parsons, Trans.). Oxford University Press. (Original work published 1922)
Weick, K. E. (1995). *Sensemaking in organizations*. Sage.
Zuboff, S. (2019). *The age of surveillance capitalism: The fight for a human future at the new frontier of power*. PublicAffairs.

Chapter 2

Purpose

Orienting Toward the Leader's True North

Introduction

Twenty-seven years behind bars in a small prison cell on Robben Island. Nelson Mandela could have emerged a broken man – bitter, angry, and prepared for revenge. Yet his compass pointed north. His purpose was not revenge but reconciliation, not personal freedom but the liberation of an entire nation. When he stood as President, he invited his jailers to his inauguration. That is what purpose looks like – something greater than the prison walls that contain you, larger than the pain that shapes you, and more profound than self-interest. Purpose is the force that transforms suffering into service and limitation into legacy.

Shakespeare reminds us that "all the world's a stage, and all the men and women merely players" (Shakespeare, 1623/2008, Act II, Scene VII), a reflection on the human search to understand not only where we stand in the world, but why we are here – our role, our purpose, upon its unfolding stage. Yet too often, individuals stumble through life as if asleep – following scripts written by others, conforming to societal templates of success, and rarely pausing to ask whether the roles they perform are authentically theirs. Living unconsciously is to surrender to default settings: study, work, accumulate, retire. Life becomes mechanical, repetitive, and hollow. One may be alive biologically, yet existentially unmotivated – the living dead of modern conformity.

To awaken is to reclaim authorship of one's own story. We are not merely actors trapped in a prewritten play but also playwrights and directors of our own script. This awakening requires courage – the courage to question assumptions, to resist inertia, and to steer our energies with conscious intent. Authentic leadership begins here. Before one can lead others, one must first lead oneself, and self-leadership begins with purpose (George, 2007; Sinek, 2011). Purpose functions as the North of the leadership compass, the orienting principle that anchors leaders amid complexity and change. It transforms work from burden into calling and life from survival into significance. When the *why* is clear, the *how* becomes not only easier but often joyful (Frankl, 1984).

The global financial crisis of 2008–2009 exposed how organisational purpose shapes leadership decisions under extreme pressure. Research on cooperative and

DOI: 10.4324/9781003766414-2

stakeholder-oriented enterprises shows that, rather than dismantling participatory ownership structures to satisfy short-term investor demands, some organisations chose to preserve commitments to human dignity, shared sacrifice, and democratic governance (Birchall & Ketilson, 2009; International Labour Organization [ILO], 2012). Such purpose-led decisions often required personal and collective cost, yet evidence suggests they strengthened long-term trust, organisational identity, and resilience, enabling these firms to recover credibility and opportunity as markets stabilised (ILO, 2016). This pattern illustrates how purpose functions as leadership's True North – not as an abstract ideal, but as a stabilising force that guides ethical action amid uncertainty.

As George (2007) observes, purpose does not provide certainty – it offers orientation. In an era defined by algorithmic speed, market volatility, and moral ambiguity, purpose serves as an anchor of meaning and direction (Rey et al., 2019). Without it, organisations drift into short-termism, cynicism, or irrelevance. This chapter explores the idea of purpose as the cardinal North of the Leadership Compass – not as rhetoric but as an orienting principle that shapes identity, culture, and legitimacy. While Chapter 1 introduced the Imagination Age, Leadership Compass and the Moral Gyroscope, this chapter dives deep into purpose. It examines how leaders can navigate such an age by anchoring their decisions in a clear sense of *why*.

Framing Purpose: Why Now?

During the industrial era, purpose could be inferred from production: companies existed to manufacture goods, deliver services, or generate profit. In the Imagination Age – when artificial intelligence (AI) accelerates creation and algorithms proliferate choices – Purpose becomes both an existential and ethical necessity (Ibarra & Rattan, 2022).

Three converging dynamics make purpose indispensable today:

1. **Proliferation of Options:** AI-driven systems produce endless alternatives – products, markets, financial scenarios. Yet possibility without purpose breeds paralysis or reckless pursuit. Purpose serves as a filter, helping leaders discern which paths align with enduring identity (Daugherty & Wilson, 2018).
2. **Erosion of Trust:** Public confidence in corporations and institutions continues to decline amid misinformation, opaque algorithms, and ethical lapses. Research indicates that purpose-driven organisations exhibit stronger reputations, resilience, and stakeholder loyalty (Hurst, 2014; Korschun et al., 2022). Purpose rebuilds legitimacy where compliance alone cannot.
3. **Changing Workforce Expectations:** Millennials and Generation Z increasingly seek meaningful work that contributes to something larger than profit (Deloitte, 2023). Purpose-driven organisations consistently outperform peers in engagement, creativity, and retention (Grant, 2008; Rosso et al., 2010; Martela & Steger, 2016). In short, talent gravitates toward purpose.

Purpose, therefore, is not a luxury or branding exercise – it is both a strategic necessity and a moral compass (Craig & Snook, 2014).

Differentiating Purpose from Mission and Vision

Although often used interchangeably, *purpose*, *mission*, and *vision* play distinct roles.

- *Mission* defines *what* an organisation does – in other words, how to manifest purpose daily, but it is not purpose.
- *Vision* articulates *where* the organisation aspires to go.
- *Purpose* clarifies *why* the organisation exists.

While missions and visions evolve over time, purpose remains enduring. Collins and Porras (1994) call it the *core ideology* – the unchanging essence that sustains identity across generations. For example, IBM shifted from punch cards to cloud computing, but its foundational purpose – *to think* – remains constant.

Purpose as Orientation in the Imagination Age

In a world where intelligence is abundant but wisdom scarce, purpose provides moral and strategic orientation. AI may optimise outcomes, but only the purpose determines which outcomes matter. Consider two trajectories:

- *Without purpose*: A bank's algorithm may maximise profit but exclude marginalised borrowers, eroding trust.
- *With purpose*: The same bank may define its purpose as *financial dignity* and design transparent, bias-tested systems. Profit remains essential, but it is subordinated to ethics and meaning.

Purpose thus clarifies not only *what* decisions are made but *why* they matter (Rey et al., 2019; Smith & Lewis 2011). Industrial-era leadership prized efficiency, control, and predictability. Yet as automation assumes these functions, *imagination* becomes the defining human asset. In this context, the purpose shifts from a peripheral statement to a central navigational tool (Hamel & Zanini, 2020).

Case Study 2.1 Winning Minds Before Hands: Leadership Purpose from Ancient Wisdom to Modern Practice

The question *"Why should people follow us?"* has occupied human thought since ancient times. Ancient philosophers argued that the legitimacy of leadership arises not from authority but from virtue – what the Greeks called aretė, the unified expression of moral character and practical competence

(Aristotle, trans. 2000). This insight remains essential in today's leadership context, where people seek purpose, integrity, and authenticity in those they choose to follow.

A compelling example comes from Xenophon, a student of Socrates, whose leadership of ten thousand Greek mercenaries during their retreat from Persia in 400 BC continues to illuminate the essence of followership.

> Strong commanders are those who can inspire upon their troops that they must be followed even through fire or danger of any kind... people follow because they recognise his qualities... great indeed is the man who can use his mind rather than his physical might for great achievement.
>
> (Xenophon, as cited in Kolenda, 2001, p. 3)

Xenophon's lesson is clear: leaders win the minds of their people before they earn their hands. Followers choose their leaders when they recognise excellence, judgement, and integrity – qualities that signal a leader is worthy of trust.

This principle is echoed across ancient thought.

- Plato argued that true leadership is guided by the highest moral purpose and a commitment to the common good, not personal ambition (Plato, trans. 1992).
- Aristotle expanded on areté by defining leadership excellence as a combination of character (who the leader is) and competence (what the leader can do) (Aristotle, trans. 2000).
- Cicero emphasised the leader's role as a guardian of justice and moral equality, responsible for the welfare of the community (Cicero, trans. 2014).

These ancient frameworks align closely with contemporary leadership expectations: followers still look for leaders who display moral clarity, competence, and a purpose beyond self-interest.

Serving aboard naval warships, I encountered the concept of watertight integrity, the requirement that a ship's hull must be free from even the smallest leak to remain seaworthy. A single breach below the waterline can place the entire crew at risk. This became a defining metaphor for leadership: just as a ship cannot endure the ocean with hidden weaknesses, leaders cannot sustain trust when their integrity is compromised. This insight cemented the idea that integrity – uncompromising honesty regardless of circumstance – is the foundation of character. This view resonates with Aristotle's conception of virtue and Cicero's insistence on justice as the basis for authority.

The implication for leadership purpose is profound. People follow leaders not because they hold power, but because they embody areté – excellence of character and competence expressed in service of a meaningful purpose. Leaders inspire followership when their values, identity, and actions align consistently over time.

In an era that demands imagination, trust, and shared direction, the ancient wisdom remains relevant: people follow leaders whose purpose is credible, whose integrity is intact, and whose excellence is visible.

Conceptualising Purpose

Having established why purpose is indispensable in the Imagination Age, it is now time to examine its conceptual, practical, and spiritual foundations. Purpose is more than motivation or mission – it is a north star of meaning that integrates cognition, ethics, and spirit, enabling leaders to navigate complexity without losing direction. The discussion begins with three foundational frameworks in leadership thought: Bill George's *True North* (2007), which grounds purpose in authentic self-awareness and moral integrity; Jim Collins's *Good to Great* (2001), which defines purpose as disciplined focus through the "hedgehog concept"; and Collins and Porras's *Built to Last* (1994), which locates purpose in enduring organisational ideology. Building on these classics, the section extends to authentic leadership theory, stakeholder theory, moral imagination, and the psychology of meaningful work, each offering a distinctive lens on how purpose animates both individuals and institutions.

Beyond these managerial perspectives, the chapter also engages a spiritual and existential lens, drawing on Joseph Jaworski's *Synchronicity: The Inner Path of Leadership* (1996) and Margaret Wheatley's *Leadership and the New Science* (2006), which portray purpose as an emergent field of meaning that connects inner consciousness with collective order. This is complemented by Morten Hansen's P-Squared framework (2018), showing how the fusion of passion and purpose enhances performance and vitality. Finally, the chapter considers purpose through sacred and philosophical traditions, where it is seen as a divine trust and a moral calling to stewardship.

Together, these perspectives reveal purpose as a multidimensional construct (Figure 2.1) – at once personal and organisational, pragmatic and transcendent. In an age marked by flux and boundless possibility, they converge into an integrated understanding of purposeful leadership, aligning head, heart, and spirit toward a coherent and ethical direction. As the most fundamental dimension of the Leadership Compass, purpose is not merely one element among others; it functions as the compass itself, orienting leaders amid complexity and guiding judgement, choice, and responsibility.

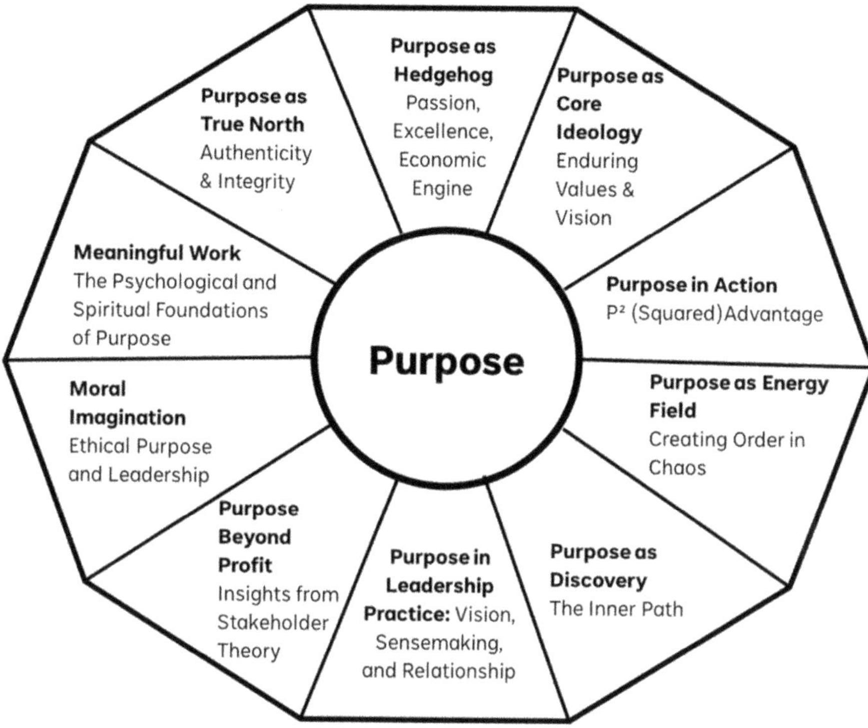

Figure 2.1 Conceptualising Purpose in Leadership.

Source: Developed by author from existing literature.

Purpose as True North

Bill George (2007) introduced a resonant metaphor: every leader possesses an inner compass that points toward their *true north* – the alignment of actions with deeply held values and authentic motivations. When leaders remain faithful to this compass, they inspire trust, legitimacy, and resilience (George, 2007).

George's model draws from the broader field of authentic leadership theory (Avolio & Gardner, 2005), which highlights four key elements:

- Self-awareness: recognising one's values, strengths, and limitations.
- Relational transparency: acting with openness and honesty.
- Balanced processing: considering diverse perspectives.
- Internalised moral perspective: adhering to internal moral standards over external pressures.

Leaders often discover their purpose not through abstract reflection but through *crucibles* – transformative life experiences that reveal what truly matters. For example, Howard Schultz's experience of his father's lack of healthcare later shaped Starbucks's commitment to employee benefits (see Case Study 2.5). In an era dominated by machine intelligence, the *True North* metaphor acquires renewed significance. Algorithms can present options, but they cannot supply moral orientation. Purpose and authenticity prevent leaders from outsourcing ethical judgment to code (Ibarra & Rattan, 2022). Purpose-centred leaders ask not only "what we can do" but "who we are becoming by doing this."

Purpose as Hedgehog

In *Good to Great*, Collins (2001) and his team studied companies that sustained superior performance across decades. Their insight – the Hedgehog Concept – rests on the intersection of three circles:

- What is the organisation deeply passionate about?
- What can it be the best in the world at?
- What drives its economic engine?

Purpose, in this model, emerges as disciplined clarity rather than vague aspiration. For instance, Walgreens thrived not by being the biggest pharmacy, but by focusing on being the *most convenient* – an expression of purpose grounded in passion, capability, and economic logic.

As AI generates an abundance of possibilities, the Hedgehog framework becomes an essential filter for focus and restraint. Purpose provides clarity in a world of technological abundance (Daugherty & Wilson, 2018). A start-up tempted to chase every opportunity must return to the single intersection of passion, capability, and sustainability – its purpose point.

Purpose as Core Ideology

In *Built to Last*, Collins and Porras (1994) examined enduring organisations that thrived for decades, even centuries. Their conclusion: visionary companies succeed by preserving a *core ideology* – a combination of purpose and values – while stimulating continuous progress.

Core ideology ensures continuity amid disruption. Hewlett-Packard's enduring purpose of making technical contributions for the advancement and welfare of humanity remained intact as its technologies evolved. When AI accelerates transformation, leaders face dual imperatives: preserve the core and stimulate progress. Purpose serves as both anchor and sail – anchoring identity while propelling adaptive innovation. Organisations that cling to outdated practices lose relevance; those that abandon their core ideology lose identity.

Purpose in Action: The P^2 (P-Squared) Advantage

If awakening from autopilot is the first step, the next challenge is to *live* purposefully daily. Hansen's (2018) research on over 5,000 professionals revealed that those who combined passion (what energises them) and purpose (how their work contributes to others) outperformed peers by an average of 18 percentile points – the *P^2 effect*. The combination is crucial as passion without purpose becomes self-indulgence; purpose without passion becomes burnout; and together, they create vitality, focus, and resilience (Hansen, 2018; Martela & Steger, 2016). Hansen (2018) recommended three ways for building P^2:

- Redefine your role to align tasks with both your interests and your contributions.
- Broaden sources of passion through learning, mentoring, and creativity.
- Climb the Purpose Pyramid: add value, find meaning, and connect to mission.

For leaders, the P^2 principle is not a motivational cliché but a performance multiplier. Leadership, in essence, is the art of awakening energy and meaning in others (Craig & Snook, 2014; Kashdan et al., 2021).

Purpose as Energy Field: Creating Order in Chaos

Wheatley (2006) reframes chaos as a generative force rather than a threat. Drawing from complexity science, she argues that living systems thrive not through rigid control but through shared meaning and purpose.

> Order is maintained not by structure, but by a compelling sense of identity and purpose that acts as an invisible field shaping behavior.
>
> (Wheatley, 2006, p. 40)

Purpose, in this sense, functions as an *energy field* that organises collective action. In turbulent systems, meaning – not management – creates coherence (Uhl-Bien & Arena, 2018). Leaders who articulate and embody purpose generate self-organisation, innovation, and trust without micromanagement. In times of volatility, rules fragment, but shared purpose holds.

Purpose as Discovery: The Inner Path

While Wheatley (2006) examines purpose as an organising field, Jaworski (1996) focuses on its interior journey. In *Synchronicity: The Inner Path of Leadership*, he argues that leadership begins not with control but with awakening, realising that life unfolds through deeper currents of meaning.

When individuals open themselves to discovery rather than forcing outcomes, *remarkable synchronicities* occur (Jaworski, 1996). Purpose is thus not invented but uncovered through reflection, dialogue, and attentiveness to experience (Scharmer, 2009). For leaders, the lesson is transformative: before mobilising others around purpose, one must first *listen inwardly*. True leadership begins with humility and awareness of one's place in the unfolding whole.

Purpose in Leadership Practice: Vision, Sensemaking, and Relationship

Purpose operates not only as philosophy but as practical leadership practice (Nohria & Khurana, 2010). Three dominant frameworks illuminate how purpose is enacted:

- Vision (Transformational Leadership): Leaders inspire when they articulate a vision that connects everyday tasks to a transcendent purpose (Bass & Riggio, 2006).
- Sensemaking: Leaders interpret uncertainty by framing stories that help people understand *what is happening and why it matters* (Weick, 1995).
- Relationship (Leader–Member Exchange): Trust and shared goals anchor collaboration; a sense of purpose strengthens these relational bonds (Graen & Uhl-Bien, 1995).

Together, these mechanisms show that purpose is not abstract – it is enacted daily through meaning-making, communication, and trust-building (Fairhurst & Uhl-Bien, 2012).

Purpose Beyond Profit: Insights from Stakeholder Theory

Freeman (1984) expanded leadership beyond shareholders to encompass a broader ecosystem of stakeholders. Purpose, in this light, is collective value creation – for employees, customers, communities, and the planet (Freeman et al., 2020). Companies like Unilever, under Paul Polman, embodied this by defining their purpose as *making sustainable living commonplace.* In the Age of Imagination, stakeholder orientation should ensure that AI and innovation serve humanity, not merely investors (Henderson, 2020).

Moral Imagination and Ethical Purpose

Werhane (1999) introduced *the concept of moral imagination* – the capacity to envision solutions that respect the dignity of all stakeholders. It enables leaders to transcend binary trade-offs between profit and ethics. In the Age of Imagination, moral imagination is essential for responsible AI and technological ethics (Brown & Treviño, 2006). Purpose acts as a moral compass, guiding leaders to ask not only *can we do something,* but *should we do that* (Mittelstadt et al., 2016).

Meaningful Work: The Psychological and Spiritual Foundations of Purpose

At the individual level, purpose intersects with the psychology of meaningful work. Rosso et al. (2010) identify four pathways to meaningfulness:

1. Self-connection: alignment between values and work.
2. Contribution: impact on others.
3. Unification: belonging to a collective.
4. Individuation: expressing uniqueness.

In the Imagination Age, as AI automates routine tasks, workers crave creativity and connection. Leaders who link organisational purpose with personal meaning cultivate engagement and innovation (Steger, 2023).

Moreover, across spiritual traditions, purpose is not self-created but divinely anchored. The Qur'an teaches, "I have not created humankind except to worship Me" (51:56). Worship here signifies alignment with the Creator's design. Humanity is entrusted as *khalifah* – a steward on Earth (2:30) – responsible for justice, compassion, and care.

Purpose, therefore, is sacred stewardship: to live without purpose is to deny the intentionality of creation itself. To lead with purpose is to fulfil the highest calling of responsibility and devotion (Al-Faruqi, 1992).

Purpose as Orientation, Meaning, and Responsibility

Taken together, the perspectives explored above reveal that purpose is not a single, static idea but functions as a multidimensional compass that operates across the inner life of leaders, the everyday practices of organisations, and the wider moral and social systems in which they are embedded. Purpose works simultaneously at multiple levels: psychological and strategic, ethical and spiritual, personal and collective. Each lens illuminates a distinct yet interconnected way in which purpose anchors judgement, guides action, and sustains coherence amid uncertainty.

Seen through these lenses, purpose functions as self-awareness and integrity, grounding leaders in values that resist distortion under pressure; as disciplined focus, helping organisations choose what to pursue – and what to decline – in a world of infinite possibility; and as an enduring core ideology, preserving meaning while enabling adaptation. Purpose also acts as an energy field for self-organisation, creating shared meaning that allows people and systems to coordinate without excessive control. At a more personal level, it emerges as discovery and synchronicity, aligning inner intention with larger patterns of meaning and contribution.

Beyond the individual and the firm, purpose expands into moral imagination, enabling leaders to envision responsible futures that honour human dignity; into stakeholder value creation, reframing success as collective and sustainable rather than extractive; and into the experience of meaningful work, where individuals find connection, contribution, belonging, and self-expression through what they do.

In the Imagination Age, leadership requires the integration of these dimensions. Leaders must combine authenticity with adaptability, ethics with innovation, and passion with contribution – using purpose not merely as an ideal, but as a living compass that aligns head, heart, and responsibility, and enables navigation through complexity with clarity, courage, and care.

Applying Purpose in Practice

Theoretical discussions illuminate *why* purpose matters and *how* it operates. Theories offer conceptual clarity, but leaders often ask: *How do we translate purpose into practice?* Without application, purpose risks being reduced to marketing slogans, posters in corridors, or executive speeches without making real impact. To be effective, purpose must be operationalised, tested, and lived. This phase explores four principles for embedding purpose in practice.

Codify but Do Not Calcify

Purpose must be articulated in clear language. Vague statements such as "to be the best" lack resonance. A strong purpose captures enduring identity and aspiration. Yet codification is not the same as calcification. A purpose statement should serve as an anchor, not a cage.

Case Study 2.2 Tesla: From Electric Cars to a Sustainable Energy Ecosystem

Tesla's founding mission was "to accelerate the world's transition to sustainable energy" (Tesla, 2020). Initially, Tesla focused on high-performance electric vehicles (EVs), launching the Roadster, Model S, and later more affordable mass-market models like the Model 3 and Model Y (Niedermeyer, 2019). However, leadership recognised that cars alone would not achieve the broader energy transition. Tesla expanded into energy generation and storage by acquiring SolarCity and developing solar panels, Solar Roof tiles, and Powerwall battery systems (Tesla, 2020). By vertically integrating – making its own batteries, owning factories, and controlling distribution – Tesla aimed to lower costs, scale production, and ensure alignment with its sustainability mission (Niedermeyer, 2019).

Lesson

A mission-driven purpose can guide a company beyond its initial product line. Embedding sustainability into the core business allows a company to build a coherent ecosystem and leverage synergy across different business units.

Align Systems with Purpose

Purpose is not credible unless embedded in systems: strategy, operations, HR, marketing, finance. When systems contradict purpose, employees and stakeholders perceive hypocrisy. For example, Patagonia's purpose – We're in business to save our home planet – is embedded into product design (repairability and durability), supply chains (traceable materials), and activism (lawsuits against environmental deregulation). Even its marketing (Don't buy this jacket) signals alignment.

Case Study 2.3 Patagonia: Purpose as Strategic Integrity in the Imagination Age

Patagonia offers a powerful illustration of purpose-led leadership that goes beyond rhetoric to shape strategy, culture, and innovation. Founded by Yvon Chouinard, the company's mission – We're in business to save our home planet – operates as a moral anchor and strategic filter rather than a marketing slogan. Purpose is embedded in daily decisions, demonstrating how values can align ethical intent with long-term competitiveness (Collins & Porras, 1994; George, 2007).

A defining moment came during Patagonia's 2011 Black Friday campaign, when the company donated 100% of sales – $10 million – to grassroots environmental initiatives. Although the decision involved a short-term financial sacrifice, it deepened stakeholder trust, strengthened brand legitimacy, and reinforced long-term resilience (Hawken, 2017). This action exemplifies moral imagination (Werhane, 1999) and a stakeholder-oriented approach (Freeman, 1984), where leadership choices reflect deeply held values rather than narrow profit maximisation. Employees reported heightened engagement and meaning, reflecting the P-Squared effect – the alignment of personal passion with contribution to a larger purpose (Hansen, 2018).

In the Imagination Age, Patagonia also demonstrates how purpose guides innovation amid technological acceleration. The company uses data analytics and AI to improve supply-chain efficiency yet evaluates all technologies through an environmental lens. Practices that threaten ecosystems are rejected, even when profitable, showing how purpose functions as an ethical filter for innovation (Ryan & Deci, 2020).

Three lessons emerge: purpose builds trust and resilience; it amplifies engagement and creativity; and it integrates ethics with strategy. Patagonia shows that when purpose is lived – not proclaimed – organisations can thrive amid complexity without compromising moral integrity.

Test Decisions Against True North

Bill George (2007) emphasises the role of crucibles in clarifying True North. Leaders can institutionalise this insight by creating purpose-tests for decisions. These tests should be practical, repeatable, and transparent. The following questions are critical:

- Traceability: Can we trace the decision back to our purpose?
- Proportionality: Does the decision serve the long-term good, not only immediate gains?
- Reversibility: Would we be proud to reverse or publicise this decision if scrutinised?

Case Study 2.4 Unilever under Paul Polman: Testing Decisions Against True North

When Paul Polman became CEO of Unilever in 2009, he inherited a global organisation under intense pressure to deliver short-term financial returns. Polman chose a different path. He committed Unilever to a broader purpose – improving people's lives while reducing environmental impact – through the launch of the Unilever Sustainable Living Plan (USLP), which embedded long-term social and environmental goals into corporate strategy (Unilever, 2010). This approach reflected the principles of *True North* leadership, which emphasise aligning decisions with deeply held purpose and values rather than short-term gain (George, 2007).

Under Polman, Unilever effectively institutionalised a *purpose test* for decision-making. Strategic choices were assessed for traceability to the company's purpose of serving people and planet (Unilever, 2010; Polman, 2011). They were evaluated for proportionality, prioritising long-term resilience over immediate profit – seen in continued investment in employees, brands, and innovation even during economic downturns (Unilever, 2020). Decisions were also tested for reversibility under public scrutiny. When Unilever faced a hostile takeover bid from Kraft Heinz in 2017, Polman rejected it, framing the bid as incompatible with the company's long-term purpose (Unilever, 2020).

By consistently applying this implicit purpose-test, Unilever resisted short-termism, aligned growth with long-term value creation, and strengthened trust among employees, partners, and consumers (George, 2007; Polman, 2011). The case demonstrates how testing decisions against *True North* can safeguard organisational identity while building enduring legitimacy and resilience.

Cultivate Personal Alignment

Organisational purpose requires leaders who embody personal alignment. When leaders' behaviour contradicts purpose, credibility collapses. George (2007) emphasises that leaders often discover personal purpose through life crucibles – formative trials. Leadership development programmes should encourage reflective storytelling to uncover these crucibles.

Case Study 2.5 Howard Schultz and Starbucks: Personal Alignment Through Crucibles

Bill George (2007) argues that authentic leadership is forged not primarily through position or skill, but through life experiences that test character. He describes these defining moments as crucibles – deeply challenging experiences that compel leaders to reflect on who they are and what they stand for. Through such trials, leaders discover their True North: an inner compass that anchors purpose, values, and leadership identity (George, 2007; George & Clayton, 2022).

The leadership journey of Howard Schultz, former CEO of Starbucks, offers a vivid illustration of this process. Schultz grew up in a working-class family in Brooklyn. When his father lost his job following a workplace injury, the family was left without health insurance and financial security. Witnessing his father's loss of dignity and vulnerability became a formative crucible that profoundly shaped Schultz's values around fairness, care, and respect for workers (George, 2007; Shortform, 2023).

When Schultz later led Starbucks, he translated these deeply personal convictions into organisational practice. He championed policies that provided health benefits even to part-time employees and sought to create a workplace grounded in dignity and mutual respect (George, 2007; Shortform, 2023). These decisions were not driven by branding or public relations; rather, they reflected Schultz's lived experience and personal alignment between values and action. As a result, his leadership carried credibility – employees and customers perceived Starbucks' stated values as authentic rather than performative.

This alignment had lasting impact. Starbucks evolved into more than a coffee retailer; it became associated with community, care, and employee wellbeing. Internally, this fostered engagement and loyalty; externally, it strengthened trust and brand affinity. As George (2007) notes, when leaders' actions are consistent with their purpose, their capacity to inspire endures – when they are not, credibility erodes.

George therefore emphasises reflective storytelling as a core leadership development practice: encouraging leaders to revisit their life stories, identify crucibles, and articulate the values that emerged (George, 2007; George & Clayton, 2022). In Schultz's case, early hardship became the moral foundation of an organisational purpose centred on dignity and care.

Reflective Exercise

Write about a time you acted against your values. What inner compass was missing? How might that experience clarify your purpose today?

Cross-Cutting Challenges in Applying Purpose

Even when leaders genuinely embrace purpose, translating it into daily practice presents significant and recurring challenges. Purpose is not a static declaration; it is a living commitment that must withstand pressure, ambiguity, and competing demands. Understanding these cross-cutting challenges enables leaders to navigate complexity while remaining authentic and credible.

One of the most visible risks is purpose-washing. When organisations articulate lofty purpose statements without corresponding changes in behaviour, stakeholders quickly detect the inconsistency. Such symbolic adoption of purpose erodes trust rather than strengthening it. As George (2007) argues, authenticity in leadership requires sustained alignment between values, decisions, and actions. Purpose must therefore be demonstrated repeatedly through choices, trade-offs, and accountability mechanisms, not merely communicated through branding.

A second challenge lies in the persistent tension between purpose and profit. Crises often force leaders to choose between short-term financial performance and long-term purpose. While empirical evidence suggests that organisations committed to sustainability and purpose outperform peers over time, maintaining this alignment demands courage and discipline, particularly under market pressure (Eccles, Ioannou, & Serafeim, 2014). Purpose-driven leadership requires resisting short-termism without abandoning economic responsibility.

Leaders must also manage conflicting stakeholder purposes. Investors may prioritise returns, employees may demand ethical practices and wellbeing, while communities emphasise social and environmental impact. These competing expectations cannot be resolved through simplistic trade-offs. Instead, leaders must exercise moral imagination to reframe dilemmas and seek integrative solutions that honour multiple values simultaneously (Werhane, 1999).

In multinational organisations, global versus local interpretation adds further complexity. A shared purpose may resonate differently across cultural contexts. Effective leaders maintain global clarity while allowing local adaptation, ensuring the purpose remains meaningful without becoming diluted or fragmented.

As illustrated earlier, Patagonia demonstrates how these challenges can be navigated when purpose functions as a true north. Guided by its mission to save our home planet (Chouinard, 2005), Patagonia aligns marketing with action, most notably through campaigns such as "Don't Buy This Jacket," which explicitly discouraged overconsumption. During economic downturns, the company has resisted cost-cutting measures that would compromise environmental or social commitments, prioritising long-term impact over short-term gain. Conflicts with suppliers over cost versus sustainability have been addressed through transparent engagement and shared purpose training, while regional adaptations – particularly in Asia – have framed environmental responsibility in culturally resonant terms without abandoning the global mission. Patagonia thus demonstrates that purpose can be globally coherent yet locally adaptable.

Because purpose is dynamic, leaders must continually revisit and operationalise it – especially as AI and machine intelligence expand decision-making capacity. Purpose ensures ethics are not outsourced to algorithms. Practical tools help sustain this alignment: purpose journals encourage weekly reflection; purpose scorecards integrate financial, stakeholder, and ethical metrics; narrative audits test whether organisational stories match lived practice; and purpose circles connect daily work to shared meaning. Codification without practice produces rhetoric, while practice without codification creates confusion. Effective leadership requires both.

Finally, leaders must confront deeper ethical provocations. Can purpose become propaganda? What happens when stakeholder purposes collide? Should AI be trained on organisational purpose, or should purpose remain a governance principle rather than code? Is purpose elitist, accessible only to large firms? Research suggests that authenticity, not scale, is decisive (Eccles, Ioannou, & Serafeim, 2014). These questions invite leaders to interrogate assumptions and test integrity. Ultimately, purpose must transcend products, withstand financial pressure, and inspire imagination – not merely constrain behaviour. When lived consistently, purpose becomes a source of resilience, legitimacy, and creative possibility.

Conclusion

Purpose functions as the *north* of the leadership compass – a fixed point of orientation amid uncertainty, acceleration, and expanding possibility. It is not a slogan or performance metric, but a multidimensional anchor that integrates authenticity, ethics, strategy, and societal contribution. From discovering one's *True North* to aligning personal passion with meaningful impact (P-Squared), purpose shapes how leaders decide, behave, and cultivate culture in the Age of Imagination.

As leaders such as Paul Polman demonstrate, when purpose is clearly articulated, embodied, and operationalised, it becomes both an anchor and a guide. It provides stability during disruption while directing innovation, creativity, and ethical action. Practical tools – reflection, stakeholder mapping, and purpose-driven storytelling – translate purpose from abstraction into everyday leadership practice.

In an era defined by AI, competing stakeholder demands, and global volatility, purpose is not a luxury but a necessity. Without it, organisations drift; with it, people, performance, and possibility gain coherence. Purpose also grounds storytelling – the quiet language of leadership – in credibility and trust.

To lead with purpose requires clarity and humility: clarity to simplify complexity, and humility to recalibrate through experience and learning. For leaders navigating the intersection of imagination and machine intelligence, purpose is both compass and ballast – steadying the organisation while enabling exploration. Discovering and living one's *True North*, personally and organisationally, remains the defining task of leadership in this era.

Reflective Questions

1. What is the deeper purpose that guides your leadership decisions, and how clearly does it align with your personal values, organisational mission, and responsibility to society?
2. When faced with pressure, incentives, or uncertainty, how do you ensure that your leadership remains anchored to purpose rather than drifting toward short-term gains or symbolic "purpose-washing"?
3. How can purpose function not only as an inspirational idea but as a daily discipline that shapes your judgement, resilience, and the long-term impact of the choices you make as a leader?

References

Al-Faruqi, I. R. (1992). *Al-tawhid: Its implications for thought and life*. International Institute of Islamic Thought.

Aristotle. (2000). *Nicomachean ethics* (R. Crisp, Trans.). Cambridge University Press. (Original work published ca. 350 BCE).

Avolio, B. J., & Gardner, W. L. (2005). Authentic leadership development: Getting to the root of positive forms of leadership. *The Leadership Quarterly, 16*(3), 315–338. https://doi.org/10.1016/j.leaqua.2005.03.001

Bass, B. M., & Riggio, R. E. (2006). *Transformational leadership* (2nd ed.). Lawrence Erlbaum.

Birchall, J., & Ketilson, L. H. (2009). *Resilience of the cooperative business model in times of crisis*. International Labour Organization.

Brown, M. E., & Treviño, L. K. (2006). Ethical leadership: A review and future directions. *The Leadership Quarterly, 17*(6), 595–616. https://doi.org/10.1016/j.leaqua.2006.10.004

Chouinard, Y. (2005). *Let my people go surfing: The education of a reluctant businessman*. Penguin Press.

Cicero, M. T. (2014). *On duties* (M. Atkins & M. Griffin, Eds. & Trans.). Cambridge University Press. (Original work published 44 BCE).

Collins, J. (2001). *Good to great: Why some companies make the leap… and others don't*. HarperCollins.

Collins, J. C., & Porras, J. I. (1994). *Built to last: Successful habits of visionary companies*. Harper Business.

Craig, N., & Snook, S. (2014). From purpose to impact. *Harvard Business Review, 92*(5), 104–111.

Daugherty, P. R., & Wilson, H. J. (2018). *Human + machine: Reimagining work in the age of AI*. Harvard Business Review Press.

Deloitte. (2023). *The Deloitte global 2023 Gen Z and Millennial survey*. Deloitte Insights.

Eccles, R. G., Ioannou, I., & Serafeim, G. (2014). The impact of corporate sustainability on organisational processes and performance. *Management Science, 60*(11), 2835–2857. https://doi.org/10.1287/mnsc.2014.1984

Fairhurst, G. T., & Uhl-Bien, M. (2012). Organizational discourse analysis (ODA): Examining leadership as a relational process. *The Leadership Quarterly, 23*(6), 1043–1062. https://doi.org/10.1016/j.leaqua.2012.10.005

Frankl, V. E. (1984). *Man's search for meaning*. Washington Square Press.

Freeman, R. E. (1984). *Strategic management: A stakeholder approach*. Pitman.

Freeman, R. E., Harrison, J. S., Wicks, A. C., Parmar, B., & de Colle, S. (2020). *Stakeholder theory: The state of the art*. Cambridge University Press.

George, B. (2007). *True north: Discover your authentic leadership*. Jossey-Bass.

George, B., & Clayton, Z. (2022). *True north: Emerging leader edition* (3rd ed.). Wiley.

Graen, G. B., & Uhl-Bien, M. (1995). Relationship-based approach to leadership: Development of leader–member exchange (LMX) theory. *Leadership Quarterly, 6*(2), 219–247. https://doi.org/10.1016/1048-9843(95)90036-5

Grant, A. M. (2008). The significance of task significance. *Journal of Applied Psychology, 93*(1), 108–124. https://doi.org/10.1037/0021-9010.93.1.108

Hamel, G., & Zanini, M. (2020). *Humanocracy: Creating organizations as amazing as the people inside them*. Harvard Business Review Press.

Hansen, M. T. (2018). *Great at work: How top performers do less, work better, and achieve more*. Simon & Schuster.

Hawken, P. (2017). *Drawdown: The most comprehensive plan ever proposed to reverse global warming*. Penguin Books.

Henderson, R. (2020). *Reimagining capitalism in a world on fire*. PublicAffairs.

Hurst, A. (2014). *The purpose economy: How your desire for impact, personal growth and community is changing the world*. Elevate.

Ibarra, H., & Rattan, A. (2022). Purpose-driven leadership for an age of flux. *MIT Sloan Management Review, 63*(4), 45–52.

International Labour Organization. (2012). *Cooperatives and the world of work*. ILO.

International Labour Organization. (2016). *Cooperatives and sustainable development: Goals, values and practices*. ILO.

Jaworski, J. (1996). *Synchronicity: The inner path of leadership*. Berrett-Koehler.

Kashdan, T. B., McKnight, P. E., & Goodman, F. R. (2021). Evolving positive psychology: A blueprint of uncharted territory. *Journal of Positive Psychology, 17*(2), 210–218. www.tandfonline.com/doi/full/10.1080/17439760.2021.2016906

Kolenda, D. K. (2001). *Leadership: The warrior's art*. The Army War College Foundation Press.

Korschun, D., Bhattacharya, C. B., & Swain, S. D. (2022). Corporate social responsibility, purpose, and trust. *Journal of Business Ethics, 181*(3), 743–760. https://doi.org/10.1007/s10551-021-04901-5

Martela, F., & Steger, M. F. (2016). The three meanings of meaning in life. *The Journal of Positive Psychology, 11*(5), 531–545. https://doi.org/10.1080/17439760.2015.1137623

Mittelstadt, B. D., Allo, P., Taddeo, M., Wachter, S., & Floridi, L. (2016). The ethics of algorithms: Mapping the debate. *Big Data & Society, 3*(2), 1–21. https://doi.org/10.1177/2053951716679679

Niedermeyer, E. (2019). *Ludicrous: The unvarnished story of Tesla Motors*. BenBella Books.

Nohria, N., & Khurana, R. (Eds.). (2010). *Handbook of leadership theory and practice*. Harvard Business Press.

Plato. (1992). *Republic* (G. M. A. Grube, Trans.; C. D. C. Reeve, Rev.). Hackett Publishing. (Original work published ca. 380 BCE).

Polman, P. (2011). *Remarks on long-term value creation and stakeholder capitalism*. Business from Purpose Interview Series.

Rey, C., Bastons, M., & Sotok, P. (2019). *Purpose-driven organizations*. Palgrave Macmillan.

Rosso, B. D., Dekas, K. H., & Wrzesniewski, A. (2010). On the meaning of work. *Research in Organizational Behavior, 30*, 91–127. https://doi.org/10.1016/j.riob.2010.09.001

Ryan, R. M., & Deci, E. L. (2020). Intrinsic and extrinsic motivation. *Contemporary Educational Psychology, 61*, 101860. https://doi.org/10.1016/j.cedpsych.2020.101860

Scharmer, O. (2009). *Theory U*. Berrett-Koehler.

Shakespeare, W. (2008). *As you like it* (J. Dusinberre, Ed.). Arden Shakespeare. (Original work published 1623).

Shortform. (2023). *Howard Schultz: Early life and leadership values*. www.shortform.com

Sinek, S. (2011). *Start with why*. Penguin.

Smith, W. K., & Lewis, M. W. (2011). Toward a theory of paradox: A dynamic equilibrium model of organizing. *Academy of Management Review, 36*(2), 381–403. https://doi.org/10.5465/amr.2009.0223

Steger, M. F. (2023). *Meaning in work and life*. Springer.

Tesla, Inc. (2020). *Impact report*. www.tesla.com/ns_videos/2020-tesla-impact-report.pdf

Uhl-Bien, M., & Arena, M. (2018). Leadership for organizational adaptability. *The Leadership Quarterly, 29*(1), 89–104. https://doi.org/10.1016/j.leaqua.2017.12.009

Unilever. (2010). *Unilever Sustainable Living Plan*. www.unilever.com/files/origin/9752ff2d82b8afabb507eb92c47b5dad795801d5.pdf/unilever-sustainable-living-plan.pdf

Unilever. (2020). *Unilever marks 10 years of the Sustainable Living Plan*. www.unilever.com/news/press-and-media/press-releases/2020/unilever-celebrates-10-years-of-the-sustainable-living-plan/

Weick, K. E. (1995). *Sensemaking in organizations*. Sage.

Werhane, P. H. (1999). *Moral imagination and management decision-making*. Oxford University Press.

Wheatley, M. J. (2006). *Leadership and the new science* (3rd ed.). Berrett-Koehler.

Chapter 3

People

Leading with Humanity, Imagination, and Emotional Intelligence

Introduction

March 2019. A gunman attacks two mosques in Christchurch. The world watches in horror. A nation mourns. And then a young Prime Minister steps forward. Jacinda Ardern does not come with policies, or speeches full of jargon. She comes with a scarf over her head. Tears in her eyes. She embraces grieving families, looks them in the eye, and says, "They are us." In that moment, she was pointing east to what we metaphorically call the *rising sun*: leadership through people, through empathy, through human connection. The *rising sun* matters because before people follow your vision, they need to feel your heart.

At dawn, the sun breaks the horizon, transforming darkness into light, uncertainty into clarity, fatigue into energy. In many cultures, sunrise is a metaphor for new beginnings, hope, and renewal. For leadership, the image of the *rising sun* captures something essential: leaders bring light to people's lives, helping them see possibilities, grow in confidence, and find meaning in their work. Without people, there is no leadership; without light, there is no dawn.

The industrial age cast people largely as resources: units of labour to be managed, optimised, and often reduced. The information age celebrated human capital and talent, elevating people to strategic assets but often reducing them to productivity metrics. In the Imagination Age, by contrast, people are recognised not only for what they can produce, but for what they can imagine, create, and inspire. Leaders today must cultivate environments where imagination flourishes and environments are defined by trust, empathy, and shared purpose.

The story of Satya Nadella's transformation of Microsoft illustrates this point vividly. When Nadella became CEO in 2014, Microsoft was widely perceived as bureaucratic, competitive internally, and slow to innovate. Instead of focusing first on technology, Nadella focused on people. He invoked a simple but profound cultural shift: from being a "know-it-all" organisation to a "learn-it-all" one. By embodying empathy shaped by his own life experiences as the father of a child with disabilities, Nadella repositioned Microsoft's leadership culture. Psychological safety grew, collaboration deepened, and innovation returned. Under his tenure, the company not only regained commercial momentum but also a renewed sense

DOI: 10.4324/9781003766414-3

of humanity (George, 2017). This example reveals a crucial insight: leadership of people is not primarily about control or charisma; it is about creating conditions where human beings can thrive. As Bill George argued in his book, *Authentic Leadership*, authenticity – self-awareness, relational transparency, and consistency of values – builds the trust that people need to bring their best selves to work (George, 2003). Transformational leadership theory reinforces this, highlighting the leader's role in providing vision, stimulation, and individual consideration (Bass, 1990). Self-determination theory adds a psychological dimension: people flourish when they experience autonomy, competence, and relatedness (Deci & Ryan, 1985; Gagné & Deci, 2005).

In other words, leadership in the Imagination Age requires the illumination of people's innate drives. Like the *rising sun*, leaders must warm the workplace with dignity, energise teams with vision, and illuminate pathways for creativity.

Why People Matter in the Imagination Age

Technology has fundamentally shifted the nature of work. Routine and repetitive tasks are increasingly automated, while algorithms now outperform humans in analytics, prediction, and optimisation. Yet the qualities machines cannot replicate such as imagination, empathy, ethical judgement, storytelling, and curiosity remain distinctly human (Orme, 2019; Goleman, 2006). When leaders fail to recognise this shift, organisations risk cultivating cultures of compliance that prioritise efficiency over meaning, and output over originality.

Consider two fictional organisations that mirror real-world responses to the Imagination Age. *DataMax Studios*, a media firm, adopted AI aggressively to streamline content production. In doing so, it marginalised human creators, reducing them to editors of machine-generated material. While efficiency initially improved, creativity declined, morale weakened, and audiences noticed the sameness in output. Innovation stalled, demonstrating how prioritising technology over people erodes organisational vitality. By contrast, *Aurora Collective* treated AI as an enabler rather than a substitute. Leaders framed technology as a tool to amplify rather than replace human creativity. Writers, designers, and musicians retained ownership of narrative and style while using AI for technical support. Experimentation was encouraged, failure was reframed as learning, and communities of practice flourished. The outcome was renewed creativity, high engagement, and a reputation for imaginative risk-taking. These contrasting examples underline a critical insight: machines may accelerate processes, but human-centred leadership sustains innovation.

Understanding why people matter requires a broader historical lens. In the industrial era, workers were treated as hands – components in mechanised systems optimised for efficiency (Taylor, 1911). The information age elevated heads, valuing knowledge and specialised expertise (Drucker, 1999). In the Imagination Age, however, what differentiates humans is not speed or calculation, but creativity, curiosity, empathy, and moral judgement (Daugherty & Wilson, 2018; Orme,

2019). Leadership must therefore shift focus from narrow productivity metrics to cultivating these uniquely human capacities.

Empathy enables leaders to build trust and relational depth, something machines can simulate but not genuinely experience (Goleman, 2006). Moral imagination – the capacity to envision ethical responses beyond existing frameworks – is increasingly vital in navigating AI-driven dilemmas (Werhane, 1999). Creativity and curiosity allow humans to contextualise, innovate, and collaborate in ways that produce original and meaningful outcomes (Amabile, 1996; Orme, 2019). Together, these capacities form the basis of human flourishing.

Flourishing, however, is culturally situated. Collectivist cultures emphasise harmony and belonging; individualist contexts prioritise autonomy and self-expression; African philosophies such as Ubuntu foreground interdependence and dignity (Mbigi, 2005); and Indigenous perspectives stress balance between people, community, and environment. Effective leadership respects these differences, enabling plural expressions of flourishing rather than imposing uniform norms.

Ultimately, the Imagination Age calls leaders to recognise people as ethical, imaginative co-creators. Technology may accelerate output, but it is human potential that illuminates possibility and sustains meaningful progress.

Theoretical Foundations of People-Centred Leadership

The foundations of people-centred leadership are grounded in several complementary perspectives. Transformational leadership (Burns, 1978; Bass, 1990) inspires followers to pursue collective goals through vision, intellectual stimulation, and individualised consideration, while authentic leadership (George, 2003, 2007; Avolio & Gardner, 2005) emphasises self-awareness and alignment between values and actions, fostering trust and commitment. Emotional intelligence (Salovey & Mayer, 1990; Goleman, 1998) operates as a critical enabling capability across these approaches, allowing leaders to recognise and regulate their own emotions, empathise with others, and sustain constructive relationships under pressure. By strengthening awareness, self-management, social awareness, and relationship management, emotional intelligence supports ethical judgement, psychological safety, and meaningful engagement. Self-determination theory (Deci & Ryan, 1985; Gagné & Deci, 2005) further highlights the importance of satisfying autonomy, competence, and relatedness to drive intrinsic motivation, while psychological safety (Edmondson, 1999) ensures a climate in which individuals can take interpersonal risks, voice ideas, and learn without fear of retribution. Complementing these perspectives, *The Human Edge* (Orme, 2019) – which reflects the spirit of the Imagination Age – underscores consciousness, curiosity, creativity, and collaboration as uniquely human capabilities. Collins' (2001) principle of "First Who, Then What" reinforces the primacy of placing the right people in the right roles, leading to purpose-aligned roles.

Taking together these perspectives, this chapter introduces a People-Centric Leadership Model (Figure 3.1), positioning people not as resources to be managed,

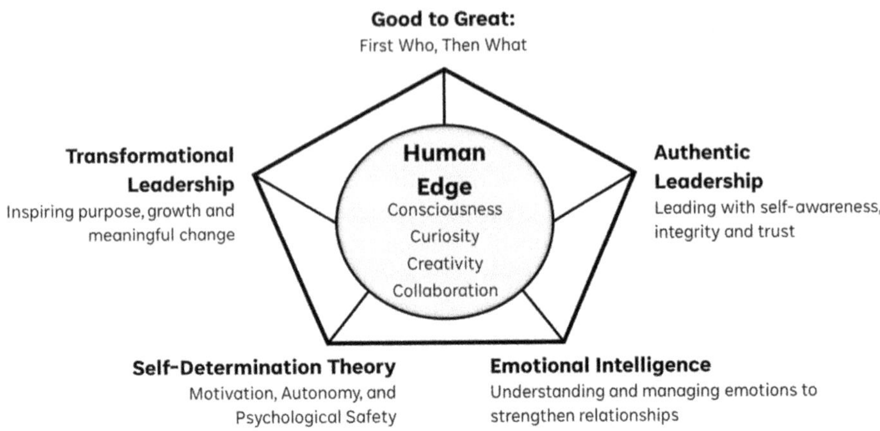

Figure 3.1 People-Centric Leadership Model.

Source: Developed by the author, informed by established leadership and organisational research.

but as emotionally intelligent, motivated, and relational co-creators of organisational success. The model illustrates how human potential is activated through emotional intelligence and leadership practices, and aligned through purpose, trust, and meaningful roles to enable sustainable performance in the Imagination Age.

Transformational Leadership

The concept of transformational leadership emerged from James MacGregor Burns' seminal work *Leadership* (1978), distinguishing transactional leaders – those who exchange rewards for compliance – from transformational leaders, who engage followers in pursuit of higher moral purpose and collective good. Bass (1990) expanded this framework with four central dimensions: idealised influence, inspirational motivation, intellectual stimulation, and individualised consideration. Judge and Piccolo's (2004) meta-analysis confirms strong correlations between transformational leadership and follower satisfaction, motivation, and performance. In creative contexts, such as Pixar Animation Studios, Ed Catmull fostered a culture of candour where all employees could contribute ideas, resulting in films like *Toy Story* and cultivating trust and psychological ownership among teams (Catmull & Wallace, 2014). Transformational leadership thus energises people, illuminates possibilities, and nurtures engagement.

Authentic Leadership

The early 2000s saw growing disillusionment with corporate scandals, leading Bill George to articulate authentic leadership as a model rooted in *integrity, self-awareness*, and *moral responsibility* (George,2003). Authentic leaders act consistently with their values, maintain transparency, and prioritise long-term stewardship over short-term gain. George (2007) emphasised that authentic leaders discover their *True North* through life experiences and crucibles that shape resilience. Avolio and Gardner (2005) situate authenticity within positive organisational scholarship, linking it to trust, hope, and psychological capital. Satya Nadella at Microsoft exemplifies this approach. His empathy, informed by personal experiences, fostered a corporate culture of humility, learning, and inclusivity, driving renewed innovation (George, 2017). Authentic leadership reassures employees that their leader is principled, trustworthy, and invested in collective growth.

The Human Edge

In the Imagination Age, human capabilities – curiosity, consciousness, collaboration, and creativity – are the primary source of competitive advantage (Orme, 2019). In his book, The Human Edge, Orme (2019) emphasises that technological proficiency alone is insufficient; organisations thrive when employees are encouraged to ask questions, challenge assumptions, and co-create solutions. Leaders who cultivate these traits empower individuals to innovate, solve complex problems, and contribute to shared purpose. For example, Atlassian encourages employees to engage in self-directed innovation through initiatives such as *ShipIt Days* (formerly *FedEx Days*), where employees are given time and autonomy to work on projects of their own choosing. These practices foster creativity, collaboration, and intrinsic motivation, leading to new products, process improvements, and organisational learning (Atlassian, 2023; Rigby et al., 2016). Integrating The Human Edge into leadership practice reinforces psychological safety, nurtures intrinsic motivation, and enhances engagement, demonstrating that human potential is both a differentiator and a driver of organisational success.

Good to Great: First Who, Then What

Collins' (2001) principle of "First Who, Then What" highlights the importance of people over strategy. Leaders must first ensure the right individuals are in the right seats before deciding on direction or strategy. The premise is simple yet powerful: talented, values-aligned employees will navigate uncertainty and generate superior outcomes even when strategy evolves. For instance, Level 5 leaders at companies like Kimberly-Clark focused on assembling teams of capable, committed individuals before executing bold strategic shifts, resulting in long-term success. By prioritising the right people, leaders create a foundation of trust, competence, and engagement, amplifying the effects of transformational, authentic, and human-centred leadership practices. This approach underscores that sustainable organisational excellence begins with people, not processes.

Emotional Intelligence

People-centred leadership depends not only on leaders' knowledge or intend, but on how they perceive, regulate, and respond to emotion in themselves and others. Emotional intelligence (EI) – commonly defined as the capacity to recognise, understand, manage, and use emotions constructively – has emerged as a foundational capability for leading human systems characterised by uncertainty, interdependence, and emotional complexity (Salovey & Mayer, 1990; Goleman, 1998).

Research consistently shows that leadership effectiveness, trust, and inclusion are deeply shaped by emotional awareness, self-regulation, empathy, and relational skill, particularly in contexts where authority alone is insufficient (Boyatzis, 2018). Within people-centred leadership, EI enables leaders to create psychological safety, sustain meaningful relationships, and respond thoughtfully rather than reactively under pressure.

It supports ethical judgement by tempering impulse, strengthens authenticity by increasing self-awareness, and enhances collaboration by fostering empathy and social attunement (Hannah et al., 2011). Importantly, leadership failure rarely stems from a lack of values or competence; it more often arises from unmanaged emotion – fear, ego, anxiety, or defensiveness – that distorts perception and erodes trust (Bandura, 1999; Tenbrunsel & Messick, 2004). Seen through this lens, emotional intelligence is not a soft interpersonal skill but a stabilising human capacity that enables leaders to lead with humanity, sustain inclusion, and translate intention into responsible action. As such, EI forms a critical theoretical pillar of people-centred leadership in the Imagination Age.

Table 3.1 summarises the main dimensions of Emotional Intelligence (EI), their meaning, and their impact on leadership, based primarily on Goleman's framework (Goleman, 1995, 1998; Goleman et al., 2002) and related scholarship.

Table 3.1 The Main Dimensions of Emotional Intelligence (EI)

EI dimensions	*What it means*	*Impact on leadership*
Self-Awareness	Understanding one's own emotions, strengths, and limitations (Goleman, 1998).	Enables authentic leadership, sound judgement, and greater credibility with others.
Self-Regulation	Managing emotions and impulses, especially under pressure (Goleman, 1998).	Helps leaders remain calm, ethical, and consistent during uncertainty or conflict.
Motivation	Inner drive to pursue goals with persistence and optimism (Goleman, 1995).	Sustains resilience, encourages innovation, and inspires commitment among teams.
Empathy	Understanding the emotions and perspectives of others (Goleman, 1998).	Builds trust, supports inclusive leadership, and strengthens relationships.
Social Skills	Ability to communicate, influence, and manage relationships effectively (Goleman et al., 2002).	Enables collaboration, conflict resolution, and alignment of teams toward shared goals.

Intellectual Adda | Emotional Intelligence in Leadership: A Conversation with S M Arifuzzaman

Professor S M Arifuzzaman's professional journey has unfolded across disciplines, sectors, and geographies. Educated at leading universities in Asia and Europe, he has taught at prominent institutions in Bangladesh while remaining deeply engaged in corporate training, executive education, and applied research. His career has not followed a linear path. Trained initially as a computer engineer, he moved into finance before transitioning fully into leadership development. Each shift added depth to his understanding of people, systems, and decision-making under pressure.

Today, Arifuzzaman is a seasoned strategist and emotional intelligence (EI) practitioner with more than two decades of experience in leadership development and organisational change. His work bridges theory and practice: from designing EI-based leadership programmes to coaching senior executives and supporting culture transformation. What distinguishes his approach is a sustained attentiveness to the human dimension of leadership – how emotions, relationships, and inner discipline shape trust, inclusion, and long-term performance. In the Imagination Age, where complexity and speed increasingly define organisational life, his work invites a deeper reflection on leadership as a people-centred practice.

Author *In today's volatile environment, leadership often feels relentless. What does emotional intelligence mean when leading people through constant disruption?*

Arifuzzaman: Disruption is no longer episodic – it is continuous. Leaders face regulatory change, market uncertainty, social pressure, and rising expectations from their people. In this context, emotional intelligence is not about being *nice*; it is about being steady. I have seen leaders lose trust not because their strategy failed, but because their emotional responses unsettled others – panic in meetings, frustration directed at teams, or emotional withdrawal when reassurance was needed. Emotional intelligence begins with self-regulation. When leaders manage themselves well, they create a sense of safety for others. That emotional steadiness becomes a form of leadership in itself.

Author: *How does emotional intelligence shape the way leaders relate to people when decisions must be made quickly, and information is incomplete?*

Arifuzzaman: Most significant decisions are made without full information. Under pressure, people tend to react – either by rushing or by freezing. Emotional intelligence creates a pause, not necessarily in action, but in awareness. That pause helps leaders distinguish between facts and assumptions, between urgency and anxiety. Leaders with strong EI listen more carefully, remain open to dissent, and avoid transferring their stress onto others. This is especially important for people-centred leadership, because how decisions are made often matters as much as the decisions themselves.

Author: *Many leadership failures seem less about competence and more about erosion of trust. What role does EI play when values and integrity are tested?*

Arifuzzaman: Ethical challenges rarely arrive as dramatic crises. They appear quietly -through pressure to take shortcuts, to stay silent, or to *adjust* decisions for convenience. In my experience, leaders do not abandon values suddenly; they drift under emotional strain.

Emotional intelligence helps leaders recognise that strain early. It builds the capacity to tolerate discomfort without compromising principles. Courage, in leadership, is often emotional before it is moral. Leaders who can sit with anxiety are far more likely to act with integrity.

Author: *As AI and automation reshape work, how can leaders remain effective without losing their humanity?*

Arifuzzaman: Technology may accelerate work, but leadership remains relational. People still need to feel seen, heard, and respected. Emotional intelligence ensures that leaders do not sacrifice human connection in the pursuit of speed or efficiency. I have worked with organisations that invested heavily in systems but struggled because leaders failed to understand what their people were feeling – fear of change, insecurity, or exhaustion. EI enables leaders to drive performance while preserving dignity. In a world increasingly shaped by algorithms, emotionally intelligent leadership reminds people that they still matter.

Closing Reflection

In this Intellectual Adda, Professor Arifuzzaman illuminates emotional intelligence not as a peripheral skill, but as a foundational capacity for people-centred leadership. His insights reveal EI as a quiet discipline that enables leaders to remain steady, humane, and trustworthy – especially when pressure is high and certainty is scarce.

Self-Determination Theory: Motivation, Autonomy, and Psychological Safety

Self-Determination Theory (SDT) provides a foundational psychological lens on motivation, identifying autonomy, competence, and relatedness as the core drivers of engagement, creativity, and sustained performance (Deci & Ryan, 1985). These motivational needs, however, do not operate in isolation; they are most effectively realised within environments of psychological safety, where individuals feel able to speak up, experiment, and learn without fear of negative consequences. Organisations such as Spotify operationalise SDT through autonomous squads that balance freedom with mastery and connectedness, fostering a culture of innovation and rapid adaptation while maintaining coordination and trust (Kniberg & Ivarsson, 2012).

Psychological safety plays a critical enabling role in this process. Edmondson (1999) demonstrated that teams with higher psychological safety often report more errors – not because they fail more frequently, but because members feel safe to admit mistakes, surface problems early, and learn collectively. This insight was reinforced by Google's multi-year Project Aristotle, which identified psychological safety as the single most important factor distinguishing high-performing teams, outweighing individual talent, seniority, or team composition (Rozovsky, 2015). The study revealed that effective teams are characterised by open communication, dependability, clarity of roles, shared meaning, and a sense of impact.

Practical illustrations further reinforce this relationship. Toyota's Andon Cord system – a primary mechanism for implementing the Jidoka principle – empowers any employee to halt production when issues arise, embedding psychological safety directly into operational practice and enhancing quality, trust, and adaptability (Toyota: Online). In the Imagination Age, leaders must therefore design environments that simultaneously satisfy the psychological needs outlined by SDT and cultivate psychological safety, recognising that innovation depends not on control, but on courage supported by trust.

Operationalising People-Centred Leadership

Leadership theories illuminate principles, but their true value emerges only when they shape everyday practice. The metaphor of the rising sun – symbolising illumination, growth, and renewal – comes alive in how leaders communicate, distribute authority, respond to difference, and balance care with accountability. In the Imagination Age, people-centred leadership is not an abstract ideal; it is enacted through disciplined practices that unlock human potential, creativity, and ethical judgement. This chapter recommends four interrelated practices that can translate philosophy into action: narrative and inspiration, distributed authority, inclusive culture, and empathetic discipline. Together, they operationalise humanity and imagination in organisational life.

Narrative and Inspiration: Harnessing the Power of Stories

Stories are powerful vehicles for meaning, connection, and shared direction (Denning, 2005). For leaders, storytelling functions as emotional data, conveying strategy and values through lived experience rather than abstract instruction. Research shows that stories enhance understanding of organisational vision (Gardner, 2011) and embed values in collective memory (Boal & Schultz, 2007). Satya Nadella's reframing of Microsoft's culture from a "know-it-all" to a "learn-it-all" organisation demonstrates how narrative can humanise leadership and energise performance (Nadella, 2017). By sharing his personal journey of empathy and learning, Nadella modelled vulnerability and reframed failure as growth.

Similarly, Anne Wojcicki at 23andMe used narrative to anchor innovation in human significance. By sharing family health stories, she framed the mission of empowering individuals with their genetic information in ethical and personal terms, not merely scientific or commercial ones. This narrative fostered cross-functional collaboration, encouraged experimentation, and reinforced responsibility for ethical data use – sustaining trust and engagement in a highly regulated industry. In practice, leaders operationalise narrative by sharing personal stories of vulnerability to model authenticity (Avolio & Gardner, 2005), celebrating collective successes to reinforce resilience, and crafting aspirational stories that invite imagination about the future.

Distributed Authority: From Control to Empowerment

Adaptive challenges cannot be solved by hierarchical expertise alone (Heifetz, 1994). Distributed authority relocates decision-making closer to the work, strengthening autonomy, motivation, and creativity (Deci & Ryan, 1985). Buurtzorg, the Dutch community nursing organisation, eliminated traditional management layers in favour of self-managed teams supported by digital tools – resulting in higher productivity, patient satisfaction, and staff retention (Kreitzer et al., 2015). Similarly, Spotify's squad model demonstrates how self-organising teams adapt rapidly while leaders act as coaches rather than controllers (Kniberg & Ivarsson, 2012). Shared leadership approaches consistently outperform rigid hierarchies in complex environments (Pearce & Conger, 2003). In practice, leaders operationalise distributed authority by empowering teams to set milestones, asking generative questions rather than issuing instructions, and legitimising initiative at every level.

Inclusive Culture: Celebrating Diversity

Diversity fuels innovation only when paired with inclusion (Shore et al., 2018). Psychological safety – the belief that one can speak up without fear – is essential for inclusion to function (Edmondson, 1999). Unilever exemplifies this by embedding equity, diversity, and inclusion into leadership development and innovation strategy. Under CEO Alan Jope, inclusion is positioned not as compliance, but as a strategic driver of performance and legitimacy (Unilever, 2021). Leaders operationalise inclusion by practising active listening, ensuring equitable policies in pay and progression, and using symbolic acts – whose voices are amplified, whose stories are told – to signal belonging.

Empathetic Discipline: Balancing Care and Accountability

People-centred leadership integrates compassion with high standards. Empathy without boundaries risks indulgence; discipline without care becomes authoritarian (Cameron, 2012). The New Zealand All Blacks illustrate how excellence can coexist with humility and respect, combining rigorous performance expectations with deep care for people (Kerr, 2013). Leaders operationalise empathetic discipline by communicating clear goals while recognising personal context, delivering feedback that affirms dignity while addressing gaps, and using restorative approaches to conflict rather than punitive ones.

Integrated Application in Practice

These four practices are most powerful when applied together. For example, leaders in an AI start-up facing rapid scaling can preserve culture by grounding growth in a founding narrative of "technology for human dignity," empowering teams to define milestones, embracing global and flexible talent, and enforcing clear ethical boundaries with accountability. In doing so, the rising sun metaphor becomes operational: leadership illuminates rather than controls, enabling imagination to become collective power (Table 3.2).

People-centred leadership is not a soft alternative to performance. It is a disciplined, integrated approach that illuminates human potential while advancing organisational goals – ensuring that, in the Imagination Age, humanity and imagination remain the sources of sustainable excellence.

Table 3.2 Practical Applications of People-Centred Leadership

Practice	*Practical applications*
Narrative & Inspiration	Share personal stories of vulnerability (Avolio & Gardner, 2005); celebrate collective wins; articulate aspirational future narratives (Denning, 2005; Gardner, 2011).
Distributed Authority	Empower self-organising teams (Kniberg & Ivarsson, 2012); practise shared leadership (Pearce & Conger, 2003); lead as coach, not commander (Heifetz, 1994).
Inclusive Culture	Foster psychological safety (Edmondson, 1999); ensure equitable policies; amplify diverse voices (Shore et al., 2018; Unilever, 2021).
Empathetic Discipline	Set clear standards with care; provide dignity-affirming feedback; use restorative conflict practices (Cameron, 2012; Kerr, 2013).

Case Study 3.1 Turning Followers into Leaders

Deep beneath the ocean's surface, where error can be fatal, Captain David Marquet confronted one of the most profound leadership challenges of his career. Appointed commander of the USS *Santa Fe* – a submarine notorious for poor performance and low morale – Marquet inherited a crew conditioned to obey orders rather than think independently. What followed became one of the most striking leadership transformations in modern naval history (Marquet, 2012).

The turning point came during a sea trial when Marquet issued an order that was technically impossible on that class of submarine. Instead of questioning it, the officer repeated the command, and a sailor attempted to execute it, despite knowing it made no sense. In that moment, Marquet realised the problem was not competence but culture. The leadership system rewarded compliance over judgement.

Marquet immediately abandoned traditional command-and-control leadership. In its place, he introduced *intent-based leadership*. Rather than issuing orders, he stated intentions – inviting sailors to decide how to achieve them. "Start the reactor" became "I intend to start the reactor." This subtle shift compelled sailors to think, understand systems, and take responsibility.

Gradually, silence gave way to initiative. Sailors began identifying risks, offering solutions, and acting with confidence. Trust and pride flourished. The *Santa Fe* evolved from one of the fleet's weakest submarines into one of its strongest, producing an extraordinary number of future captains.

Marquet's lesson is enduring: treat people as followers and they remain so; treat them as leaders and they rise. Leadership, at its best, is not about exercising power, but about releasing it in others (Marquet, 2012).

Leadership as Illumination: Reflection and Renewal

The People-Centric Leadership model provides structure, but leadership comes alive only in daily practice. The metaphor of the rising sun reminds us that leadership is not a static achievement or a positional entitlement; it is a continuous act of illumination. Just as the sun rises each day to energise life, leaders must repeatedly renew their commitment to human dignity, imagination, and ethical responsibility. Leadership in the Imagination Age is therefore less about control and more about creating the conditions in which people can flourish.

From Concept to Daily Practice

Leadership in the Imagination Age cannot be reduced to policies, frameworks, or strategies alone. It demands relational attention and moral presence. Leaders shape environments in which imagination, empathy, and courage either emerge naturally or are quietly suppressed. Human action gains meaning when people come together to speak, reflect, and create and leaders resemble the rising sun: they do not force growth but illuminate possibilities, invite dialogue, and enable ethical reflection. Leadership shifts from directing outcomes to cultivating human capacity, where success is measured not only by outputs, but by the quality of human thriving within the system.

Daily Disciplines of Renewal

The rising sun metaphor also underscores rhythm and renewal. Trust, inspiration, and engagement are not achieved once and sustained indefinitely; they must be renewed daily. Small acts – listening with attention, recognising effort, celebrating learning, and creating space for creativity – accumulate into cultures of light rather than exhaustion. Kouzes and Posner (2017) describe leadership as a set of ordinary, consistent practices that produce extraordinary cultures over time. People-centred leadership is sustained through such disciplines, inviting leaders to reflect continually on whether their words and actions energise or deplete those around them.

Leadership Beyond the Organisation

Illumination does not stop at organisational boundaries. In times of inequality, polarisation, and technological disruption, leadership in civic, educational, and political spheres carries similar moral weight. New Zealand Prime Minister Jacinda Ardern's response to the Christchurch mosque shootings demonstrated people-centred leadership at a societal scale. Her empathetic language, inclusive symbolism, and visible solidarity fostered trust and collective healing, reinforcing leadership as a relational and ethical act rather than a display of authority (Wilson, 2020). Leadership, wherever it occurs, becomes an invitation to dignity, imagination, and shared humanity.

Reframing Success: Trust, Dialogue, and the Legacy of Developing People

People-centred leadership fundamentally reframes what success means. Traditional metrics – profit, efficiency, market share – capture only part of organisational vitality. Research on flourishing suggests that wellbeing, meaning, and trust are not peripheral but central to sustainable performance (Cameron, 2012; Seligman, 2011). Organisations such as Patagonia illustrate how embedding ethical purpose and empowerment strengthens resilience and innovation.

Trust becomes the core currency of leadership. Maxwell (2013) argues that authentic influence begins at the permission level, where people follow because they "want to," not because they "have to." Wheatley (2006) similarly emphasises that organisations thrive through networks of trust and meaning rather than control. High-quality leader–member relationships consistently predict stronger commitment and performance (Graen & Uhl-Bien, 1995, as cited in Nohria & Khurana, 2010).

Case Study 3.2 Climbing Maxwell's Five Levels: Leading for Productivity and People

John Maxwell's Five Levels of Leadership offer a practical lens for understanding how leadership matures from authority to authentic influence: Position, Permission, Production, People Development, and Pinnacle (Maxwell, 2013). The model is particularly useful for navigating a central leadership tension in the Imagination Age – the balance between human care and performance.

Consider Alex, a composite figure reflecting the journeys of many contemporary leaders. When Alex was promoted to manager in a mid-sized technology firm, he entered leadership at Level 1: Position. His authority derived solely from his title. Team members complied, but motivation was limited. Under pressure to deliver results, Alex focused heavily on deadlines and metrics, often overlooking emotional wellbeing and individual differences within the team.

Realising the limits of positional authority, Alex moved to Level 2: Permission, where relationships become central. He invested time in one-to-one conversations, listened actively, and sought to understand each person's strengths and challenges. Trust grew, and the team began to engage more openly. As Maxwell (2013) suggests, at this level people follow because they "want to," not because they "have to."

With trust established, the team progressed to Level 3: Production. Clear goals, stronger collaboration, and mutual accountability led to tangible results, including the successful early delivery of a major project. Performance improved precisely because people felt valued, reinforcing Maxwell's (2013) argument that results and relationships are mutually reinforcing.

Over time, Alex progressed into a senior leadership role. Now he has focused on Level 4: People Development, mentoring emerging leaders and delegating meaningful responsibility. Leadership capacity spread across the team. Over time, Alex experienced moments of Level 5: Pinnacle, where his influence shaped culture beyond his formal role. The organisation he leads is known for both high performance and psychological safety.

Alex's journey illustrates that leadership growth is not linear but relational. The Five Levels show that effective leadership does not require choosing between productivity and humanity; it requires cultivating both simultaneously (Maxwell, 2013).

Trust deepens through dialogue. Jaworski (1996) describes dialogue as a space where purpose is discovered collectively rather than imposed. Through dialogue, people-centred leaders co-create meaning, surface imagination, and enable ethical sense-making. Ultimately, leadership is measured by the people it develops. At Level 4 of Maxwell's model, leaders shift focus from personal success to investing in others' growth (Maxwell, 2013). Transformational leadership reinforces this emphasis on development, inspiration, and individualised consideration (Bass & Riggio, 2006, as cited in Nohria & Khurana, 2010).

Leadership grounded in trust, dialogue, and development leaves a lasting legacy. As Jaworski (1996) reminds us, leaders participate in a story larger than themselves. When leaders illuminate people rather than overshadow them, they create cultures – and futures – that endure.

Case Study 3.3 Bob Chapman and Barry-Wehmiller – Truly Human Leadership

Bob Chapman, CEO of Barry-Wehmiller, provides a compelling example of people-centred leadership grounded in dignity, care, and shared responsibility. As documented in *Everybody Matters*, Chapman reframed leadership around a simple yet radical belief: "everyone deserves to be cared for" (Chapman & Sisodia, 2015). This philosophy was put to the test during the recession, when Barry-Wehmiller experienced a sharp decline of approximately 35% in orders. Conventional business logic pointed towards layoffs. Chapman, however, posed a different question: *What would a caring family do in this situation?* (Chapman & Sisodia, 2015).

Rather than dismissing employees, Chapman introduced a series of collective sacrifices. All employees participated in mandatory four-week unpaid furloughs, spreading the burden across the organisation. Retirement matching and executive bonuses were suspended, and Chapman himself took a significant personal pay cut. Throughout this period, leadership communicated transparently, emphasising trust, shared sacrifice, and collective survival rather than fear or blame.

The outcomes were striking. Instead of declining morale, employees reported feeling valued rather than expendable. Trust deepened, strengthening psychological safety and reinforcing a sense of belonging. When economic conditions improved, Barry-Wehmiller emerged stronger, continuing to grow and successfully acquire new firms.

This case illustrates that people-centred leadership is neither naïve nor sentimental. As Barry-Wehmiller demonstrates, leadership rooted in human dignity can generate strategic resilience, loyalty, and long-term organisational strength (Chapman & Sisodia, 2015).

The Shadows of the Rising Sun: Tensions and Challenges

The metaphor of the rising sun evokes warmth, renewal, and illumination. Yet every sunrise also casts shadows. Leadership that places people at the centre inevitably encounters tensions and contradictions that cannot be wished away. The tensions, however, do not undermine people-centred leadership; rather, they reveal its complexity and the vigilance it demands.

People versus Productivity: The Dilemma

One of the most enduring leadership tensions is balancing care for people with demands for productivity. People flourish when their needs for autonomy, relatedness, and recognition are met (Deci & Ryan, 1985), yet organisations operate under pressure for efficiency, shareholder returns, and competitive performance. Walton (1985) described this oscillation as a shift between "control" systems, focused on efficiency, and "commitment" systems, focused on trust and development. Empirical evidence suggests that pursuing both simultaneously often generates contradictions (Boxall & Purcell, 2016).

The case of Amazon illustrates this tension vividly. Its relentless focus on customer obsession and operational excellence has driven extraordinary value creation, yet it has also attracted criticism for warehouse environments where metrics-driven productivity can overshadow worker wellbeing (Bensinger, 2021). The dilemma is real, but it is also false to frame it as an either–or choice. Pfeffer (1998) demonstrated that high-performance work systems can integrate productivity with people development through participation, training, and supportive culture. People-centred leaders do not deny the tension; they continuously negotiate it, recognising that long-term performance depends on human sustainability.

Empathy Fatigue: The Risk of Over-Identification

Empathy is central to people-centred leadership, but it carries risks. Psychologists describe empathy fatigue or compassion fatigue as emotional exhaustion resulting from prolonged exposure to others' distress (Figley, 2002). Leaders, particularly in caring professions or crisis contexts, may over-identify with their teams and neglect their own limits. During the COVID-19 pandemic, many healthcare leaders faced precisely this dilemma. While supporting frontline staff with compassion, they struggled with personal exhaustion, moral distress, and resource scarcity. Shanafelt et al. (2020) documented high levels of burnout among leaders linked to emotional overextension.

Sustainable people-centred leadership therefore requires empathic regulation – distinguishing between empathy (feeling with) and compassion (caring without being consumed). It also requires peer support networks where leaders themselves receive care, and clear boundaries that acknowledge leaders cannot carry every emotional burden personally. Empathy must be paired with self-care and structural support.

Cultural Variability: Flourishing Across Cultures

The meaning of flourishing varies across cultures, creating another tension. Practices that empower in one context may alienate in another. Distributed authority may be celebrated in Scandinavia but viewed with suspicion in high power-distance cultures (Hofstede, 2001). Google's Project Aristotle identified psychological safety as critical to team effectiveness (Rozovsky, 2015), yet its enactment differs markedly between contexts such as Japan – where indirect communication prevails – and the United States, where direct expression is valued.

People-centred leaders must therefore practise cultural humility: recognising the limits of their own assumptions and adapting principles sensitively to local contexts (Hook et al., 2013). This involves dialogue with cultural insiders, attentiveness to norms, and flexibility in application rather than rigid standardisation.

Technology Temptation: People versus Algorithms

The rise of AI introduces a further challenge: the temptation to delegate people leadership to algorithms. In gig-economy platforms, automated systems allocate work, monitor performance, and even terminate contracts, often without human dialogue. Such algorithmic management risks stripping people of dignity, agency, and voice (Rosenblat & Stark, 2016). Scheduling algorithms in retail, designed to optimise labour costs, frequently produce unstable shifts that undermine wellbeing and work–life balance (Kantor, 2014). While efficient, these practices erode trust and long-term commitment. Technology should augment humanity, not replace it. Leaders must retain responsibility for feedback, recognition, conflict resolution, and ethical judgement. Data can inform decisions, but only humans can provide meaning.

Navigating the Tensions: Towards Paradoxical Leadership

These challenges call for what Smith and Lewis (2011) describe as paradoxical leadership: the capacity to hold competing demands without prematurely resolving them. Paradoxical leaders recognise that productivity and people are interdependent, empathy requires boundaries, cultural universals coexist with local particularities, and technology offers both promise and peril. The rising sun illuminates potential while casting shadows. People-centred leadership does not eliminate these tensions; it navigates them with humility, reflection, and adaptability. It is in negotiating these contradictions that leaders reveal their deepest humanity and their greatest capacity to inspire.

Conclusion

To lead people is to face the east – to stand where light breaks through and possibility begins. In the Imagination Age, people-centred leadership is not a set of techniques but a way of seeing: a commitment to dignity, creativity, and human flourishing. As technology amplifies capability, it is empathy, moral judgement, imagination, and trust that ultimately define leadership effectiveness.

The metaphor of the rising sun clarifies this role. Leaders do not command growth; they create the conditions in which it emerges. Through trust, psychological safety, authentic dialogue, and development, leaders enable performance, innovation, and commitment to arise naturally. This work is neither sentimental nor episodic. Like the daily sunrise, people-centred leadership depends on continual renewal – listening deeply, recognising contributions, embracing vulnerability, and sustaining meaningful conversation.

Within the leadership compass, the east animates the whole journey. Purpose gives direction, but people give it life. Performance follows when people are energised, and possibility is reached only through collective effort. Storytelling binds these dimensions, aligning meaning with action.

Ultimately, leadership begins and ends with people. When leaders turn towards the east, they accept the responsibility to illuminate human potential – ensuring that, in the Imagination Age, progress remains grounded in humanity and the future is shaped together.

Reflective Questions

1. How consciously do you recognise and respond to the emotional realities of the people you lead, and how does your emotional awareness influence the culture of trust and psychological safety within your team?
2. In what ways do your everyday leadership practices – such as listening, feedback, storytelling, and empowerment – help people feel valued, inspired, and connected to a shared purpose?
3. Do you see people primarily as resources to achieve performance targets, or as the true source of creativity, resilience, and innovation within your organisation – and how does this belief shape the way you lead?

References

Amabile, T. M. (1996). *Creativity in context*. Westview Press.

Atlassian. (2023). *ShipIt days: Innovating at Atlassian*. www.atlassian.com/company/shipit

Avolio, B. J., & Gardner, W. L. (2005). Authentic leadership development: Getting to the root of positive forms of leadership. *The Leadership Quarterly, 16*(3), 315–338. https://doi.org/10.1016/j.leaqua.2005.03.001

Bandura, A. (1999). Moral disengagement in the perpetration of inhumanities. *Personality and Social Psychology Review, 3*(3), 193–209. https://doi.org/10.1207/s15327957pspr0303_3

Bass, B. M. (1990). From transactional to transformational leadership: Learning to share the vision. *Organizational Dynamics, 18*(3), 19–31. https://doi.org/10.1016/0090-2616(90)90061-S

Bass, B. M., & Riggio, R. E. (2006). *Transformational leadership* (2nd ed.). Lawrence Erlbaum Associates.

Bensinger, G. (2021, March 11). Amazon's great labour awakening. *The New York Times*.

Boal, K. B., & Schultz, P. L. (2007). Storytelling, time, and evolution: The role of strategic leadership in complex adaptive systems. *The Leadership Quarterly, 18*(4), 411–428. https://doi.org/10.1016/j.leaqua.2007.04.008

Boxall, P., & Purcell, J. (2016). *Strategy and human resource management* (4th ed.). Palgrave Macmillan.

Boyatzis, R. E. (2018). *The competent manager: A model for effective performance* (2nd ed.). Wiley.

Burns, J. M. (1978). *Leadership*. Harper & Row.

Cameron, K. S. (2012). *Positive leadership: Strategies for extraordinary performance*. Berrett-Koehler.

Catmull, E., & Wallace, A. (2014). *Creativity, Inc.: Overcoming the unseen forces that stand in the way of true inspiration*. Random House.

Chapman, B., & Sisodia, R. (2015). *Everybody matters: The extraordinary power of caring for your people like family*. Portfolio/Penguin.

Collins, J. (2001). *Good to great: Why some companies make the leap—and others don't*. HarperBusiness.

Daugherty, P. R., & Wilson, H. J. (2018). *Human + machine: Reimagining work in the age of AI*. Harvard Business Review Press.

Deci, E. L., & Ryan, R. M. (1985). *Intrinsic motivation and self-determination in human behavior*. Springer.

Denning, S. (2005). *The leader's guide to storytelling*. Jossey-Bass.

Drucker, P. F. (1999). *Management challenges for the 21st century*. HarperCollins.

Edmondson, A. C. (1999). Psychological safety and learning behavior in work teams. *Administrative Science Quarterly, 44*(2), 350–383. https://doi.org/10.2307/2666999

Figley, C. R. (2002). Compassion fatigue: Psychotherapists' chronic lack of self-care. *Journal of Clinical Psychology, 58*(11), 1433–1441. https://doi.org/10.1002/jclp.10090

Gagné, M., & Deci, E. L. (2005). Self-determination theory and work motivation. *Journal of Organizational Behavior, 26*(4), 331–362. https://doi.org/10.1002/job.322

Gardner, H. (2011). *Leading minds: An anatomy of leadership*. Basic Books.

George, B. (2003). *Authentic leadership: Rediscovering the secrets to creating lasting value*. Jossey-Bass.

George, B. (2007). *True north: Discover your authentic leadership*. Jossey-Bass.

George, B. (2017). Microsoft's Nadella reframed leadership with empathy. *Harvard Business Review*.

Goleman, D. (1995). *Emotional intelligence*. Bantam Books.

Goleman, D. (1998). *Working with emotional intelligence*. Bantam Books.

Goleman, D. (2006). *Social intelligence: The new science of human relationships*. Bantam.

Goleman, D., Boyatzis, R., & McKee, A. (2002). *Primal leadership: Realizing the power of emotional intelligence*. Harvard Business School Press.

Graen, G. B., & Uhl-Bien, M. (1995). Relationship-based approach to leadership: Development of leader–member exchange (LMX) theory of leadership over 25 years. *The Leadership Quarterly, 6*(2), 219–247. https://doi.org/10.1016/1048-9843(95)90036-5

Hannah, S. T., Avolio, B. J., & May, D. R. (2011). Moral maturation and moral conation. *Academy of Management Review, 36*(4), 663–685. https://doi.org/10.5465/amr.2010.0128

Heifetz, R. A. (1994). *Leadership without easy answers*. Harvard University Press.

Hofstede, G. (2001). *Culture's consequences: Comparing values, behaviors, institutions and organizations across nations* (2nd ed.). Sage.

Hook, J. N., Davis, D. E., Owen, J., Worthington, E. L., & Utsey, S. O. (2013). Cultural humility. *Journal of Counseling Psychology, 60*(3), 353–366. https://doi.org/10.1037/a0032595

Jaworski, J. (1996). *Synchronicity: The inner path of leadership*. Berrett-Koehler.

Judge, T. A., & Piccolo, R. F. (2004). Transformational and transactional leadership. *Journal of Applied Psychology, 89*(5), 755–768. https://doi.org/10.1037/0021-9010.89.5.755

Kantor, J. (2014, August 13). Working anything but 9 to 5. *The New York Times*.

Kerr, J. (2013). *Legacy: What the all blacks can teach us about the business of life*. Constable.

Kniberg, H., & Ivarsson, A. (2012). *Scaling agile at Spotify*. Spotify Engineering.

Kouzes, J. M., & Posner, B. Z. (2017). *The leadership challenge* (6th ed.). Wiley.

Kreitzer, M. J., Monsen, K. A., Nandram, S., & de Blok, J. (2015). Buurtzorg Nederland. *Global Advances in Health and Medicine, 4*(1), 40–44. https://doi.org/10.7453/gahmj.2014.030

Marquet, L. D. (2012). *Turn the ship around!: A true story of turning followers into leaders*. Portfolio/Penguin.

Maxwell, J. C. (2013). *The 5 levels of leadership: Proven steps to maximize your potential*. Center Street.

Mbigi, L. (2005). *The spirit of African leadership*. Knowledge Resources.

Nadella, S. (2017). *Hit refresh*. Harper Business.

Nohria, N., & Khurana, R. (Eds.). (2010). *Handbook of leadership theory and practice*. Harvard Business Press.

Orme, G. (2019). *The human edge: How curiosity and creativity are your superpowers in the digital economy*. FT Publishing International.

Pearce, C. L., & Conger, J. A. (Eds.). (2003). *Shared leadership: Reframing the hows and whys of leadership*. Sage.

Pfeffer, J. (1998). *The human equation: Building profits by putting people first*. Harvard Business School Press.

Rigby, D. K., Sutherland, J., & Takeuchi, H. (2016). Embracing agile. *Harvard Business Review, 94*(5), 40–50.

Rosenblat, A., & Stark, L. (2016). Algorithmic labor and information asymmetries. *International Journal of Communication, 10*, 3758–3784.

Rozovsky, J. (2015). *The five keys to a successful Google team*. re:Work (Google).

Salovey, P., & Mayer, J. D. (1990). Emotional intelligence. *Imagination, Cognition and Personality, 9*(3), 185–211. https://doi.org/10.2190/DUGG-P24E-52WK-6CDG

Seligman, M. E. P. (2011). *Flourish*. Free Press.

Shanafelt, T., Ripp, J., & Trockel, M. (2020). Understanding and addressing sources of anxiety among health care professionals during COVID-19. *JAMA, 323*(21), 2133–2134. https://doi.org/10.1001/jama.2020.5893

Shore, L. M., Cleveland, J. N., & Sanchez, D. (2018). Inclusive workplaces: A review and model. *Human Resource Management Review, 28*(2), 176–189. https://doi.org/10.1016/j.hrmr.2011.07.003; Science direct link: www.sciencedirect.com/science/article/abs/pii/S1053482217300529?via%3Dihub

Smith, W. K., & Lewis, M. W. (2011). Toward a theory of paradox. *Academy of Management Review, 36*(2), 381–403. https://doi.org/10.5465/amr.2009.0223

Taylor, F. W. (1911). *The principles of scientific management*. Harper & Brothers.

Tenbrunsel, A. E., & Messick, D. M. (2004). Ethical fading. *Social Justice Research, 17*(2), 223–236. https://doi.org/10.1023/B:SORE.0000027411.35832.53

Toyota Motor Corporation. (n.d.). *The Toyota production system*. https://global.toyota/en/company/vision-and-philosophy/production-system/

Unilever. (2021). *Equity, diversity and inclusion strategy*. www.unilever.com

Walton, R. E. (1985). From control to commitment in the workplace. *Harvard Business Review, 63*(2), 77–84.

Werhane, P. H. (1999). *Moral imagination and management decision-making*. Oxford University Press.

Wheatley, M. J. (2006). *Leadership and the new science* (3rd ed.). Berrett-Koehler.

Wilson, S. (2020). Pandemic leadership: Lessons from New Zealand's approach to COVID-19. *Leadership, 16*(3), 279–293. https://doi.org/10.1177/1742715020929151

Chapter 4

Performance

Building a Culture of Excellence

Introduction

When Indra Nooyi assumed leadership of PepsiCo, she understood an essential truth about performance: results achieved without integrity rarely endure. Her *performance with purpose* strategy – reducing sugar content, expanding healthier product lines, and embedding sustainability into core operations – demonstrated that disciplined execution and moral clarity are not opposing forces but mutually reinforcing ones. Under her leadership, PepsiCo grew to more than $63 billion in revenue while strengthening trust, reputation, and long-term viability. Her example captures the essence of the midday sun: a leadership orientation where clarity, accountability, and structured execution illuminate the path from intention to impact.

At noon, the sun stands at its highest point, revealing everything with uncompromising clarity. In the leadership compass, this southern point represents the disciplined domain of performance – the place where goals become commitments, plans become processes, and values take operational form. If north provides purpose and east energises through people, then south is where work becomes real. It is the manager's realm: organising, coordinating, prioritising, and sustaining the efforts that make organisations function. Drucker (1999) reminds us, strategy alone is never enough; even the most compelling ideas demand disciplined effort to make a real difference.

While often overshadowed by the inspirational power of purpose or the imaginative spark of vision, the southern domain is indispensable. Without disciplined execution, vision drifts into ideology and purpose dissolves into sentiment. Leadership requires not only aspiration but also the capacity to create order, maintain focus, and guide others through the practical realities of delivering results. Thinkers from Taylor and Weber, who emphasised the architecture of systems and structure (Taylor, 1911; Weber, 1947), to Mintzberg, who revealed the complexity of managerial work (Mintzberg, 1973), have long shown that leadership cannot exist without a strong operational backbone.

In the Imagination Age, this operational backbone must evolve. Organisations face unprecedented complexity: dispersed teams, rapid technological change,

DOI: 10.4324/9781003766414-4

heightened transparency, and accelerated cycles of innovation. These forces require a mode of performance that is both disciplined and adaptive – rigorous enough to provide stability, humane enough to sustain energy, and flexible enough to respond to continual flux. The midday sun captures this duality: illumination paired with intensity and structure balanced with responsiveness.

Industrial logic once equated performance with output, reducing humans to instruments of efficiency (Braverman, 1974). But modern performance is not a race for maximisation; it is a practice of alignment. It requires the steady conversion of shared purpose into coordinated action, the integration of processes with behaviours, and the cultivation of accountability that empowers rather than constrains. Performance becomes the disciplined capacity to deliver outcomes that matter – not only to shareholders, but to society, employees, and the organisation's enduring mission.

Technological advancements intensify this challenge. Algorithmic management can drive precision and speed, yet it can also erode autonomy and meaning when applied without care. Leaders must therefore harness the strengths of digital systems while safeguarding the humanity of work. In this sense, the midday sun calls for leaders who are both managers and stewards: custodians of clarity, architects of process, and guardians of dignity.

Several forces make the southern domain more essential than ever. Global complexity demands disciplined coordination; innovation requires structures that turn creativity into impact; employees seek autonomy grounded in clear expectations; and ethical scrutiny requires that organisational values be enacted, not merely declared. Standing in the light of the midday sun means embracing this visibility and accountability – recognising that execution is not a mechanical function but a moral one.

Thus, performance in the Imagination Age is not defined by speed alone, nor by scale alone, but by the capacity to translate purpose into disciplined action while preserving the humanity of the people who make that action possible. It is the grounded force that holds the compass steady, allowing organisations to move with coherence, integrity, and sustained excellence.

Theoretical Foundations of Performance

The pursuit of performance has been a central concern for leaders and scholars for more than a century. Performance, once narrowly equated with output or efficiency, has evolved into a multidimensional construct integrating results, human experience, and organisational purpose. As the world of work has shifted from industrial factories to knowledge economies, the theories underpinning performance have similarly transformed, offering leaders both guidance and caution. The evolution is as much philosophical as it is practical: from Taylor's time-and-motion studies to contemporary adaptive frameworks, each stage reflects a recalibration of the relationship between people, process, and outcomes. Understanding this evolution is essential for leaders striving to cultivate sustainable performance in the Imagination Age.

Scientific Management and the Pursuit of Efficiency

Frederick Winslow Taylor's *Principles of Scientific Management* (1911) marked the first systematic attempt to study work scientifically. Taylor believed that by decomposing tasks into discrete elements, measuring motions, and standardising procedures, organisations could optimise efficiency and predictability. His work transformed how work was conceptualised: no longer a set of routines, but a system capable of being measured, analysed, and improved.

The impact of Taylorism was profound. Factories became more productive, costs dropped, and managers gained tools to control variability. Yet, Taylor's methods often dehumanised workers, reducing them to mechanical cogs in a vast industrial machine (Braverman, 1974). The emphasis on efficiency frequently ignored creativity, intrinsic motivation, and the social dimension of work. Workers were expected to follow prescribed motions precisely, leaving little room for improvisation or initiative.

Modern applications of Taylorism principles appear in lean manufacturing, six sigma, and business process reengineering. These approaches retain the analytical rigour and clarity Taylor advocated, but with a crucial difference: human agency is recognised as a necessary ingredient for innovation and adaptability. Leaders today must learn from Taylor's successes and failures: clarity and standardisation are critical, but they must be coupled with trust, autonomy, and ethical oversight. Efficiency is no longer the sole measure of performance – it must be balanced with the human experience, a lesson that resonates more than a century after Taylor's experiments.

Bureaucracy and Rational Authority

Building on the quest for predictability, Max Weber conceptualised bureaucracy as a rational means of achieving organisational order (Weber, 1947). Bureaucracy codifies roles, responsibilities, decision rights, and formal processes. It ensures consistency, reduces ambiguity, and establishes accountability which are essential foundations for scaling operations beyond small teams or local markets. In essence, bureaucracy was the next evolutionary step after Taylorism: if Taylor clarified the *how* of work at the *individual* level, Weber clarified it at the *organisational* level.

Yet, as with Taylor, there were trade-offs. Excessive bureaucracy can stifle creativity, slow decision-making, and alienate employees. In a world increasingly defined by complexity, volatility, and innovation, rigid hierarchies undermine the very performance they are intended to support. The modern leader's challenge is to cultivate what can be called *enabling bureaucracy*: structures that provide clarity and accountability without constraining initiative. Here, performance is not merely about adherence to rules but about creating systems in which people can act effectively and responsibly. The midday sun metaphor is particularly suitable: like sunlight that illuminates without burning, enabling bureaucracy provides visibility and direction while leaving room for growth, creativity, and human judgment.

Human Relations, Motivation, and Positive Psychology

By the mid-20th century, scholars recognised that purely mechanistic approaches were insufficient to sustain high performance. The Human Relations Movement highlighted the social and emotional dimensions of work, demonstrating that productivity is inseparable from human engagement. Herzberg's (1966) distinction between hygiene factors (e.g., pay, safety) and motivators (e.g., recognition, autonomy, purpose) clarified that optimal performance arises from meaningful work experiences rather than simply better working conditions.

Deci and Ryan's (1985) Self-Determination Theory further demonstrated that intrinsic motivators – competence, autonomy, and relatedness – are key drivers of sustained engagement and creativity. These theories signalled a paradigm shift: performance is not merely the result of control, incentives, or rules, but emerges from a system that nurtures human potential.

Seligman's (2011) PERMA model adds an additional dimension by linking performance to flourishing. Positive emotion, engagement, relationships, meaning, and accomplishment are not optional; they are essential drivers of sustainable performance. Leaders who integrate these principles create environments in which employees are not only productive but resilient, innovative, and committed to the organisation's mission. The evolution from Taylorism efficiency to positive psychology illustrates a profound expansion in the understanding of performance: it is as much about people as it is about process.

Contemporary Management Models

As organisations evolved beyond the industrial paradigm, scholars and practitioners recognised that performance was no longer a linear function of efficiency or hierarchy. The complexity, speed, and interconnectivity of modern work demanded new frameworks that could account for human behaviour, emergent challenges, and adaptive decision-making. Contemporary management models therefore shift the focus from rigid control and standardised processes to dynamic systems that balance structure, autonomy, and purpose. These models emphasise that performance is not only about outputs, but also about the orchestration of people, information, and decisions in real time – requiring leaders to act less as controllers and more as integrators of multiple, often competing, demands.

It is within this context that the work of Mintzberg on managerial roles as a dynamic practice, Drucker's emphasis on the discipline of execution, Locke and Latham's goal-setting and measured impact, Galbraith's insights on organisational design and information flow, the principles of lean, agile, and adaptive performance, and Smith and Lewis's paradox theory on balancing competing demands collectively provide a comprehensive lens for understanding how leaders orchestrate complexity, align people and processes, and sustain high performance

Henry Mintzberg's (1973) research reframed the managerial role as dynamic, adaptive, and complex. Managers must balance multiple roles – leader, monitor, negotiator, and decision-maker – while coordinating teams, resources, and information. Performance, therefore, is not a static metric but a dynamic interplay of tasks, relationships, and decisions. This perspective aligns with the midday sun metaphor: like the sun's light, managerial attention must be distributed wisely, illuminating priorities without causing burnout or neglect. Leaders must navigate competing demands continuously, calibrating effort to maximise clarity, alignment, and impact. The evolution here is from viewing performance as output to understanding it as a living, responsive system requiring judgment, adaptation, and skilful management.

Drucker (1999) reframed performance as a responsibility of disciplined execution. Plans, no matter how visionary, are meaningless unless translated into results. Drucker emphasised alignment, focus, and accountability, insisting that leaders connect the "why" of strategy with the "how" of execution. In practice, this means that leaders must ensure organisational efforts are coordinated, that goals are clear and aligned, and that work is conducted ethically and purposefully. Drucker's insights highlight a critical evolutionary argument: efficiency is insufficient without direction, and output is hollow without alignment to values and purpose.

Goal-setting theory (Locke & Latham, 2002) provides operational clarity to performance. Specific, challenging, and measurable goals create focus and accountability while enabling creativity within constraints. Tools like Objectives and Key Results (OKRs) translate strategy into tangible actions, allowing teams to track progress while maintaining autonomy. Modern leaders can thus create scaffolding that structures effort without stifling innovation – a delicate balance that reflects the evolution of performance thinking from rigid control to guided empowerment.

Galbraith's (2014) Star Model situates performance within the systemic alignment of strategy, structure, processes, rewards, and people. Leaders act as architects, designing organisations where information flows freely, responsibilities are clear, and accountability is embedded. High performance arises not from isolated individual output but from the orchestration of collective effort. The midday sun metaphor is again illustrative: performance illuminates the system, but its impact depends on the design, timing, and calibration of organisational levers.

The Toyota Production System (Liker, 2004) exemplifies disciplined performance that respects human dignity. Kaizen (continuous improvement) encourages incremental progress while empowering employees to identify problems and propose solutions. Agile methodologies extend this principle, emphasising iterative cycles, autonomy, and responsiveness to changing conditions. In the Age of Imagination, leaders must cultivate a dual capability: structure enough to provide clarity and control, yet flexible enough to enable innovation and adaptation. Performance is no longer a static output but a dynamic equilibrium between freedom and discipline, speed and reflection, exploration and execution.

Finally, Smith and Lewis (2011) highlight the inherently paradoxical nature of performance. Leaders must simultaneously manage competing demands – efficiency and creativity, short-term outcomes and long-term sustainability, structure and autonomy. Performance is a dynamic balancing act rather than a linear process. The midday sun metaphor captures this nuance: light provides clarity, but intensity must be managed; exposure can energise or burn. Leaders must embrace tension, not eliminate it, cultivating adaptive practices that reconcile competing imperatives.

Rethinking Performance

For many years, performance in organisations has been synonymous with results – higher output, lower costs, greater efficiency. The industrial-era mindset was built on the logic that predictable environments reward control, standardisation, and speed. Yet this view now feels inadequate. Today's organisations operate in conditions defined by complexity, transparency, and rapid interconnectedness. As a result, the simple equation of performance with output no longer reflects what enables success or sustainability.

A growing body of thinking suggests that performance depends as much on *how* results are achieved as on the *results* themselves. Drucker (1999) famously warned that doing things efficiently that should not be done at all is pointless. In the digital era, the consequences of poor judgment can scale globally within minutes, damaging reputation, morale, and long-term value. Leaders who chase results at any cost often discover that short-term wins conceal deeper fragilities – burnout, ethical lapses, or eroded trust.

By contrast, organisations that focus on integrity, culture, and trust tend to generate performance that compounds over time. They may appear slower at first, but their outcomes endure because they build systems where people can innovate, learn, and take responsibility. Two companies may pursue growth: one through pressure and corner-cutting, another through fair processes, transparency, and investment in people. Although the first may see quick revenue lifts, the second typically proves more resilient, adaptive, and trusted – qualities that underpin long-term performance.

This shift in thinking is reflected in the work of several leadership theorists. Seidman (2011) argues that in a hyperconnected world, behaviour has become a central driver of performance. With employees documenting their working conditions and customers instantly sharing experiences, organisations can no longer hide behind branding or polished narratives. How work is done is now visible, assessable, and consequential. Trust, therefore, becomes what Seidman (2011) calls the only legal performance-enhancing drug, because it enables collaboration, information flow, and responsible autonomy.

Integrity plays a similar role. When words and actions align, employees can make decisions confidently without heavy oversight. This allows capacity to scale through shared values rather than through control mechanisms. Compliance may prevent failure, but character fuels excellence. Seidman (2011) urges organisations to move from rule-based systems toward principle-based cultures that encourage self-governance and authentic accountability.

Where Seidman focuses on behaviour, Birkinshaw (2012) highlights the organisational structures that shape it. Traditional management models, influenced by Taylorism, were designed for stable environments where efficiency mattered most. Today's performance, however, relies on creativity, discretionary effort, and rapid learning. Birkinshaw identifies four dimensions – coordination, decision-making, objectives, and motivation – that determine how well an organisation adapts and performs.

He describes four management archetypes: the Planning Model (tight control), the Science Model (analytical optimisation), the Quest Model (purpose-driven), and the Discovery Model (decentralised, experimental). High-performing organisations intentionally choose and adapt these models, while low performers remain trapped in outdated designs. Crucially, Birkinshaw stresses the balance between freedom and discipline: too much freedom breeds chaos, while too much discipline suppresses initiative. Examples such as the Toyota Production System illustrate how autonomy and structure can coexist to support consistent, high-quality performance.

Agile methodologies similarly reflect this balance, empowering teams while providing cycles of reflection and alignment. For leaders, the key question becomes: *Are we managing by design or by default?* Adjustments in decision rights, feedback systems, or goal-setting practices can dramatically strengthen performance when grounded in trust and shared purpose.

Ultimately, performance in the 21st century is a multidimensional concept. Results still matter, but they are only one part of the equation. Sustainable performance depends on the quality of behaviour, the integrity of systems, and the capacity of people to work creatively and ethically. When leaders align results with trust, culture, and human potential, they create performance that not only delivers today but strengthens the organisation for tomorrow.

Singing the Song of Significance

Performance in the Imagination Age is more than the achievement of targets or the efficient completion of tasks; it is the art and discipline of transforming purpose into meaningful results while nurturing human potential. Leaders who, as Godin (2023) describes, sing the song of significance recognise that people are not merely contributors to performance – they are its source, its expression, and its purpose. The midday sun – the south of the leadership compass – illuminates clarity, grounded execution, and the disciplined pursuit of excellence. Yet performance, as contemporary scholars have argued, is not simply a matter of output; it is defined by how results are achieved, how people are engaged, and how ethical, human-centred practices are embedded into organisational life (Birkinshaw, 2012; Seidman, 2011; Seligman, 2011). Leading in this quadrant requires holding the paradox of discipline and freedom, rigour and imagination, metrics and meaning, shaping performance cultures that are both productive and humane. Table 4.1 illustrates the theoretical foundations underpinning the midday sun.

Table 4.1 Theoretical Grounding of the Midday Sun

Model element	*Key theories/ authors*	*Leader actions*	*Practical implication*
Significance Orientation	Seidman (2011); Seligman (2011); Godin (2023)	Communicate purpose; model value-aligned behaviour; link daily tasks to impact	Anchors performance in purpose and human flourishing; motivates intrinsically
Clarity of Goals & Metrics	Drucker (1999); Locke & Latham (2002)	Set measurable, aspirational goals; align objectives across teams; review progress regularly	Reduces ambiguity, focuses collective effort, illuminates the path
Discipline with Freedom	Collins (2001); Bass (1990)	Establish structured processes without micromanagement; empower decision-making within boundaries; reward disciplined initiative	Creates an environment where structure enables creativity rather than stifling it
Alignment with Strengths & Passion	Collins (2001); Orme (2019)	Identify strengths and interests; assign tasks that leverage intrinsic motivation; foster learning and curiosity	Increases engagement, energy, and innovation; harnesses human potential
Continuous Feedback & Adaptation	Liker (2004); Kniberg & Ivarsson (2012a,2012b); Birkinshaw (2012)	Implement regular feedback loops; encourage experimentation and learning; monitor trends and adapt	Ensures performance is dynamic, responsive, and continuously improving
Ethical & Trust-Based Execution	Seidman (2011)	Model ethical behaviour; empower teams via principles; build psychological safety	High-trust environments accelerate collaboration, decision-making, and resilience
Measured Impact & Recognition	Godin (2023)	Track outcomes that matter; celebrate contributions; combine qualitative and quantitative metrics	Reinforces significance orientation, sustains motivation, embeds culture of excellence

Source: Author's synthesis based on the literature.

Significance Orientation: Anchoring Performance in Meaning

The foundation of the Midday Sun Model is *significance orientation*, which links daily tasks to purpose and values. When people understand why their work matters, motivation shifts from compliance to contribution (Seidman, 2011; Seligman, 2011). Significance is communicated not only through mission statements but through leaders' everyday behaviour – how they explain decisions, recognise effort, and role-model ethical judgment.

A powerful illustration is Patagonia, where performance is inseparable from environmental stewardship. Every employee – from designers to retail staff – can articulate how their work contributes to ecological responsibility. The company's "Don't Buy This Jacket" campaign, which discouraged unnecessary consumption, demonstrated organisational integrity while increasing long-term loyalty. Here, significance fuels both engagement and performance: people work not just to complete tasks but to protect something they value.

Effective leaders therefore make the "why" visible, linking each role to impact and demonstrating that performance and purpose strengthen one another.

Clarity of Goals and Metrics: Illuminating the Path

If significance provides meaning, clarity provides direction. People perform best when expectations are visible, measurable, and connected across teams. Foundational research on goal setting (Locke & Latham, 2002) and Drucker's (1999) work on management by objectives both highlight the power of specific, aspirational goals.

A well-known example is Google's Objectives and Key Results (OKRs). While the organisation encourages innovation and experimentation, OKRs translate bold vision into transparent metrics. Teams have autonomy, yet progress is visible and aligned. This balance – freedom guided by clarity – reduces ambiguity and builds collective focus.

Leaders who embrace the midday sun must therefore set measurable goals, review progress frequently, and ensure everyone understands not only *what* success looks like but *how* it will be measured.

Discipline with Freedom: Structured Autonomy

Modern performance leadership requires a simultaneous embrace of structure and autonomy. Excessive control stifles creativity while excessive freedom leads to chaos. Sustainable performance emerges when clear processes coexist with empowered decision-making (Bass, 1990; Collins, 2001).

The Toyota Production System (TPS) is a classic example of structured autonomy. Workers follow rigorous processes but possess the authority to stop production when quality is at risk. This combination ensures high standards while unleashing employee problem-solving capabilities (Liker, 2004). It transforms discipline into a platform for creativity rather than a constraint.

Under the midday sun, leaders clearly define expectations and boundaries while trusting teams to act within them. Freedom becomes safe, and discipline becomes enabling.

Strengths and Passion: Harnessing Human Potential

Performance improves when people work from their strengths and passions. Leaders who understand individual talents and interests unlock energy that cannot be generated by pressure alone (Collins, 2001; Orme, 2019).

The transformation of Microsoft under Satya Nadella illustrates this principle. Nadella shifted the culture from internal competition to collective learning and curiosity. Instead of rewarding technical brilliance alone, he encouraged growth mindsets and placed people in roles that leveraged their unique strengths. This created a surge in innovation, employee engagement, and market performance.

In the Midday Sun Model, aligning work with strengths is not a luxury. It is a strategic driver of creativity, engagement, and resilience.

Continuous Feedback and Adaptation: Making Performance a Living System

Performance today is dynamic. Markets shift, technology evolves, and expectations change. A static performance system becomes obsolete. Leaders must therefore implement regular reflection cycles, feedback loops, and learning processes that allow teams to adapt (Birkinshaw, 2012; Kniberg & Ivarsson, 2012a, 2012b; Liker, 2004).

The Spotify squad model provides a strong example. Squads operate like mini startups within the organisation, using iterative cycles to adjust based on user feedback and data. Regular retrospectives enable rapid improvements, making performance responsive rather than reactive.

Midday sun leadership embeds learning into everyday work through coaching, reviews, experimentation, and open dialogue.

Ethical and Trust-Based Execution: Performing with Integrity

Trust accelerates performance. It reduces friction, improves collaboration, and supports autonomy (Seidman, 2011). When leaders act with integrity – saying what they mean and doing what they promise – employees feel safe to commit fully.

Barry-Wehmiller CEO Bob Chapman exemplifies trust-based execution. During recession, instead of layoffs, he introduced shared furloughs: Everyone suffers a little so that no one suffers a lot. This choice strengthened loyalty and became a defining cultural milestone. Chapman's commitment to caring leadership transformed trust into a performance multiplier. The midday sun does not scorch – it illuminates. Ethical execution ensures that performance is both effective and humane.

Measured Impact and Recognition: Reinforcing Excellence

Measured impact and recognition reinforces the connection between purpose, contribution, and performance. Godin (2023) emphasises that significance is created when organisations prioritise outcomes that matter – those that enhance contribution, deepen engagement, and strengthen community. Recognition, therefore, is not merely symbolic; it validates behaviours aligned with shared purpose and fosters intrinsic motivation. Leaders who track qualitative and quantitative indicators, celebrate meaningful progress, and highlight contributions that reflect core values embed a culture of excellence that endures. By reinforcing what truly matters, leaders create an upward spiral of motivation, ownership, and commitment.

The Performance Triangle for the Imagination Age

Performance today demands a shift from industrial efficiency to a multidimensional view that integrates results, behaviours, and the human meaning behind work. This view aligns with the shift Seth Godin (2023) calls the move toward *significance*: work that enables human contribution, dignity, and shared purpose. To support such significance-driven work, leaders need a performance model suited for complexity, transparency, and human creativity. To that end, this chapter introduces the Performance Triangle (Figure 4.1) – a proposed framework for the Imagination Age that integrates three essential dimensions of sustainable performance: Results (What), Processes and Behaviours (How), and People and Purpose (Who/Why). Together, these dimensions form a balanced system that supports the creation of meaningful, coherent, and high-value organisational performance.

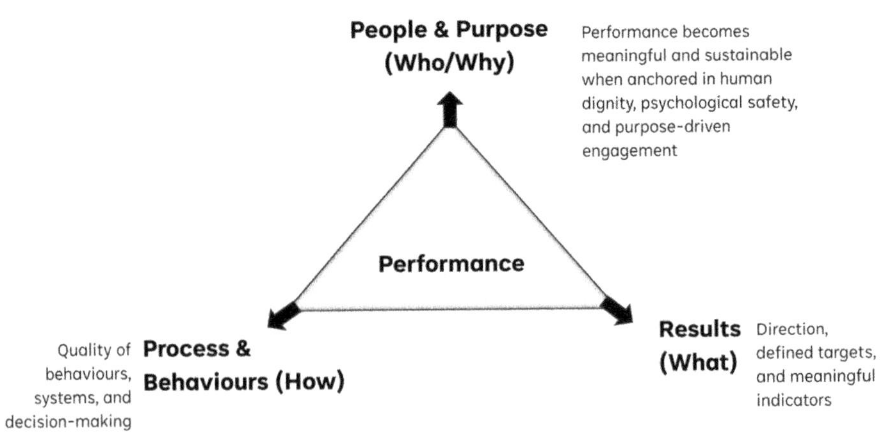

Figure 4.1 Performance Triangle.

Source: Developed by the author, informed by leadership and organisational literature.

Results

Clear goals, measurable outcomes, and shared expectations establish direction. Without clarity on results, organisations drift or fracture. But results alone are insufficient – they must be contextualised within ethical processes and meaningful purpose with a long-term focus.

Case Study 4.1 Blockbuster: Performance Undone by Inertia

Blockbuster illustrates how an overemphasis on short-term results (What) combined with rigid management processes can undermine long-term viability. Through the 1990s, Blockbuster's model delivered strong revenue, but its structures – hierarchical decision-making, centralised control, and a heavy reliance on late fees – discouraged innovation (Birkinshaw, 2012).

Although profitable, the company's processes and culture were misaligned with emerging technological realities. When Netflix approached Blockbuster in 2000, leadership declined, prioritising established revenue streams over strategic adaptation. Risk aversion and outdated behavioural norms made the organisation slow, inward-looking, and unable to pivot.

Blockbuster's collapse underscores that results alone cannot sustain performance; without adaptive behaviours and purpose-aligned culture, success becomes temporary and brittle.

Processes and Behaviours

Systems, practices, and norms determine *how* work is performed. Trust, learning, adaptability, and ethical discipline shape behaviour. When "how" is misaligned with purpose or incentives, performance quality deteriorates even if results appear strong in the short term.

Case Study 4.2 The Excel Communications Phenomenon: Incentives, Culture, and the Fragility of Fast Growth

Excel Communications offers a powerful illustration of how performance systems driven primarily by incentives can generate extraordinary momentum – and equally extraordinary vulnerability. Founded on a multilevel marketing model, Excel tightly aligned financial rewards with recruitment and sales activity. The result was spectacular early growth, with rapid expansion fuelled by clear, immediate incentives and a strong sense of opportunity (Robinson, 1997a).

These incentives acted as potent behavioural levers. Sales activity intensified, recruitment accelerated, and success reinforced itself through visible rewards and social proof. However, the very behaviours that were incentivised also planted the seeds of fragility. Growth became increasingly dependent on constant recruitment rather than sustainable customer value. Ethical lapses emerged as pressure mounted to meet targets, and the organisation's long-term viability became vulnerable to regulatory scrutiny and reputational risk (Robinson, 1997a).

Importantly, Excel's success was not driven by incentives alone. The company invested heavily in cultural rituals – large rallies, motivational events, shared language, and collective identity – which created emotional commitment and a powerful sense of belonging (Robinson, 1997b). This highlights a critical insight for leadership: behaviour is always shaped by an interaction between structural drivers (such as incentives) and cultural narratives (such as meaning, identity, and aspiration).

Yet culture, when detached from ethical purpose, proved insufficient as a stabilising force. Excel's experience demonstrates that high-speed performance built primarily on incentives can deliver output, but not resilience. Without alignment to deeper questions of *who the organisation is*, *why it exists*, and *what kind of behaviour it seeks to honour*, systems may scale rapidly while quietly undermining trust, legitimacy, and sustainability.

For leaders in the Imagination Age, the Excel phenomenon serves as a cautionary tale: incentives shape action, culture amplifies it, but purpose and ethics are what ultimately sustain it.

People and Purpose

The human dimension – commitment, meaning, identity, autonomy, and moral purpose – forms the deepest layer of organisational performance. As Godin (2023) argues, significance emerges when people are treated not as resources but as contributors whose humanity and creativity elevate the system. These three angles of the triangle determine whether performance is fast, scalable, and sustainable, rather than brittle, extractive, or short-lived.

Case Study 4.3 Howard Schultz and People-Centred Performance at Starbucks

Howard Schultz's leadership exemplifies how the "who/why" dimension becomes a cornerstone of sustainable performance. Schultz's childhood memory of his father losing both work and dignity shaped his belief that organisations must honour the humanity of their people (Gallo, 2016).

From early on, Starbucks introduced health insurance and stock options for all employees – including part-time baristas. Although costly, these choices proved strategically prescient: employee turnover decreased, service quality improved, and the company developed a reputation for warmth, stability, and trust.

Schultz created structural trust (policies that treat people with dignity) and cultural trust (stories that give work meaning). During crises like 2008, this trust acted as organisational resilience; Schultz even closed stores for retraining to reinforce quality and values, prioritising long-term culture over short-term optics.

Starbucks shows that when leaders invest in people and purpose, the "who/why" dimension strengthens the entire performance system (Schultz & Gordon, 2011). Performance becomes humane, regenerative, and strategically durable.

The performance triangle has been derived from the theoretical foundations underpinning the midday sun concept discussed before. First, the emphasis on *clarity of goals and measurable outcomes* (Drucker, 1999; Locke & Latham, 2002) establishes the Results (What) dimension. These theories insist that performance must have direction, defined targets, and meaningful indicators – precisely the apex of the performance triangle.

Second, the literature on disciplined execution, adaptive learning, and continuous improvement (Collins, 2001; Liker, 2004; Kniberg & Ivarsson, 2012a, 2012b; Birkinshaw, 2012) forms the Processes and Behaviours (How) dimension. These scholars show that high performance does not emerge from goals alone but from the quality of behaviours, systems, and decision-making that bring those goals to life.

Finally, the works of Seidman (2011), Seligman (2011), Orme (2019), and Godin (2023) emphasise significance, intrinsic motivation, ethical action, strengths, and human flourishing where Consciousness, Curiosity, Creativity, and Collaboration are not only welcomed but celebrated. These form the People and Purpose (Who/Why) dimension. Their insights affirm that performance becomes both meaningful and sustainable only when anchored in human dignity, psychological safety, and purpose-driven engagement.

Taken together, these theoretical strands naturally converge into a three-part structure:

What we are trying to achieve (Results)
How we carry out the work (Processes and Behaviours)
Who is doing the work and **why** it matters (People and Purpose)

The Performance Triangle thus synthesises decades of research into a coherent, actionable framework suited to the Imagination Age that balances clarity with adaptability, discipline with creativity, and purpose with measurable impact.

From Performance to Mastery: Applying the Performance Triangle

Mastery in the Imagination Age is not the relentless pursuit of metrics; it is the disciplined orchestration of the conditions under which people, processes, and purpose converge. The midday sun symbolises this integrative clarity – when intentions, values, and actions align to illuminate a path forward. Leaders move from managing performance to shaping performance ecosystems and creating a culture of excellence. This includes:

- Purpose made actionable.
- Processes that promote trust, learning, and ethics.
- People empowered with autonomy, significance, and belonging.

Leaders convert clarity into coordinated action and human potential into sustained impact to create their song of significance (Godin, 2023). The three case studies reveal three distinct but connected insights. The Starbucks case study demonstrates that when organisations invest deeply in people and purpose, performance becomes resilient and regenerative. The Excel case study shows that incentives can power rapid growth but become unstable without ethical grounding and intrinsic motivation. The Blockbuster case study warns of the dangers of prioritising short-term results while neglecting adaptive processes and meaningful culture. Together, they illustrate the central proposition of the performance triangle: sustainable performance emerges from the dynamic balance of What, How, and Who/Why. In the Imagination Age, organisations cannot choose between speed, scale, and sustainability – they must integrate all three. The performance triangle offers a guideline; the midday sun offers the discipline of application; and significance – as Godin (2023) argues – offers the moral and human horizon toward which performance should ultimately rise.

Conclusion

Charlie Chaplin once observed that power is needed only to cause harm, whereas love is enough to accomplish anything. While poetic, this insight captures a central truth of contemporary leadership. Performance driven by fear, pressure, or control may secure short-term compliance, but performance grounded in trust, care, and shared purpose generates commitment, creativity, and endurance. Performance is not a mechanical output; it is a living expression of organisational character – shaped by the alignment of purpose, people, and process.

When performance is reduced to targets alone, effort becomes transactional and fragile. By contrast, when leaders understand performance as alignment between values, behaviours, and outcomes, they unlock a deeper and more sustainable source of energy. As Seidman (2011) reminds us, in a transparent and interdependent world, how results are achieved matters as much as the results themselves. Birkinshaw (2012) similarly shows that performance architectures – how decisions are made, motivation is cultivated, and work is coordinated – must evolve with context. Rigid, control-heavy systems suppress initiative; trust-based systems release ownership and ingenuity.

Great leaders understand that pressure generates heat, but purpose generates light. When people understand why their work matters, they contribute rather than comply. This is the essence behind the song of significance: balancing speed, scale, and sustainability by continuously returning to purpose and people as stabilising forces. Performance, therefore, is not the endpoint of leadership but the bridge between purpose and possibility. When integrity, trust, and meaning guide action, performance gains a soul – and leadership becomes an act of creation rather than control.

Reflective Questions

1. How effectively do your leadership practices translate purpose and vision into clear systems, structures, and daily behaviours that enable consistent and meaningful performance?
2. When pursuing results, how do you balance disciplined execution with humanity, ensuring that performance cultures energise people rather than exhaust them?
3. To what extent does your organisation's performance emerge from intentional design – alignment, shared accountability, and systems thinking – rather than from pressure, urgency, or short-term targets?

References

Bass, B. M. (1990). From transactional to transformational leadership: Learning to share the vision. *Organizational Dynamics, 18*(3), 19–31. https://doi.org/10.1016/0090-2616(90)90061-S

Birkinshaw, J. (2012). *Reinventing management: Smarter choices for getting work done* (Rev. ed.). Jossey-Bass.

Braverman, H. (1974). *Labor and monopoly capital*. Monthly Review Press.

Collins, J. (2001). *Good to great: Why some companies make the leap... and others don't*. HarperCollins.

Deci, E. L., & Ryan, R. M. (1985). *Intrinsic motivation and self-determination in human behavior*. Springer.

Drucker, P. F. (1999). *Management challenges for the 21st century*. HarperBusiness.

Galbraith, J. R. (2014). *Designing organizations: Strategy, structure, and process at the business unit and enterprise levels* (3rd ed.). Jossey-Bass.

Gallo, C. (2016). *The storyteller's secret: How TED speakers and inspirational leaders turn their passion into performance*. Macmillan.

Godin, S. (2023). *The song of significance: A new manifesto for teams*. Penguin Random House.
Herzberg, F. (1966). *Work and the nature of man*. World Publishing.
Kniberg, H., & Ivarsson, A. (2012a). *Scaling Agile @ Spotify with tribes, squads, chapters and guilds*. Crisp AB. https://blog.crisp.se/wp-content/uploads/2012/11/SpotifyScal ing.pdf
Kniberg, H., & Ivarsson, A. (2012b). *Scrum and XP from the trenches* (2nd ed.). C4Media.
Liker, J. K. (2004). *The Toyota way: 14 management principles from the world's greatest manufacturer*. McGraw-Hill.
Locke, E. A., & Latham, G. P. (2002). Building a practically useful theory of goal setting and task motivation: A 35-year odyssey. *American Psychologist, 57*(9), 705–717.
Mintzberg, H. (1973). *The nature of managerial work*. Harper & Row.
Orme, J. (2019). *The human edge: Cultivating curiosity and creativity at work*. Routledge.
Robinson, A. (1997a). *Corporate culture and the rise and fall of Excel Communications*. Wiley.
Robinson, J. W. (1997b). *The Excel phenomenon: The astonishing success story of the fastest-growing communications company*. Prima Lifestyles.
Schultz, H., & Gordon, J. (2011). *Onward: How Starbucks fought for its life without losing its soul*. Rodale.
Seidman, D. (2011). *How: Why how we do anything means everything* (Expanded ed.). Wiley.
Seligman, M. E. P. (2011). *Flourish: A visionary new understanding of happiness and well-being*. Free Press.
Smith, W. K., & Lewis, M. W. (2011). Toward a theory of paradox: A dynamic equilibrium model of organizing. *Academy of Management Review, 36*(2), 381–403.
Taylor, F. W. (1911). *The principles of scientific management*. Harper & Brothers.
Weber, M. (1947). *The theory of social and economic organization* (A. M. Henderson & T. Parsons, Trans.). Free Press.

Chapter 5

Possibility

Envisioning the Futures

Introduction

In September 1962, standing before 40,000 people at Rice University, John F. Kennedy declared one of the boldest visions in modern history: "We choose to go to the Moon in this decade and do the other things, not because they are easy, but because they are hard." At that moment, the United States had no rockets powerful enough to reach the moon, no computers capable of managing space navigation, and no certainty that a human could even survive the journey. Yet Kennedy's declaration reframed the national imagination. It was not a statement of what was *possible now*; it was a call to *make possible what did not yet exist*.

That is the essence of leadership in the west – the leadership of *Possibility*. It is where vision replaces fear, imagination replaces inertia, and courage replaces certainty, setting to explore the territories of uncertainties. Kennedy did not offer a detailed plan – he offered a direction, a dream, and a belief that human ingenuity, collaboration, and purpose could turn that dream into reality. Within seven years, his words had manifested into footprints on lunar soil. This is the *alchemy of possibility*: transforming imagination into achievement through conviction, courage, and collective will.

Visionary leadership begins with sight – not only the ability to look beyond the horizon but also the courage to see what others cannot yet imagine. Visionary leaders do not merely react to reality; they reinterpret it, creating new frames of meaning and new futures that seem impossible until they become inevitable. This is the essence of *possibility leadership*: leading from imagination, not imitation.

In the late 1970s, when computers were still massive machines reserved for corporations and research labs, a young man named Bill Gates envisioned a computer on every desk. At the time, that idea was perceived illogical. Experts at IBM estimated that global demand for personal computers would not exceed five (Isaacson, 2011). Yet Gates and his small team at Microsoft chose to see a different world – one where computing was not a luxury, but a language of empowerment.

Similarly, Steve Jobs of Apple dreamed not of machines, but of "bicycles for the mind" – elegant, intuitive tools that would amplify human creativity (Isaacson, 2011). Both men shared one trait that defines the leadership of possibility: they

DOI: 10.4324/9781003766414-5

could envision a future before others could imagine it. Where conventional managers respond to trends, possibility leaders not only envision the future – they also *create them.* Possibility thinking begins in the imagination, but it does not stay there. It is both art and discipline – the art of perceiving what is latent, and the discipline of nurturing it into being. It requires what futurist Joel Barker called the "paradigm shift" – the willingness to question deeply held assumptions and to imagine alternatives beyond existing boundaries (Barker, 1992).

Framing Possibility: Horizons of the Setting Sun for Reflection and Rekindling

If the south is the noonday sun – direct, focused, and grounded in discipline – the west is the setting sun, casting long shadows, colouring the sky, and inviting pause while igniting the imagination. The setting sun marks not an end but a transition: a moment when day gestures toward night, inviting reflection, foresight, and the ability to see beyond the immediate horizon. For leaders, west symbolises vision: the capacity to imagine futures that do not yet exist, craft possibility in the present, and inspire others to move toward that horizon. Vision is a critical aspect of leadership, creating an image of an achievable future that motivates collective endeavour (Bennis, 1994).

Collins and Porras (1994) describe the "Big Hairy Audacious Goal" (BHAG) as a central driver of enduring organisations: goals bold enough to inspire, yet concrete enough to guide action. Vision is the westward gaze – simultaneously poetic and practical. The setting sun metaphor captures this tension: it illuminates what is visible while revealing what lies just beyond the horizon, bridging imagination with actionable direction.

Vision as the Realm of Possibility

Unlike purpose (north), which provides direction, or productivity (south), which delivers results, vision (west) is inherently about possibility. It is future-oriented, transcending present constraints to imagine what could be. Kouzes and Posner (2017) argue that leaders must envision exciting and ennobling possibilities, lifting people beyond immediate limitations. Yet vision is not fantasy. Bennis and Nanus (1985) define it as a *realistic, credible, attractive future* for an organisation, anchored in both imagination and credibility.

In the Imagination Age, where human creativity intersects with artificial intelligence, vision becomes both more urgent and complex. Leaders craft futures that integrate human values with technological possibilities as Nadella (2017) argues, the technology industry is fundamentally driven by innovation rather than by tradition. Leaders must articulate visions that are technologically feasible, ethically grounded, and socially desirable (Werhane, 1999). The westward horizon, in this context, requires both foresight and moral imagination: seeing beyond the immediate while considering what kind of future is worth building.

The Psychological and Neuroscientific Foundations of Vision

Vision inspires because it activates both cognition and emotion. Snyder's (2002) theory of hope defines hope as the combination of agency – the belief that goals can be achieved – and pathways – the perceived routes to reach them. Vision functions as a multiplier of hope, strengthening agency and clarifying pathways. Neuroscience further reveals how resonant leadership alters follower perception. Boyatzis and McKee (2005) argue that leaders who communicate vision authentically activate positive emotional attractors, releasing dopamine, broadening attention, and enhancing motivation. Vision, therefore, is not merely an abstract idea but a transformative force that shifts perception and opens the mind to possibility.

Vision is also inseparable from emotion. Leaders who communicate vision effectively evoke awe, trust, and aspiration, mobilising collective energy toward a shared horizon (Boyatzis et al., 2015; Goleman, 1998). The westward gaze metaphor captures this interplay: vision is both seen and felt, blending imaginative foresight with emotional resonance.

Theoretical Foundations of Vision and Possibility

Leadership, at its deepest level, transcends management. While management is primarily concerned with order, stability, and efficiency, leadership is fundamentally concerned with transformation – interpreting present realities, imagining alternative futures, and mobilising collective energy toward shared horizons (Kotter, 1990; Bass, 1990). Visionary leadership does not merely respond to what is; it redefines what could be. As Bennis and Nanus (1985) argue, authentic vision does not impose ambition from above but reveals what is latent within collective purpose, giving form to emergent possibility. Vision, in this sense, becomes the primary mechanism through which transformational leadership unfolds.

Foundational Frameworks of Visionary Leadership

Several influential frameworks illuminate how leaders construct, communicate, and sustain compelling visions. Bennis and Nanus's (1985) seminal work identifies four interdependent strategies of visionary leadership: creating a compelling image of the future, communicating it clearly, building trust in its feasibility, and sustaining confidence over time. Vision operates simultaneously as cognition and emotion – engaging logic through strategy and meaning through values. Leaders focus attention by articulating a vivid and desirable future, create meaning by shaping shared interpretation, establish trust through consistency and reliability, and deploy the self through continuous learning and resilient confidence – what Bennis and Nanus describe as positive self-regard and the "Wallenda factor."

Complementing this, Collins and Porras (1994) introduce the notion of Big Hairy Audacious Goals (BHAGs), arguing that catalytic, long-term aspirations can galvanise organisational imagination more powerfully than incremental objectives. BHAGs stretch collective capacity and provide moral momentum, enabling organisations to orient themselves toward futures that feel both ambitious and meaningful.

Yet vision achieves its fullest power only when it becomes shared. Kouzes and Posner (2017) emphasise that leaders must enlist others in co-creating the horizon, while Senge (1990) frames vision as a discipline of collective meaning-making. When vision is co-owned rather than imposed, it generates commitment, aligns values, and converts abstract possibility into a lived organisational trajectory.

Vision as Strategic and Ethical Practice

Visionary leadership is neither poetic escapism nor rhetorical flourish; it is both strategic and ethical. Strategically, vision provides direction, while strategy provides the pathway. As Nanus (1992) cautions, vision without strategy risks fantasy, while strategy without vision lacks purpose. The two are symbiotic: vision defines the destination, strategy maps the journey.

Ethically, vision must be grounded in moral responsibility. Burns (1978) distinguishes transformational leadership by its capacity to connect present action with morally grounded future possibilities. Vision must therefore address not only what is achievable, but what is desirable. Werhane's (1999) concept of moral imagination underscores leaders' responsibility to envision futures that respect human dignity, ecological balance, and social justice. Visionary leadership demands creativity disciplined by ethical discernment, ensuring that possibility is aligned with responsibility.

Vision in Practice: Creativity, Experimentation, and Uncertainty

In contexts of volatility and disruption, vision requires creativity, experimentation, and adaptive resilience. Pink (2008) argues that contemporary leadership depends increasingly on right-brain capacities – design, narrative, empathy, synthesis, and meaning-making – which enable leaders to imagine non-obvious futures and communicate them in human terms. Orme (2019) further emphasises conscious creativity, where curiosity is grounded in awareness rather than novelty for its own sake.

Vision must also be tested through action. Transformational leaders translate insight into practice through experimentation, prototyping, and iterative learning (Bass, 1990; Orme, 2019). These processes surface assumptions, mitigate risk, and gradually align organisational capabilities with aspirational futures. In uncertain environments, antifragility – the capacity to grow stronger through disruption – becomes a defining advantage (Taleb, 2012). Visionary organisations embed feedback loops, decentralised experimentation, and adaptive learning, ensuring that vision remains responsive rather than rigid.

Vision, therefore, is neither prophecy nor abstraction. It is a dynamic practice – strategic, ethical, creative, and adaptive. When grounded in shared meaning, moral purpose, and disciplined experimentation, vision shapes not only organisational goals, but organisational becoming.

Distinguishing Vision: From Imagination to Execution

Vision is often conflated with strategy, mission, or goals, yet each serves a distinct leadership function. Mission articulates present purpose; strategy defines pathways; goals measure progress. Vision alone articulates the desired future state toward which all others align (Nanus, 1992). It functions as the guiding compass, shaping strategy, animating mission, and orienting milestones toward a coherent horizon.

Vision is inseparable from imagination, values, and emotion. Imagination enables leaders to perceive emergent possibilities and reframe constraints as opportunities (Follett, 1924). Values anchor vision ethically, ensuring that aspiration does not erode integrity or sustainability (George, 2007; Werhane, 1999). Emotion mobilises commitment and collective energy, transforming vision from statement to movement (Boyatzis & McKee, 2005). Mandela's vision of a "rainbow nation" exemplifies this emotional resonance, translating moral imagination into national transformation.

However, vision carries risks when misapplied. Tourish (2013) warns against over-personalised vision that creates dependency or ethical blind spots, as illustrated by Enron's charismatic yet destructive leadership (Sims & Brinkmann, 2003). Vagueness erodes credibility; exclusivity marginalises voices; overstretch occurs when ambition outpaces grounding (Mintzberg, 2009). Theranos stands as a cautionary tale of vision untethered from reality – rhetorically powerful but scientifically unsound.

Effective visionary leadership therefore balances imagination with execution, ambition with credibility. Vision must be inclusive, actionable, ethically grounded, and strategically disciplined.

Vision as the Westward Gaze

Vision represents the westward gaze of leadership – the capacity to orient toward a future that is both aspirational and grounded. Like the setting sun, it marks endings and beginnings, inviting reflection while illuminating possibility. Vision functions simultaneously as compass and canvas: directing collective movement while inspiring creative participation.

Sinek (2020) identifies three qualities of enduring vision: resilience amid turbulence, inclusivity across stakeholders, and service beyond self-interest. When vision embodies these qualities, it transcends rhetoric and becomes a living force. Collins and Porras (2005) further distinguish between charismatic visionary leaders and those who build enduring institutions. While charisma may ignite momentum, lasting impact emerges when vision is embedded in culture, values, and systems.

In the Imagination Age, visionary leadership is no longer optional. As creativity, technology, and complexity converge, leaders must craft horizons that stretch imagination while respecting reality. Vision bridges ethics and strategy, inspiration and execution, hope and discipline. Visionary leaders do not merely point toward distant futures; they cultivate conditions in which others can see, inhabit, and co-create them. In doing so, vision transforms possibility into shared reality – and leadership into an act of collective becoming.

The Horizon-Making Model: Leading with Vision

Visionary leadership is not a single flash of insight, nor a charismatic declaration of intent. Rather, it is a disciplined, cyclical practice through which leaders perceive emerging futures, shape them into meaningful direction, and mobilise collective action over time (Bennis & Nanus, 1985; Bass, 1990). In the Imagination Age – marked by uncertainty, technological acceleration, and social complexity – leaders must do more than announce a future. They must create the conditions in which many people can imagine, test, and realise that future together.

The Horizon-Making Model (Figure 5.1) provides a practical framework for this work. It conceptualises vision not as a static statement but as an ongoing process of *horizon construction*. Leaders continually move through five interdependent processes – Sensing, Framing, Storying, Co-creating, and Enacting – as contexts evolve. The model is intentionally recursive: enactment generates new signals that

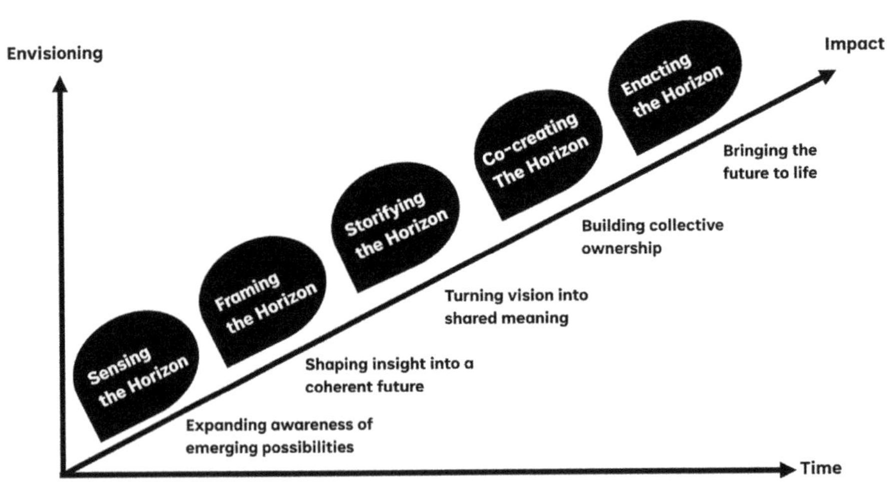

Figure 5.1 Horizon-Making Model.

Source: Developed by the author, informed by leadership and organisational literature.

demand renewed sensing; stories invite further co-creation; and framing is refined through experimentation and learning (Bass, 1990; Bennis & Nanus, 1985; Senge, 1990; Hines & Bishop, 2015; Pink, 2008).

Each process is explained and illustrated with examples as follows, demonstrating how leaders translate vision from personal insight into shared reality.

Sensing the Horizon: Expanding Awareness

Sensing is the practice of widening perceptual range – attending to weak signals, anomalies, emerging trends, and shifting stakeholder expectations (Weick, 1995; Hines & Bishop, 2015). It blends analytical foresight with imaginative curiosity, enabling leaders to notice what may not yet be fully visible (Pink, 2008).

Leadership practices include the following:

- Environmental and horizon scanning.
- Scenario planning and trend analysis.
- Reverse mentoring and frontline listening.
- Engagement with diverse knowledge sources (customers, regulators, researchers, communities).

Shell's scenario planning in the 1970s illustrates the power of sensing. By exploring multiple plausible energy futures, Shell was better prepared for oil shocks than many competitors (Wack, 1985). More recently, Adobe sensed the decline of perpetual licensing and the rise of cloud-based delivery, informing its strategic shift to Creative Cloud (McKinsey & Company, 2015).

Robust sensing reduces surprise, surfaces early options, and builds the confidence required to frame ambitious yet credible futures.

Framing the Horizon: Discipline in Imagination

Framing converts raw signals into purposeful direction. It synthesises complexity into a coherent aspiration that is strategic, morally grounded, and stretch-oriented (Bennis & Nanus, 1985; Burns, 1978; Collins & Porras, 1994).

Leadership practices include the following:

- Articulating a clear north star or BHAG.
- Anchoring ambition in values and purpose.
- Clarifying what will change, why it matters, and how success will be recognised.

Satya Nadella reframed Microsoft's future by integrating cloud strategy with a humanistic purpose of global empowerment, aligning culture, investment, and innovation (Nadella, 2017). Similarly, Unilever, under Paul Polman, reframed corporate success by embedding sustainability and social responsibility within long-term value creation.

Effective framing creates coherence – guiding resource allocation, shaping incentives, and providing a durable reference point for storytelling and co-creation.

Storifying the Horizon: From Vision to Shared Meaning

Vision becomes actionable when it is emotionally compelling. Storying translates abstraction into narrative, metaphor, and symbol – forms through which humans make sense of possibility and sustain commitment (Denning, 2011; Weick, 1995).

Leadership practices include the following:

- Use of lived stories, metaphors, and rituals.
- Repetition with variation across contexts.
- Embedding vision in symbols, ceremonies, and everyday language.

Nelson Mandela's "rainbow nation" metaphor offered an inclusive narrative for reconciliation, enabling collective movement beyond apartheid. Howard Schultz used his father's story to frame Starbucks' commitment to dignity and healthcare benefits, transforming policy into moral purpose (Gallo, 2016).

Storying builds emotional ownership and social identity, making the horizon tangible and worth pursuing.

Co-creating the Horizon: From Vision to Collective Ownership

Co-creation shifts vision from leader proclamation to shared authorship. As Senge (1990) argues, shared vision is a discipline of practice that requires structures for participation and dialogue.

Leadership practices include the following:

- Participatory foresight and design workshops.
- Cross-functional future teams.
- Distributed authority for local experimentation.
- Inclusion of marginalised or dissenting voices.

Pixar institutionalised candid "Braintrust" sessions, enabling collective critique without hierarchy and strengthening creative outcomes (Catmull, 2014). Grameen Bank co-created microfinance systems with communities, embedding ownership and dignity into local institutions (Yunus, 2007).

Co-creation deepens alignment, strengthens intrinsic motivation, and multiplies the cognitive resources devoted to the future.

Enacting the Horizon: Experimentation and Learning

Enactment is where imagination meets disciplined action. Leaders translate vision into capability through experimentation, learning loops, and adaptive scaling (Argyris & Schön, 1978; Heifetz et al., 2009).

Leadership practices include the following:

- Sponsoring small, reversible bets.
- Hypothesis-driven experimentation.
- Rapid feedback loops.
- Metrics that capture learning as well as performance.

SpaceX's iterative testing – accepting failed prototypes in pursuit of reusable rockets – demonstrates disciplined experimentation aligned with long-term vision (Vance, 2015). Adobe similarly tested and scaled its subscription model while balancing present revenue with future growth.

Enactment converts possibility into capability. It builds credibility, generates learning, and enables continual recalibration of the horizon as new evidence emerges.

A Living Cycle of Vision

These five processes are not linear steps to be completed once. They form a living cycle in which action generates new signals, stories evolve with context, and shared meaning is continually renewed. Through horizon-making, leaders do not merely point toward the future – they *build it with others*, transforming uncertainty into collective movement.

Creating a Culture of Possibility: From Vision to Shared Imagination

A leader's vision, however compelling, rarely transforms an organisation unless it becomes *shared imagination* – a lived, collective sense of what could be. This shift from individual insight to collective possibility is what separates charismatic dreamers from transformative leaders. Steve Jobs, Elon Musk, and Nelson Mandela are often cited not simply because they could *see* a different future, but because they cultivated environments where others could *feel* it, believe it, and act upon it (Isaacson, 2011; Vance, 2015). Senge (1990) calls this a *shared vision*: a collectively held picture of the future that generates meaning, energy, and commitment. Importantly, shared vision cannot be imposed; it emerges through dialogue, trust, and emotional connection (Senge, 1990). In systems terms, Wheatley (1999) describes this as a self-organising field – people align not primarily through coercion, but through resonance with purpose and possibility.

Building such a culture is not accidental. It is intentionally designed through relational conditions, leadership choices, and narrative meaning-making. Three foundations are especially decisive: psychological safety, shared power, and storytelling.

Psychological Safety: The Soil of Innovation

Possibility thrives where people can take interpersonal risks without fear. Edmondson (2018) defines psychological safety as a shared team belief that individuals can take interpersonal risks without fear of negative consequences. Without it, people self-censor, hide uncertainty, and protect status; with it, experimentation, dissent, and learning become normalised. Google's Project Aristotle similarly concluded that psychological safety was the most important factor distinguishing high-performing teams (Rozovsky, 2015). Seidman (2011) reframes trust and openness as practical necessities rather than aspirational values in contemporary organisations. Psychological safety, therefore, should be understood not as a soft cultural add-on, but as the invisible infrastructure that sustains learning, innovation, and collective sensemaking.

Power With, Not Power Over

A culture of possibility is inherently inclusive: it relies on "power with" rather than "power over." Living systems do not flourish through dominance but through interdependence, relationships, and mutual responsiveness (Wheatley, 1999). Leaders who share power do not weaken authority; they expand capacity – turning followers into co-creators. Chapman and Sisodia (2015) illustrate this through Barry-Wehmiller's "Truly Human Leadership," where treating people with dignity and care strengthens commitment and unlocks discretionary energy. Maxwell (2011) similarly argues that leadership maturity is measured not by personal achievement alone, but by people development – growing others into capability, confidence, and contribution.

Stories That Mobilise Collective Movement

Even strong structures and inclusive power can remain inert without meaning. Cultures are sustained by stories more than policies. Gallo (2016) argues that narratives communicate possibility more effectively than slides or slogans because they translate abstract goals into human significance. Storytelling functions as emotional architecture: it makes a future feel inhabited and morally worth building. In practice, possibility-oriented leaders repeatedly narrate "why" before "what," linking organisational aspiration to lived values and human dignity – thereby generating commitment rather than compliance.

When these three conditions converge – psychological safety, shared power, and meaning-rich storytelling – collective intelligence becomes an organisational norm. Catmull (2014) attributes Pixar's creative endurance to a culture of candour where every voice can challenge assumptions, and where systems are designed to convert vulnerability into learning. Similarly, Nadella's transformation of Microsoft is widely associated with a cultural shift from "know-it-all" to "learn-it-all," rooted in curiosity, empathy, and growth mindset (Nadella, 2017). The common thread is not heroism, but design: leaders construct environments where imagination can circulate, evolve, and compound.

The Courage to Imagine: Leading Beyond the Known

Creating possibility demands courage because imagination unsettles what feels safe and familiar. Brown (2018) highlights that such courage arises through vulnerability rather than certainty, a view echoed in Steve Jobs' refusal to smooth out his differences or conform to existing expectations. Imaginative leadership, therefore, requires the willingness to remain exposed and distinctive in order to create what does not yet exist. Apple's *Think Different* advertising campaign celebrated non-conformity and bold imagination:

> Here's to the crazy ones. The misfits. The rebels. The troublemakers. The round pegs in the square holes. The ones who see things differently. They're not fond of rules. And they have no respect for the status quo. You can quote them, disagree with them, glorify or vilify them. About the only thing you can't do is ignore them. Because they change things. They push the human race forward. And while some may see them as the crazy ones, we see genius. Because the people who are crazy enough to think they can change the world, are the ones who do. – Steve Jobs
>
> (Apple *Think Different* campaign, 1997 | Isaacson, 2011)

Possibility-driven leadership therefore involves normalising fear as part of learning – then converting that fear into disciplined experimentation. This is why "how" matters as much as "what": cultures that optimise efficiency at the expense of humanity often become brittle, risk-averse, and creatively exhausted (Seidman, 2011). Courageous leaders, by contrast, invite better questions, not just better answers. Berger (2014) shows how question discipline expands the imaginable – shifting from "Can we?" to "How might we?" – which keeps organisations mentally agile under uncertainty.

The Possibility Matrix

To translate imagination into organisational movement, leaders need tools that bridge aspiration and execution. The Possibility Matrix (Table 5.1) offers one such diagnostic. It maps two dimensions – *mindset* (scarcity to abundance) and *courage* (fear to imagination) – to illuminate four leadership zones. This matrix has been *developed by the author*, synthesising and extending established scholarship on mindset, vulnerability and courage, systems thinking, and strategic transformation (Anthony et al., 2017; Brown, 2018; Dweck, 2006; Wheatley, 1999).

Possibility leadership aims to move individuals and systems toward the Creative Zone, where imagination is paired with discipline, where the *Dual Transformation* concept becomes practically useful.

Table 5.1 The Possibility Matrix

	Courage/imagination	*Fear*
Abundance	Creative Zone: visionary, experimental, co-creative	Comfort Zone: stable but risk-averse
Scarcity	Dreamer Zone: ideas without execution	Survival Zone: reactive, compliance-driven

Source: Developed by author.

Dual Transformation

Anthony et al. (2017) – in Dual Transformation – clarifies how leaders can *reposition today's core* (Transformation A) while *building tomorrow's growth engine* (Transformation B), connected by capabilities that bridge present strengths and future opportunities. Together, the Possibility Matrix (diagnosis) and Dual Transformation (pathway) help leaders design cultures where the future can be explored without abandoning present responsibilities.

Ultimately, a culture of possibility is not built by charisma alone. It is built when leaders design the conditions in which shared imagination becomes normal: people feel safe to speak, empowered to shape outcomes, and inspired by stories that make the future worth the effort. In the Imagination Age, visionary leadership is increasingly less about heroic individuals and more about visionary systems – cultures where possibility can self-organise into collective movement (Senge, 1990; Wheatley, 1999).

Systems Thinking as Courageous Imagination

Systems thinking embodies the courage to imagine beyond the known, requiring leaders to relinquish linear certainty and engage with complexity, interdependence, and long-term consequence. It transforms imagination from speculative vision into responsible leadership practice. Systems thinking emerged as a response to the limits of linear, reductionist approaches to leadership and organisation. Rather than treating problems as isolated events or discrete variables, systems thinking invites leaders to see organisations as dynamic, interconnected wholes – shaped by feedback loops, time delays, and patterns that unfold over time (Senge, 1990; Meadows, 2008). This perspective requires a different kind of courage: the willingness to move beyond simple cause-and-effect explanations and confront complexity without premature closure.

The intellectual roots of systems thinking can be traced to General Systems Theory, which challenged mechanistic assumptions by arguing that living and social systems cannot be understood by analysing their parts in isolation. Meaning arises from relationships rather than components, and behaviour emerges from interaction rather than control. This insight fundamentally questioned managerial models built on predictability, optimisation, and decomposition.

Building on this foundation, *The Fifth Discipline* introduced systems thinking as a core leadership discipline – a way of seeing patterns rather than snapshots, structures rather than events (Senge, 1990). Senge demonstrated how well-intentioned actions often generate unintended consequences because leaders fail to recognise reinforcing and balancing feedback loops embedded within organisational systems. Imagination, in this sense, is not fantasy but disciplined perception – the ability to see what is shaping outcomes beneath the surface.

Donella Meadows (2008) advanced this thinking by identifying leverage points – places within a system where small shifts can produce disproportionate change. Crucially, she argued that the most powerful leverage points are not policies or structures, but mindsets, goals, and paradigms. This insight is especially salient in the Imagination Age, where technological capability often outpaces moral and systemic understanding. Courageous leadership, therefore, involves challenging underlying assumptions, not merely adjusting processes.

Systems thinking has also been reframed as a leadership sensemaking practice. Weick (1995) emphasised that leaders do not simply respond to environments; they actively enact them through interpretation, framing, and action. From this view, leadership is less about control and prediction, and more about orchestrating meaning across complex, evolving systems.

Intellectual Adda | System Leadership: A Conversation with S M Zillur Rahman

S M Zillur Rahman is passionate about leadership in the context of the fourth industrial revolution. His consultancy work focuses on the role of leaders in a world experiencing paradigm shifts, where systems thinking has become essential for creating harmony and coherence in how twenty-first-century leaders think and act. A former Army officer, Zillur's leadership was tested not only in high-pressure conflict zones during United Nations peacekeeping operations, but also in developing leaders within complex organisational environments. After voluntarily retiring from military service, he transitioned into the corporate sector to apply his experience at scale. Today, he is a specialist in Industry 4.0 leadership, supporting organisations in leadership development, talent management, and navigating systemic change in technologically accelerated contexts.

In this Intellectual Adda, the author engages in a reflective and exploratory dialogue with Zillur Rahman to conceptualise the role of systems thinking in shaping leadership for the Imagination Age.

Author: *Imagination Age driven by fourth industrial revolution (Industry 4.0) has transformed organisations into complex socio-technical systems where technology,* *people, culture, and markets interact continuously. From your perspective, what fundamentally distinguishes leadership in this era from leadership in earlier industrial ages?*

Zillur: Leadership in the Imagination Age is fundamentally distinguished by the level of complexity, interdependence, and speed of change that leaders navigate. In earlier industrial ages, organisations operated largely as linear systems: inputs were transformed into outputs through relatively predictable processes. Leadership focused on efficiency, control, and optimisation of individual functions. In contrast, Industry 4.0 organisations are socio-technical ecosystems, where digital technologies, human behaviours, organisational culture, external stakeholders, and global forces continuously interact. A change in one element instantly influences others, often in unpredictable ways. This means leadership today is less about controlling parts and more about understanding relationships, managing interdependencies, anticipating ripple effects, and guiding adaptive systems. Leaders must move from being commanders of processes to architects of systems – shaping structures, cultures, and feedback mechanisms that enable sustainable performance and innovation.

Author: *Many organisational problems today appear as isolated events – declining performance, resistance to change, technology failures. How does systems thinking help leaders move beyond surface symptoms to understand the deeper structures and interdependencies producing these outcomes?*

Zillur: Systems thinking helps leaders shift from reacting to events toward understanding the underlying structures and dynamics that generate those events. Instead of asking, "What went wrong here?", systems thinkers ask: What patterns are recurring over time? What structures are shaping these patterns? How are different parts of the system influencing each other? For example, resistance to change is rarely just an employee attitude problem. It often emerges from deeper systemic factors such as misaligned incentives, lack of trust, poor communication, leadership behaviours, and workload pressures. Similarly, technology failures are frequently not technical issues alone, but outcomes of misalignment between systems of people, processes, and culture. By mapping interconnections and feedback loops, leaders can identify root mechanisms rather than treating symptoms. This enables more sustainable solutions, redesigning systems instead of repeatedly fixing surface problems.

Author: *You have emphasised that leaders must act as synthesisers rather than mere analysts. How does systems thinking enable leaders to see the "big picture" and become truly visionary in environments characterised by rapid technological and social change?*

Zillur: Systems thinking cultivates the leader's ability to integrate diverse elements into a coherent whole, which is the foundation of vision. Analytical thinking breaks problems into parts, which is essential for expertise and operational excellence. But leadership requires synthesis – seeing how those parts interact over time within a larger system. Through systems thinking, leaders recognise patterns across departments, markets, and technologies; understand how short-term decisions shape long-term outcomes; anticipate unintended consequences; connect technological trends with human and organisational dynamics. This holistic perspective allows leaders to imagine future states of the organisation – not just incremental improvements. Visionary leadership emerges when leaders can perceive emerging system-wide shifts, integrate multiple forces into strategic direction, guide the organisation toward sustainable futures. In essence, systems thinking transforms leaders from problem-solvers into system shapers.

Author: *When leaders are trained in linear, silo-based thinking, what concrete practices can leaders adopt to begin cultivating a system-thinking mindset in everyday decision-making?*

Zillur: Leaders can cultivate system-thinking through several practical habits:

- Shift from event focus to pattern focus. Instead of reacting to individual issues, examine trends over time.
- Map interconnections. Use simple causal loop diagrams or stakeholder maps to visualise how actions in one area affect others.
- Ask systemic questions. What are the root structures driving this issue? Who else is affected by this decision? What might be the long-term consequences?
- Encourage cross-functional dialogue. Break silos by involving diverse perspectives in problem-solving.
- Test decisions through system impact thinking. Before acting, consider second- and third-order effects.

Over time, these practices retrain leaders to naturally think in terms of wholes rather than fragments.

Author: *Based on your experience, what typically happens when leaders intervene in complex systems with linear solutions? And conversely, what becomes possible when leaders design actions with systemic interconnections in mind?*

Zillur: When leaders apply linear solutions to complex systems, several patterns commonly emerge, problems shift rather than disappear, new unintended issues arise, short-term gains lead to long-term instability, and organisations enter cycles of recurring crises. For example, cutting costs may boost short-term profitability but erode morale, reduce innovation, and increase turnover – ultimately harming performance. Conversely, when leaders intervene systemically, solutions address root causes; improvements reinforce each other through positive feedback loops; change becomes more sustainable; and organisations become more adaptive and resilient. Systemic leadership enables alignment across people, processes, technology, and strategy – creating conditions where success compounds over time.

Author: *Some scholars argue that modern leadership requires understanding not just events, but the deeper structures and mechanisms shaping organisational behaviour. How does this deeper, systemic perspective change the way leaders diagnose problems and lead transformation?*

Zillur: A deeper systemic perspective fundamentally transforms leadership diagnosis and action. Rather than attributing outcomes to individual performance or isolated decisions, leaders focus on organisational structures, cultural norms, power relationships, incentive systems, and information flows. This leads to a shift from blame to design. For example, instead of disciplining employees for poor performance, a systemic leader examines whether goals are realistic, systems support success, feedback is effective, and resources are adequate. In transformation efforts, leaders move beyond superficial change – such as new policies or technologies – and redesign the deeper systems that shape behaviour.

This results in more enduring organisational change and stronger alignment between strategy, culture, and performance.

From Manager to Enterprise Leader: The Seven Seismic Shifts

The Seven Seismic Shifts from Manager to Enterprise Leader were originally articulated by Watkins (2012) in his analysis of how managers evolve into enterprise leaders. While Watkins presents these shifts as changes in mindset, scope, and influence, they can also be read through a systems thinking lens. Viewed this way, the shifts represent a developmental journey from linear, functionally bounded thinking toward systemic awareness – where leaders learn to see interdependencies, patterns over time, and the broader organisational and societal ecosystems in which they operate.

As Watkins (2012) outlines, enterprise leadership requires a series of fundamental transitions, each of which aligns closely with core principles of systems thinking (Senge, 1990; Meadows, 2008):

- The shift from **Specialist to Generalist** reflects the systems insight that no single function can be optimised in isolation without harming the whole (Senge, 1990).
- Moving from **Analyst to Integrator** mirrors the core systems task of synthesising diverse perspectives and reconciling competing feedback loops.
- The transition from **Tactician to Strategist** requires seeing patterns over time, anticipating second-order effects, and understanding how external systems – markets, regulators, societies – interact with the organisation.
- Becoming an **Architect rather than a Bricklayer** is explicitly systemic: leaders design structures, processes, and cultures so that desired behaviours emerge naturally rather than being enforced through control.
- The shift from **Problem Solver to Agenda Setter** aligns with Meadows' (2008) argument that the most powerful interventions lie in deciding which questions deserve sustained attention.
- Moving from **Warrior to Diplomat** reflects systemic awareness of inter-organisational and societal ecosystems, where influence depends on relationships rather than authority.
- Finally, the transition from **Supporting Cast Member to Lead Role** underscores the symbolic dimension of systems: leaders shape collective sensemaking through presence, narrative, and example (Weick, 1995).

Taken together, these shifts are not discrete competencies but expressions of a deeper transformation – from linear thinking to systemic awareness. Enterprise leaders succeed not because they know more, but because they see more: connections, consequences, and possibilities that remain invisible to those trapped in silos.

In the Imagination Age – where organisations are embedded within technological, social, ecological, and ethical systems of unprecedented complexity – systems thinking becomes indispensable. It is the cognitive and moral foundation that enables leaders to integrate imagination with responsibility, and possibility with stewardship.

Risks, Shadows, and Ethical Guardrails

Visionary leadership carries inherent risks when imagination is left untethered. Storytelling can slide into manipulation, as seen in the Theranos scandal; bold, aspirational goals can become reckless overreach, as illustrated by WeWork's collapse; and exclusionary visions can silence marginalised voices when leaders mistake dominance for direction. These cases remind us that imagination, while generative, is never neutral. Without ethical grounding, it can distort reality as easily as it can reshape it. For this reason, leaders must anchor imaginative practice in empirical testing, plural perspectives, and moral accountability (Seidman, 2011; Denning, 2011). Vision must be continuously interrogated through questions that serve as ethical guardrails: *Who benefits? Who bears the risk? Whose voices are absent? What evidence supports this move?* Imagination matures into leadership only when it is disciplined by responsibility.

History offers powerful examples of imagination held in ethical tension. Nelson Mandela's vision of a "rainbow nation" functioned as both political horizon and moral bridge. Through symbolic acts – most notably sport diplomacy – Mandela sustained a shared narrative that enabled reconciliation while mobilising collective participation across a fractured society. The horizon he articulated healed even as it inspired action.

In contrast, Elon Musk's ambition to make humanity multi-planetary demonstrates a different mode of visionary courage. SpaceX's audacious goal pushed the boundaries of engineering, yet its progress depended not on rhetoric alone but on relentless experimentation, public learning, and iterative failure. Here, imagination was enacted through disciplined prototyping rather than blind belief.

Satya Nadella's leadership at Microsoft illustrates how vision can be renewed from within. By reframing the organisation's purpose and practising inclusive storytelling, Nadella aligned cultural renewal with strategic transformation. The result was not only a technological pivot to the cloud, but a measurable organisational turnaround rooted in empathy and learning.

Similarly, Muhammad Yunus reimagined economic possibility for the poor by reframing credit as a human right rather than a privilege. Through small-scale pilot loans that respected local context, Grameen Bank co-created systems that later scaled into institutional practice, demonstrating how imagination grounded in dignity can transform entire ecosystems.

Corporate contrasts further sharpen the lesson. Adobe's shift to Creative Cloud exemplifies dual transformation – protecting core value while inventing a new future. Kodak, by contrast, illustrates the cost of comfort-zone thinking and the failure to co-create a new horizon despite possessing the underlying technology.

These examples converge on a final insight: imagining the future is never a solitary act. As Duarte and Sanchez (2016) describe through the metaphor of the *torchbearer*, the future begins as an unformed space – an unknown terrain that requires someone to see possibility where others see uncertainty.

> The future is a formless void,
> A blank space waiting to be filled.
> And then a Torchbearer envisions a new possibility.
> The vision is your dream, your calling,
> And it burns like a fire in your belly.
> But you cannot create the future alone.
> You need Travelers to come along.

Yet the path through the unknown is dark and unclear.
You have to illuminate the path for travelers.
Torchbearers communicate in a way that conquers fear and inspire hope.
Some say being a torchbearer is a burden.
Some say it's blessing.
Either way, those who light the path are the ones who change the world.

(Duarte and Sanchez, 2016, p.7)

Yet torchbearers do not walk alone. They invite others to travel with them, illuminating the path through fear and ambiguity with clarity, meaning, and hope. To carry the torch is both burden and blessing. But history suggests that those willing to light the way – while remaining accountable to those who follow – are the ones who truly change the world. These are the leaders who are inspired by the west – The Setting Sun.

Conclusion

The setting sun in the Leadership Compass symbolises far more than a picturesque destination or a poetic ending. It represents the westward gaze of leadership – the disciplined art of horizon-making in a world defined by uncertainty, complexity, and rapid transformation. This horizon is not fixed or final; it is continuously shaped through attentive practice. Leaders are called to sense emerging signals at the edges of systems, frame these insights into meaningful and ethical direction, translate abstraction into shared meaning through story, invite others into co-ownership, and enact possibilities through disciplined experimentation. These practices form a living cycle rather than a linear process.

In the Imagination Age, leadership work is both aesthetic and operational. Leaders must imagine futures that are compelling, just, and plausible, while simultaneously designing structures, routines, and cultures that allow those futures to be explored and realised collectively. Vision, in this sense, is neither prophecy nor performance – it is a craft grounded in curiosity, moral responsibility, and learning. When leaders practise horizon-making with humility rather than certainty, courage rather than control, and empirical rigour rather than wishful thinking, vision becomes actionable. It moves from rhetoric to reality, from individual insight to shared endeavour. The setting sun thus reminds leaders that endings are also beginnings – and that leadership is ultimately about enabling others to walk toward horizons worth inhabiting.

Reflective Questions

1. How do you cultivate the imaginative and foresightful capacity to sense emerging possibilities, rather than simply reacting to changes already unfolding around you?

2. When you communicate a vision of the future, how effectively does it inspire shared commitment while remaining ethically grounded and practically achievable?
3. In your leadership practice, how do you translate vision into action – ensuring that imagination is supported by strategy, experimentation, and learning so that possibility becomes reality?

References

Anthony, S. D., Trotter, D., & Schwartz, E. I. (2017). *Dual transformation: How to reposition today's business while creating the future*. Harvard Business Review Press.

Apple Inc. (1997). *Think different* [Advertising campaign].

Argyris, C., & Schön, D. A. (1978). *Organizational learning: A theory of action perspective*. Addison-Wesley.

Barker, J. A. (1992). *Paradigms: The business of discovering the future*. HarperBusiness.

Bass, B. M. (1990). *Bass & Stogdill's handbook of leadership: Theory, research, and managerial applications* (3rd ed.). Free Press.

Bennis, W. (1994). *On becoming a leader* (Rev. ed.). Addison-Wesley.

Bennis, W., & Nanus, B. (1985). *Leaders: Strategies for taking charge*. Harper & Row.

Berger, W. (2014). *A more beautiful question: The power of inquiry to spark breakthrough ideas*. Bloomsbury Publishing.

Boyatzis, R. E., & McKee, A. (2005). *Resonant leadership: Renewing yourself and connecting with others through mindfulness, hope, and compassion*. Harvard Business School Press.

Boyatzis, R. E., Rochford, K., & Taylor, S. N. (2015). The role of the positive emotional attractor in vision and shared vision. *Frontiers in Psychology, 6*, Article 670. https://doi.org/10.3389/fpsyg.2015.00670

Brown, B. (2018). *Dare to lead: Brave work. Tough conversations. Whole hearts*. Random House.

Burns, J. M. (1978). *Leadership*. Harper & Row.

Catmull, E., & Wallace, A. (2014). *Creativity, Inc.: Overcoming the unseen forces that stand in the way of true inspiration*. Random House.

Chapman, B., & Sisodia, R. (2015). *Everybody matters: The extraordinary power of caring for your people like family*. Portfolio.

Collins, J. C., & Porras, J. I. (1994). *Built to last: Successful habits of visionary companies*. HarperBusiness.

Collins, J. C., & Porras, J. I. (2005). *Built to last: Successful habits of visionary companies*. Random House Business/ HarperBusiness.

Denning, S. (2011). *The leader's guide to storytelling* (2nd ed.). Jossey-Bass.

Duarte, N., & Sanchez, P. (2016). *Illuminate: Ignite change through speeches, stories, ceremonies, and symbols*. Wiley.

Dweck, C. S. (2006). *Mindset: The new psychology of success*. Random House.

Edmondson, A. C. (2018). *The fearless organization: Creating psychological safety in the workplace for learning, innovation, and growth*. Wiley.

Follett, M. P. (1924). *Creative experience*. Longmans, Green & Co.

Gallo, C. (2016). *The storyteller's secret*. Macmillan.

George, B. (2007). *True north: Discover your authentic leadership*. Jossey-Bass.

Goleman, D. (1998). *Working with emotional intelligence*. Bantam Books.
Heifetz, R. A., Grashow, A., & Linsky, M. (2009). *The practice of adaptive leadership: Tools and tactics for changing your organization and the world*. Harvard Business Press.
Hines, A., & Bishop, P. (2015). *Thinking about the future*. Social Technologies.
Isaacson, W. (2011). *Steve Jobs*. Simon & Schuster.
Kotter, J. P. (1990). *A force for change: How leadership differs from management*. Free Press.
Kouzes, J. M., & Posner, B. Z. (2017). *The leadership challenge* (6th ed.). Wiley.
Maxwell, J. C. (2011). *The 5 levels of leadership*. Center Street.
McKinsey & Company. (2015). *Reborn in the cloud*. www.mckinsey.com/capabilities/tech-and-ai/our-insights/reborn-in-the-cloud
Meadows, D. H. (2008). *Thinking in systems: A primer*. Chelsea Green Publishing.
Mintzberg, H. (2009). *Managing*. Berrett-Koehler Publishers.
Nadella, S. (2017). *Hit refresh: The quest to rediscover Microsoft's soul and imagine a better future for everyone*. HarperBusiness.
Nanus, B. (1992). *Visionary leadership*. Jossey-Bass.
Orme, G. (2019). *The human edge: How curiosity and creativity are your superpowers in the digital economy*. FT Publishing.
Pink, D. H. (2008). *A whole new mind: Why right-brainers will rule the future*. Marshall Cavendish Business.
Rozovsky, J. (2015). *The five keys to a successful Google team*. re:Work (Google).
Seidman, D. (2011). *How: Why how we do anything means everything*. Wiley.
Senge, P. M. (1990). *The fifth discipline: The art and practice of the learning organization*. Doubleday.
Sims, R. R., & Brinkmann, J. (2003). Enron ethics. *Journal of Business Ethics, 45*(3), 243–256. https://doi.org/10.1023/A:1024194519384
Sinek, S. (2020). *The infinite game*. Penguin.
Snyder, C. R. (2002). Hope theory: Rainbows in the mind. *Psychological Inquiry, 13*(4), 249–275. https://doi.org/10.1207/S15327965PLI1304_01
Taleb, N. N. (2012). *Antifragile: Things that gain from disorder*. Random House.
Tourish, D. (2013). *The dark side of transformational leadership*. Routledge.
Vance, A. (2015). *Elon Musk*. HarperCollins.
Wack, P. (1985). Scenarios: Uncharted waters ahead. *Harvard Business Review, 63*(5), 72–89. https://hbr.org/1985/09/scenarios-uncharted-waters-ahead
Watkins, M. D. (2012). How managers become leaders. *Harvard Business Review, 90*(6), 64–72.
Weick, K. E. (1995). *Sensemaking in organizations*. Sage.
Werhane, P. H. (1999). *Moral imagination and management decision-making*. Oxford University Press.
Wheatley, M. J. (1999). *Leadership and the new science: Discovering order in a chaotic world* (2nd ed.). Berrett-Koehler Publishers.
Yunus, M. (2007). *Creating a world without poverty: Social business and the future of capitalism*. PublicAffairs.

Chapter 6

Storytelling as the Needle

The Secret Language of Leadership

Introduction

At the heart of the Leadership Compass lies not another cardinal direction, but the element that makes navigation possible: the needle. That needle is storytelling. Just as a compass needle magnetises north, south, east, and west into a navigable whole, storytelling aligns purpose, people, performance, and possibility into a lived and coherent practice of leadership. Without the needle, the compass is inert. Without stories, leadership fragments – unable to inspire belief, cultivate connection, sustain performance, or imagine futures beyond the immediate horizon.

Humans are, at their core, storytelling beings. Anthropological research suggests that the capacity for narrative is among the most defining features of our species (Boyd, 2009). Stories are not mere embellishments to rational life; they are the primary way humans make sense of complexity, transmit values across generations, and bind individuals into communities of meaning (Moin, 2025). As Fisher's (1984) narrative paradigm compellingly asserts, humans are *Homo narrans* – storytelling animals – whose judgments and actions are shaped less by abstract logic than by the coherence and credibility of the stories they encounter and inhabit.

Leadership, therefore, is inherently a narrative act. Leaders do not simply manage systems or allocate resources; they frame reality, interpret experience, and invite others into shared meaning. Denning (2011) identifies storytelling as the leader's most powerful instrument – one that communicates vision, builds trust, and mobilises collective action. Bennis (1994) similarly reminds us that leadership is fundamentally about meaning-making, and meaning, in human culture, is always constructed through story.

This chapter contends that storytelling is not a peripheral skill but the central axis of leadership itself. It is the needle of the Leadership Compass – the force that aligns purpose with people, translates vision into action, shapes cultures of excellence, and renders the future imaginable. Without storytelling, leaders may possess noble intentions and ambitious visions, yet these remain disconnected from human experience – like isolated points without orientation. Storytelling creates the magnetic field of leadership and essential for organisations (Brown et al., 2009). It transforms purpose into inspiration, relationships into trust, performance

DOI: 10.4324/9781003766414-6

into shared endeavour, and possibility into believable horizons. In the Imagination Age, leaders who master authentic storytelling will not only navigate complexity but will also awaken the collective courage to pursue futures worth reaching.

Storytelling as Navigation: Introducing the Needle

The compass metaphor helps illuminate the role of storytelling as navigation. Each cardinal point of leadership is essential: purpose (north) gives direction, people (east) provide energy, performance (south) grounds execution, and possibility (west) paints horizons – the futures. Yet, without a needle, these directions cannot be aligned. Storytelling is the navigational force that ensures all four points cohere.

North (Purpose): A leader may know their True North, but it becomes compelling only when shared through story. For example, Patagonia's narrative of "business unusual." Their purpose of saving the planet is not conveyed in strategy documents alone, but in founder Yvon Chouinard's stories of climbing, conservation, and anti-consumerist ethos (Chouinard & Stanley, 2012).

East (People): Connection with people is emotional, not transactional. Howard Schultz of Starbucks told his story of growing up in a poor neighbourhood in Brooklyn to build empathy with employees, transforming corporate culture through shared humanity (Gallo, 2016).

South (Performance): Efficiency and systems are often thought of as dry, yet stories embed values into daily practices. Toyota's Kaizen philosophy thrives not through procedures alone, but through stories of workers solving small problems and leaders celebrating incremental improvements (Imai, 1986; Liker, 2004).

West (Possibility): Possibility is vision, but stories are the bridge between present and future. Kennedy's 1962 "moonshot" speech remains iconic because it framed space exploration not merely as engineering but as a collective human adventure (Denning, 2011).

In each case, the story is the magnetic field aligning the compass – turning isolated points into a meaningful journey.

Theoretical Foundations of Storytelling in Leadership

Although storytelling often appears as a natural skill, a wide body of research across communication, psychology, anthropology, and management reveals that its power is grounded in deep theoretical foundations. When leaders understand these foundations, storytelling becomes not an ad hoc performance but a disciplined practice for shaping meaning, aligning people, and mobilising collective action. Storytelling is thus not an embellishment to leadership but a core mechanism through which leaders coordinate understanding, identity, and future possibility.

The Narrative Paradigm

Walter Fisher's narrative paradigm helps explain why storytelling is effective. Fisher (1984) argues that humans are essentially storytelling beings (*Homo narrans*), and that narrative – rather than technical rationality – is our primary way of communicating and making judgments. He suggests that people evaluate stories using two key criteria: narrative coherence and narrative fidelity. Narrative coherence asks whether the story holds together logically, with consistent characters, events, and reasoning. Narrative fidelity asks whether the story feels true and aligns with people's lived experiences and values. In leadership, this means that followers respond not to the sophistication of a leader's argument but to whether the leader's narrative feels believable and aligned with their own hopes, concerns, and moral intuitions. Paul Polman's story of Unilever's *Sustainable Living Plan* illustrates this well: it resonated because it cohered with Unilever's historical identity and aligned with broader societal values around environmental stewardship and long-term value creation (Polman & Winston, 2021). A vision statement, however inspiring, fails if it is not lived and does not generate authentic stories. Yuval Noah Harari's work further reinforces Fisher's (1984) insights by showing that human civilisation itself is built on shared stories – from religions and nations to corporations and currencies (Harari, 2014). These "collective fictions" enable large-scale cooperation. Leadership storytelling, therefore, is not a modern management fad but a continuation of the deep human tendency to organise around shared narratives.

Storytelling as Sensemaking

Weick (1995) expands the role of storytelling into the domain of organisational sensemaking. Organisations operate in conditions of uncertainty, ambiguity, and constant change. In such environments, leaders help people interpret events by offering narratives that create meaning and direction. Stories are thus functional: they help employees make sense of complexity, especially during transitions or crises. Satya Nadella's early leadership at Microsoft exemplifies this dynamic. By reframing the company's identity from a *know-it-all* culture to a *learn-it-all* culture, Nadella offered a unifying narrative that made sense of Microsoft's prior stagnation while legitimising and inspiring experimentation, curiosity, and renewal as the pathway forward (Nadella et al., 2017). In Weick's (1995) terms, sensemaking is social and retrospective: people understand what is happening through the stories leaders tell about what happened.

Storytelling and Organisational Culture

Schein (2010) identifies stories as one of the most powerful cultural artefacts in organisations. Stories communicate what the organisation values, rewards, tolerates, and aspires to. They transmit norms far more effectively than manuals or policies. The iconic 3M story of Art Fry inventing the Post-it Note while experimenting with weak adhesive illustrates the culture of experimentation and risk-taking that 3M holds dear. Denning (2011) builds on this by categorising leadership stories into several types: springboard stories that spark change, knowledge-sharing stories, value stories, and vision stories, etc. Each form supports different cultural functions, from preserving collective memory to motivating innovation. Leaders who fail to tell stories leave cultural meaning-making to chance, allowing fragmented or competing narratives to fill the void. Aaker (2018) adds a crucial dimension through his concept of signature stories – authentic, memorable narrative assets that convey an organisation's purpose, value, and strategic direction. Signature stories like Airbnb's founding tale or Patagonia's environmental activism help organisations differentiate themselves, build emotional resonance, and embed identity in concrete, relatable narratives. They become cultural cornerstones.

Psychology and Neuroscience of Storytelling

Psychology explains *why* stories work so effectively. Heath and Heath (2007) argue that stories are *sticky* because they transform abstract ideas into concrete, emotionally resonant narratives. People are more likely to remember stories than principles or strategies. Neuroscience supports this. Zak (2014) demonstrates that emotionally engaging stories increase oxytocin, enhancing empathy and cooperation. Stephens et al. (2010) show that storytelling produces neural coupling – synchronisation between the storyteller's and listener's brain patterns – which facilitates shared understanding and trust. Mandela's *rainbow nation* metaphor or Nadella's empathy-driven narratives are powerful precisely because they activate both cognitive and emotional pathways. Data may inform, but stories transform.

Authenticity and the Leadership Narrative

Authentic leadership theory emphasises that storytelling is not performative but identity-forming. George (2003) argues that leaders develop authenticity through reflecting on and sharing personal life stories. This resonates with Erikson's (1968) theory of identity development: narrative integration is essential to forming a coherent self. Howard Schultz's story of his father losing his job and healthcare benefits became the foundation of Starbucks' employee-centred philosophy (Gallo, 2016). Authentic stories meet Fisher's (1984) test of fidelity; fabricated stories do not. Leaders who bend or invent stories for influence risk violating trust, which is the core currency of leadership.

Storytelling and Strategic Vision

Visionary leadership is inseparable from storytelling. Bennis and Nanus (1985) emphasise that leaders articulate visions that serve as focal points for collective energy and commitment. But visions inspire only when narrated as compelling, shared journeys – not as lists of goals.

John F. Kennedy's moonshot speech was effective because it embedded a technical objective within a narrative of exploration, national ambition, and human possibility (Kennedy, 1962). It passed Fisher's (1984) tests of coherence (a believable plan) and fidelity (alignment with American values of progress). Harari's (2014) insight reinforces this: visions are shared fictions that enable large groups to act together toward futures that do not yet exist.

Storytelling as Relational Practice

Leadership is fundamentally relational, and stories are a primary medium of human connection. Kouzes and Posner (2017) highlight that leaders inspire a shared vision and encourage the heart, both of which require storytelling. Research on psychological safety (Edmondson, 1999) shows that when leaders share personal stories – including vulnerability – teams become more open, trusting, and cohesive. In diverse or cross-cultural teams, inclusive narratives are essential for belonging and shared identity.

Critical Perspectives: Storytelling's Shadow

Despite its power, storytelling carries risks. Boje (1991) warns that organisations contain multiple, fragmented narratives that can compete and confuse. Gabriel (2000) cautions that stories may romanticise leaders, obscure structural problems, or manipulate emotions. Corporate scandals, political propaganda, and the Theranos collapse case demonstrate storytelling's dark potential when narrative fidelity is violated. Ethical awareness is essential.

Case Study 6.1 When Vision Becomes Deception: The Fall of Theranos

The collapse of Theranos represents a profound failure of leadership storytelling. More than a technological or financial breakdown, it illustrates how vision, when detached from truth, can become ethically dangerous. The case highlights the shadow side of storytelling – when persuasive narratives silence dissent and obscure reality.

Founded in 2003 by Elizabeth Holmes, Theranos promised to revolutionise blood testing through a device capable of running hundreds of tests from a few drops of blood. Holmes framed this vision as a moral mission to democratise healthcare and reduce patient suffering. This compelling story resonated strongly with Silicon Valley's disruption culture and attracted significant investment, despite the absence of transparent scientific validation (Carreyrou, 2018).

Theranos raised over $700 million and reached a valuation of $9 billion, sustained largely by narrative dominance rather than operational performance. Internally, the technology failed to deliver on its promises, and employees who raised concerns were marginalised. From a leadership perspective, the story retained *narrative coherence* but lost *narrative fidelity* – it sounded convincing while being disconnected from reality (Denning, 2007).

The narrative began to collapse in 2015 when investigative journalist John Carreyrou exposed the company's practices through a series of reports (Carreyrou, 2015). As counter-stories gained credibility, trust eroded rapidly. Theranos shut down in 2018, and Holmes was later convicted of investor fraud and sentenced to prison (U.S. Department of Justice, 2022).

This case demonstrates a critical leadership lesson: storytelling is never neutral. Visionary leadership demands imagination, but it also requires honesty, accountability, and ethical responsibility. When storytelling loses fidelity to truth, leadership itself collapses.

The Needle in the Age of Imagination and AI

The Imagination Age has dramatically expanded who can tell stories and how stories are created, opening new spaces for creativity, meaning-making, and narrative expression (Moin, 2025). Yet the rise of artificial intelligence introduces a profound leadership challenge. As AI systems generate persuasive texts, images, and simulations at scale, the risk of eroding trust, authenticity, and shared meaning intensifies (Denning, 2007; Floridi et al., 2018). Leadership storytelling must therefore evolve – from crafting compelling narratives to protecting credibility, ethical responsibility, and human presence.

In this context, the needle of the Leadership Compass must do more than align purpose, people, performance, and possibility; it must safeguard truth. While machines can now produce fluent and polished stories, credibility remains a human achievement. Trust, empathy, and moral meaning arise from lived experience and relational presence, not from algorithmic sophistication. The paradox of the Imagination Age is clear: technology may accelerate storytelling, but belief still depends on human authenticity (Moin, 2025).

Research in neuroscience and narrative shows that stories shape how people interpret complexity, build trust, and coordinate collective action (Zak, 2014). Storytelling is therefore not a soft leadership add-on but a core mechanism of culture, identity, and mobilisation. Yet narrative power is ethically double-edged. As Denning (2007) warns, the same stories that inspire can also manipulate. In an era of synthetic narratives and deepfakes, leaders must develop narrative literacy – understanding how stories influence belief.

The leadership task today is not to compete with machines as storytellers, but to use technology in service of human meaning. Leaders who treat storytelling as the compass needle – anchored in authenticity, coherence, and ethical responsibility – can navigate uncertainty without sacrificing trust. In doing so, they preserve storytelling as a distinctly human act: one that aligns purpose with people, embeds values into performance, and renders future possibilities believable rather than merely imaginable.

Case Study 6.2 Accenture and the Limits of AI-Generated Leadership Narratives

As generative AI surged in 2023–2024, Accenture rapidly integrated AI into proposals, reports, and client communications, positioning itself as a leader in "GenAI-powered reinvention" (Accenture, 2023). While AI-produced narratives were fast and polished, internal reviews and client feedback revealed a limitation: they often lacked contextual depth, emotional resonance, and situational credibility in high-stakes transformation work (Iansiti & Lakhani, 2024).

In response, Accenture reframed AI as a co-pilot rather than a storyteller-in-chief. AI supported analysis and scenario modelling, while human consultants retained responsibility for sensemaking, framing, and narrative judgment. This shift reflected a key insight: clients resist not data, but stories that do not feel true to their lived experience (Accenture, 2024). The case illustrates a central lesson of the Imagination Age – AI can generate plausible stories, but leadership depends on believable ones grounded in human insight and trust.

Storytelling for Leaders: A Conceptual Model

Storytelling is the needle that aligns purpose, people, performance, and possibility. Each compass point calls for a distinct kind of story, grounded in different theoretical literatures and serving a particular function. The four-story-type model (Figure 6.1) provides both conceptual guides and practical templates.

Purpose Stories That Anchor Meaning and Moral Direction

North-facing stories answer the question: *Why do we exist?* They provide existential grounding and moral clarity. From Smith's (2019) taxonomy, the following stories align strongly with Purpose:

Origin Story: Where the company came from.
Corporate Values Story: What the company believes.
Leadership Philosophy Story: Why the leader leads as they do.

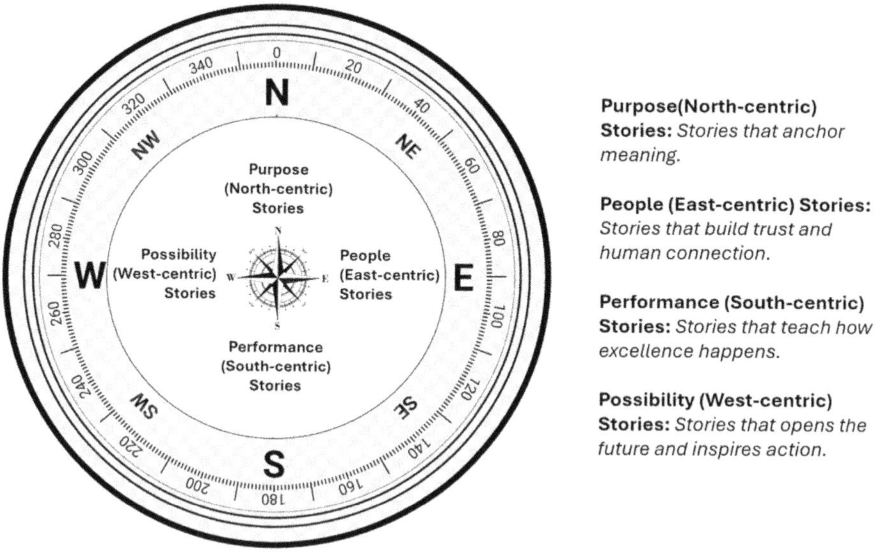

Figure 6.1 Stories Leaders Tell – The Four-Story-Type Model.

Source: Developed by the author through synthesis of leadership and organisational literature.

These stories establish continuity between past, present, and future. They explain not only *what* the organisation does, but *why it matters*. Smith (2019) argues that leaders who fail to tell these stories leave a vacuum that gets filled by cynicism or transactional thinking. Simmons (2006) complements the list with the following:

Who I am stories: The stories that humanise the leader and establish credibility.
Why I am here stories: The stories that openly acknowledge motives and intent.

Stephen Denning's purpose stories perform the same function: they articulate shared values and framework as contribution rather than compliance (Denning, 2011). Together, these stories orient the organisation morally. They are not aspirational fantasies; they are identity anchors. Without North-facing stories, organisations drift – busy, productive, but unmoored.

Case Study 6.3 Muhammad Yunus and the Origin of Grameen Bank

The founding story of Muhammad Yunus offers a powerful example of purpose-driven leadership rooted in human dignity and social entrepreneurship. Yunus's journey began in the 1970s not in policy circles, but in the village of Jobra near the University of Chittagong, where he taught economics. Confronted by famine and extreme poverty in Bangladesh, Yunus recognised a deep dissonance between elegant economic theory and the suffering he witnessed beyond the classroom (Yunus, 2007). Purpose emerged from this lived tension, not abstraction.

During visits to Jobra, Yunus met women who crafted bamboo stools yet remained trapped by exploitative moneylenders who controlled their output. He discovered that freeing forty-two women from this cycle required just US$27 in credit. This moment crystallised a radical insight: poverty was not caused by laziness or lack of ability, but by exclusion from fair financial systems (Yunus, 2007). From this insight, Grameen Bank was born.

Yunus's purpose story meets Fisher's (1984) tests of narrative coherence and fidelity. The story holds together logically – access to small loans enables dignity and self-reliance – and it resonates with universal values of fairness and opportunity. Crucially, the narrative centres the women of Jobra as agents of change, not Yunus himself as a hero.

The story also reflects authentic leadership grounded in experience rather than image (George, 2003). Grameen operationalised this purpose through trust-based microfinance, enabling millions of women to build enterprises and transform communities (Armendáriz & Morduch, 2010). As Harari (2014) suggests, such shared stories enable large-scale cooperation. Yunus's narrative redefined poverty as a solvable structural challenge, offering a compelling compass for purpose-led organisations.

People Stories That Create Trust, Belonging, and Connection

East-facing stories answer the question: *Who are we to each other?* They build relationships, psychological safety, and social cohesion. From Smith's (2019) framework, the strongest People stories include:

Customer Story: Who the company serves and its impact.
Recruiting Story: Why talented people should join.

These stories signal who belongs and why. They communicate inclusion, dignity, and mutual commitment. Adding more to the list, Simmons' (2006) contribution is especially powerful here:

Someone has to go first stories: The stories that model vulnerability and courage.
I know what you're thinking stories: The stories that surface unspoken fears and objections.

These stories reduce distance between leader and follower. They invite dialogue rather than obedience. Denning's relationship-building stories similarly foster trust by sharing lived experience rather than abstract authority (Denning, 2007). East-facing stories are essential in diverse, hybrid, and psychologically fragile workplaces. Without them, purpose becomes rhetoric and performance becomes coercive.

Case Study 6.4 Brian Chesky: Belonging Born on an Air Mattress

In 2008, during the global financial crisis, Brian Chesky was unemployed, struggling to pay rent in San Francisco, and facing personal uncertainty. What followed became one of the most recognisable origin stories in contemporary entrepreneurship – not because of technological innovation, but because of its grounding in hospitality, trust, and human connection (Gallagher, 2017).

When a major design conference left local hotels fully booked, Chesky and his roommate Joe Gebbia placed three air mattresses in their apartment, offered breakfast, and invited strangers to stay. They called the experiment *AirBed & Breakfast*. What surprised Chesky was not that people paid to sleep on the floor, but the sense of community that emerged. Guests shared stories, vulnerabilities, and late-night conversations, creating an unexpected feeling of belonging. As Chesky later reflected, they began by solving a personal problem but uncovered a deeper human need: the desire for connection (Gallagher, 2017).

This moment became the emotional foundation of Airbnb. The story exhibits what Fisher (1984) terms *narrative fidelity* – it resonates because it reflects a universal truth about wanting to feel welcomed and safe. Chesky transformed this experience into what Aaker (2018) calls a *signature story*: authentic, emotionally charged, and value-driven. Rather than prescribing culture through rules, Chesky shared the lived moment that defined it, reinforcing Schein's (2010) view that stories function as powerful cultural artefacts.

The founding narrative also guided Airbnb through later crises, including the COVID-19 pandemic. By returning to the core story of belonging, Chesky helped employees and hosts make sense of disruption and loss, exemplifying leadership sensemaking (Weick, 1995). What began as an improvised act of survival became Airbnb's enduring compass – *belong anywhere* – not as a slogan, but as a lived experience that continues to shape the company's identity.

Performance Stories That Drive Execution and Excellence

South-facing stories answer the question: *How do we get results?* They translate values into behaviour and vision into discipline, contributing to creating a culture of excellence. Smith's (2019) performance-oriented stories include:

Strategy Story: How to get there.
Case-for-Change Story: Why change is necessary.
Sales Story: What the company does for customers.

These stories clarify cause-and-effect. They explain trade-offs, priorities, and expectations.

Simmons (2006) adds the following:

Teaching stories: The stories that communicate practical wisdom.
Values-in-action stories: The stories that show – not tell – what excellence looks like.

Denning's change stories and knowledge-sharing stories are central here. His "springboard stories" help people *see* a new way of working without prescribing it bureaucratically (Denning, 2011). South-facing stories are where storytelling meets accountability. They confront reality, name constraints, and still sustain belief. Without them, vision remains theatrical, and culture deteriorates into slogans.

Case Study 6.5 Reed Hastings, the $40 Late Fee, and the Birth of a Culture of Excellence

Reed Hastings often anchors his leadership narrative in a small but formative failure: forgetting to return a rented copy of *Apollo 13* and being charged a $40 late fee. He accepts responsibility, acknowledging that the penalty was justified. Yet the incident prompted a deeper question. Shortly afterward, he noticed that gym members were not fined for staying longer than scheduled. The contrast sparked the original idea for Netflix, but Hastings emphasises that the lasting lesson was not about innovation – it was about accountability and performance (Hastings & Meyer, 2020).

This insight gained clarity through reflection on an earlier leadership failure. Hastings later admitted that in his previous company, rigid policies rewarded compliance rather than excellence. Creative talent left, innovation slowed, and the organisation became efficient but stagnant, ultimately forcing its sale.

> Policies and control processes became so foundational to our work that those who were great at coloring within the lines were promoted, while many creative mavericks felt shifted and went to work elsewhere. I was sorry to see them go, but I believed that this was what happens when a company grows up… we failed to innovate quickly. We had become increasingly efficient and decreasingly creative… we were unable to adapt, and in 1997, ended up selling the company to our largest competitors.
>
> (Hastings & Meyer, 2020, p. xix)

From this experience, Hastings drew a stark conclusion: control without trust suppresses creativity, and efficiency alone cannot sustain performance. The late-fee story evolved into a foundational performance narrative shaping Netflix's *freedom and responsibility* culture. Instead of rules and approvals, Hastings designed systems based on high talent density, radical candour, and personal ownership. Employees are trusted to make decisions – and held accountable for results (Hastings & Meyer, 2020). Excellence is expected, not enforced.

From a leadership perspective, this functions as a *springboard story* – a short, relatable narrative that challenges entrenched assumptions and invites new ways of thinking (Denning, 2011). It also reflects the discipline of confronting failure honestly while maintaining belief in future potential (Collins, 2001). Ultimately, the $40 late fee story is not about a missed deadline, but about learning in public. Hastings demonstrates that cultures of excellence emerge not from avoiding mistakes, but from designing systems that transform failure into insight.

Possibility Stories That Open Horizons and Inspire the Future

West-facing stories answer the question: *What could we become?* They stretch imagination and mobilise hope. Smith's (2019) vision story – where the organisation is going – sits squarely here. It provides a compelling future image that is emotionally resonant yet credible.

Simmons' (2006) vision story plays the same role – painting a future people want to inhabit. Denning's springboard stories are the archetypal West-facing narratives. They do not dictate change; they *invite* it by reframing what is possible (Denning, 2007). These stories are especially vital in the Imagination Age, where uncertainty is constant and technological acceleration destabilises identity. West-facing stories convert anxiety into curiosity and fear into forward motion. Without them, organisations optimise themselves into irrelevance.

Case Study 6.6 Elon Musk, Explosions at SpaceX, and Vision Through Failure

When Elon Musk founded SpaceX in 2002, his vision was audacious: drastically reduce the cost of space travel and ultimately make human life on Mars possible. The early reality, however, was defined by repeated and public failure. Between 2006 and 2008, the first three Falcon 1 launches failed catastrophically, pushing SpaceX to the edge of collapse. After the third rocket crashed, Musk recalled that the company might have had one month of cash left (Vance, 2015).

Rather than treating these failures as terminal, Musk reframed them as learning events. This approach reflects Taleb's (2012) concept of antifragility – systems that grow stronger through stress and disorder. Each explosion was rigorously analysed, designs were rapidly revised, and teams returned to testing with urgency. Musk's visible commitment – working alongside engineers and scrutinising technical details – demonstrated how leaders shape culture through action, not rhetoric (Schein, 2010). Failure was not denied; it was interrogated.

The breakthrough came on 28 September 2008, when Falcon 1 Flight 4 successfully reached orbit, becoming the first privately funded liquid-fuelled rocket to do so. The success triggered a vital NASA contract that secured SpaceX's survival and legitimised its mission (Vance, 2015). More importantly, it validated a leadership narrative grounded in perseverance.

This story exemplifies Snyder's (2002) theory of hope: effective leaders sustain agency and pathways even when outcomes are uncertain. Musk consistently communicated that setbacks were expected and instructive.

By framing failure as fuel for imagination rather than proof of inadequacy, he made the vision credible.

SpaceX's early explosions ultimately strengthened belief – showing that enduring failure can be the very process through which bold visions become believable.

Each framework – Smith's (2019) ten stories, Simmons' (2006) six story types, and Denning's (2007, 2011) leadership narratives – captures a different facet of storytelling power. But their true strength emerges when integrated.

Smith provides strategic breadth.
Simmons provides emotional depth.
Denning provides transformational leverage.

Mapped onto the Leadership Compass, they reveal a central truth: Leaders are not storytellers of one kind – they are narrative integrators.

As Steve Jobs famously observed, the leader's role is to conduct the corporate orchestra – aligning purpose, people, performance, and possibility into a coherent whole. Storytelling is the baton. It is the needle that keeps the compass aligned.

Leaders who master only one direction – purpose without people, performance without vision, or vision without discipline – create imbalance. Those who learn to tell the *right story in the right direction at the right moment* create organisations that are meaningful, humane, excellent, and future-ready.

Case Study 6.7 Al Gore and the Power of Leadership Storytelling

Al Gore's public career offers a powerful illustration of how leadership effectiveness rises or falls on storytelling capability. His evolution – from a respected but uninspiring political communicator to one of the most influential narrative leaders of the twenty-first century – reflects how leadership is exercised less through authority or logic than through stories that mobilise meaning and action (Denning, 2007). Crucially, Gore did not fundamentally change the substance of his message on climate change; rather, he transformed the *story* through which that message was communicated.

When Expertise Was Not Enough

During his years as a U.S. Senator and Vice President, Gore was widely regarded as intelligent, diligent, and deeply informed. Yet he struggled to inspire broad public engagement. His communication style was heavily analytical, grounded in data, charts, and rational argument. From a leadership storytelling perspective, this approach reflected what Denning (2007) warns against: an overreliance on explanation at the expense of imagination. Gore sought to convince audiences that climate change was real, but he did not help them imagine *what it meant* for their lives or *why they should act*.

This early failure can be understood as an absence of several enabling conditions for leadership storytelling. Gore lacked a springboard story – a short, authentic narrative that allows listeners to envisage a different future and see themselves participating in it (Denning, 2007). His message, while scientifically credible, struggled with emotional resonance and narrative fidelity. Climate change remained abstract, distant, and cognitively overwhelming, rather than immediate and human. As a result, his leadership language failed to mobilise collective energy.

The Narrative Turn: From Politician to Witness

Gore's transformation began after he exited electoral politics and culminated in *An Inconvenient Truth* (Guggenheim, 2006). This shift marked a decisive move from managerial communication to narrative leadership. Rather than positioning himself as an expert persuading an audience, Gore reframed himself as a *witness* telling a story – one that integrated scientific evidence with personal experience, moral urgency, and shared responsibility.

In Denning's (2007) terms, Gore learned to articulate a clear and inspiring change idea: climate change is real, human-caused, and solvable – but only if people choose to act together. This idea anchored his storytelling in purpose rather than politics. Importantly, Gore committed personally to this story, embodying it through sustained advocacy, repeated public engagement, and personal vulnerability. His credibility no longer rested solely on data, but on visible alignment between belief, narrative, and behaviour.

Gore also demonstrated growing narrative intelligence. He came to understand the audience's story – the fears, scepticism, and fatigue surrounding environmental discourse – and adapted his storytelling accordingly. Instead of confronting resistance with more facts, he reframed climate change through lived human experiences: melting glaciers, threatened communities, and personal reflections on his family history, including his son's near-fatal accident and his father's environmental values. These stories functioned as springboards, enabling audiences to move mentally from "this is happening" to "this requires action."

Storytelling as Continuing the Conversation

A defining feature of Gore's later leadership was his shift from prescription to enlistment. Rather than dictating solutions, he invited participation. His narrative did not close debate; it opened space for dialogue, local action, and innovation. This reflects Denning's (2007) emphasis on continuing the conversation – using storytelling to spark movement rather than impose compliance.

Equally important was the truthfulness of Gore's stories. Denning argues that leadership storytelling must be grounded in reality and lived experience to sustain trust. Gore's willingness to acknowledge uncertainty, failure, and past communication shortcomings strengthened narrative fidelity. His calm, earnest presence – voice, posture, and delivery – reinforced the sincerity of the message, illustrating how leadership presence amplifies narrative impact.

Why Gore Succeeded as a Narrative Leader

Gore's evolution exemplifies Denning's (2007) model of leadership storytelling that explains how narratives become effective when certain enabling conditions are present. At its core, the model emphasises leaders must articulate a clear and inspiring change idea, personally commit to that story, understand the audience's existing narratives, communicate truthfully, and embody the message through congruent presence and behaviour. When these conditions align, storytelling shifts from explanation to enlistment – inviting people to imagine a different future and choose to act within it.

Gore's later success reflects this alignment. He articulated a simple yet powerful change idea: climate change is real, human-caused, and solvable through collective action. Rather than framing this as a political argument, he anchored it in shared human purpose (Denning, 2007). His credibility deepened through authenticity and truthfulness; by sharing personal loss, doubt, and moral motivation, Gore moved from expert authority to moral witness. This fidelity to lived experience strengthened trust and emotional resonance.

Equally important was Gore's growing narrative intelligence – the ability to understand how audiences make sense of their own lives and concerns. He shifted from confronting scepticism with more data to engaging values, emotions, and moral imagination, meeting people where they were rather than where he wished them to be. In doing so, Gore exemplified Denning's principle of *continuing the conversation*: instead of prescribing solutions, he invited participation, local experimentation, and dialogue, allowing the story to live beyond the speaker.

Gore's effectiveness, therefore, was not the result of rhetorical flair alone. It emerged from storytelling as an integrative leadership practice that can be explained by the model introduced in this book – one that aligned with:

- Purpose (why climate change matters)
- People (who is affected)
- Performance (what actions are required)
- Possibility (what future can still be created)

However, in Denning's terms, storytelling became the mechanism through which these dimensions cohered into a shared narrative capable of mobilising sustained action. Gore's journey demonstrates that when leaders master both the substance of their message and the narrative conditions that give it life, complex global challenges can be reframed as collective human responsibilities rather than distant technical problems.

Lessons for Leaders

Al Gore's journey offers a critical lesson for contemporary leaders: expertise without narrative competence rarely inspires movement. In complex, emotionally charged contexts, data may inform, but stories mobilise. As Denning (2007) demonstrates, storytelling is not a decorative skill – it is the language through which leadership is enacted. Leaders who learn to tell truthful, audience-centred stories do more than communicate change; they enable others to imagine themselves as agents of that change.

Storytelling in the Imagination Age: Leaders as Custodians of Truth

Throughout this chapter, storytelling has been positioned not as an accessory to leadership but as its navigational core. Purpose (north), people (east), productivity (south), and possibility (west) represent essential dimensions of leadership. Yet without a force to align them, these dimensions risk remaining fragmented. Storytelling functions as that force – the needle that brings coherence, direction, and shared meaning. Purpose becomes inspirational when it is told as a journey rather than reduced to a slogan. People become engaged when their lived experiences are acknowledged and woven into the collective narrative. Productivity matures into excellence when values are embedded in everyday practice through stories that model behaviour, not mandate it. Vision becomes compelling when it is narrated as a visible horizon rather than a distant abstraction. Like sailors navigating uncertain seas, leaders rely on stories to interpret complexity and chart direction. Without storytelling, there is drift; with it, there is orientation and momentum.

This need for narrative navigation intensifies in the Imagination Age – an era shaped by the convergence of human creativity and the power brought forth by the fourth industrial revolution and particularly artificial intelligence. Today, machines can generate persuasive narratives at scale, creating abundance but also fragility of trust. While technology can accelerate storytelling, belief still depends on human authenticity. Neuroscientific research shows that stories rooted in lived experience foster empathy and trust, whereas synthetic narratives lack moral weight. The central leadership challenge is not that AI can tell stories, but that it may erode confidence in all stories. Leadership's task, therefore, is to safeguard meaning.

Storytelling is also ethically double-edged. As cases such as Theranos demonstrate, compelling narratives detached from truth can mislead and harm. In an era of deepfakes and algorithmic persuasion, leaders must act as custodians of stories – anchored in truth, transparency, and humility. The compass needle must point not merely north, but true north.

Conclusion

Looking ahead, leadership storytelling will increasingly take hybrid forms – oral, digital, visual, and immersive. Technology may extend reach and engagement, but it remains only a medium. The essence of storytelling is profoundly human: connection, belonging, and shared meaning.

Leaders in the Imagination Age must therefore master two simultaneous arts: harnessing technology to amplify narratives, and preserving humanity to sustain trust and ethical grounding. Those who achieve this balance will not merely navigate complexity; they will chart new horizons.

We return, finally, to the image of the compass. Purpose without people is hollow. People without productivity lack grounding. Productivity without vision becomes mechanical. Vision without purpose dissolves into fantasy. And without the needle – storytelling – the compass cannot guide.

Storytelling is the invisible current that aligns direction, energy, discipline, and horizon into a coherent journey. Leadership, in this sense, is narrative navigation. Leaders are storytellers not by choice, but by necessity. The stories they tell shape not only where we go, but who we become along the way.

Reflective Questions

1. How consciously do you use storytelling in your leadership to communicate purpose, connect with people, reinforce performance values, and inspire a shared vision of the future?
2. In an age of AI-generated narratives and synthetic media, how can leaders ensure that their stories remain authentic, ethical, and grounded in genuine human experience?
3. What stories are currently shaping the culture of your organisation – and how might you intentionally craft new narratives that align purpose, people, performance, and possibility?

References

Aaker, D. A. (2018). *Creating signature stories: Strategic messaging that energizes, persuades, and inspires*. Morgan James Publishing.
Accenture. (2023). *Reinventing enterprise value with generative AI*. Accenture Insights.
Accenture. (2024). *Generative AI: From productivity to trust*. Accenture Leadership Brief.
Armendáriz, B., & Morduch, J. (2010). *The economics of microfinance* (2nd ed.). MIT Press.
Bennis, W. (1994). *On becoming a leader*. Addison-Wesley.
Bennis, W., & Nanus, B. (1985). *Leaders: Strategies for taking charge*. Harper & Row.
Boje, D. M. (1991). The storytelling organization: A study of story performance in an office-supply firm. *Administrative Science Quarterly, 36*(1), 106–126.
Boyd, B. (2009). *On the origin of stories: Evolution, cognition, and fiction*. Harvard University Press.
Brown, J. S., Denning, S., Groh, K., & Prusak, L. (2009). *Storytelling in organizations: Why storytelling is transforming 21st-century organizations and management*. Routledge.
Carreyrou, J. (2015). Hot startup Theranos has struggled with its blood-test technology. *The Wall Street Journal*.
Carreyrou, J. (2018). *Bad blood: Secrets and lies in a Silicon Valley startup*. Knopf.
Chouinard, Y., & Stanley, V. (2012). *The responsible company: What we've learned from Patagonia's first 40 years*. Patagonia Books.
Collins, J. (2001). *Good to great: Why some companies make the leap…and others don't*. HarperBusiness.
Denning, S. (2007). *The secret language of leadership: How leaders inspire action through narrative*. Jossey-Bass.
Denning, S. (2011). *The leader's guide to storytelling: Mastering the art and discipline of business narrative*. Jossey-Bass.

Edmondson, A. C. (1999). Psychological safety and learning behavior in work teams. *Administrative Science Quarterly, 44*(2), 350–383.
Erikson, E. H. (1968). *Identity: Youth and crisis*. W. W. Norton & Company.
Fisher, W. R. (1984). Narration as a human communication paradigm: The case of public moral argument. *Communication Monographs, 51*(1), 1–22. https://doi.org/10.1080/03637758409390180
Floridi, L., Cowls, J., Beltrametti, M., et al. (2018). AI4People – An ethical framework for a good AI society. *Minds and Machines, 28*(4), 689–707.
Gabriel, Y. (2000). *Storytelling in organizations: Facts, fictions, and fantasies*. Oxford University Press.
Gallagher, L. (2017). *The Airbnb story: How three ordinary guys disrupted an industry, made billions…and created plenty of controversy*. Houghton Mifflin Harcourt.
Gallo, C. (2016). *The storyteller's secret*. Macmillan.
George, B. (2003). *Authentic leadership: Rediscovering the secrets to creating lasting value*. Jossey-Bass.
Guggenheim, D. (Director). (2006). *An inconvenient truth* [Film]. Paramount Classics.
Harari, Y. N. (2014). *Sapiens: A brief history of humankind*. Harper.
Hastings, R., & Meyer, E. (2020). *No rules rules: Netflix and the culture of reinvention*. Penguin Press.
Heath, C., & Heath, D. (2007). *Made to stick: Why some ideas survive and others die*. Random House.
Iansiti, M., & Lakhani, K. R. (2024). *Competing in the age of AI*. Harvard Business Review Press.
Imai, M. (1986). *Kaizen: The key to Japan's competitive success*. McGraw-Hill.
Kennedy, J. F. (1962, September 12). *Address at Rice University on the nation's space effort*. John F. Kennedy Presidential Library and Museum. www.jfklibrary.org/archives/other-resources/john-f-kennedy-speeches/rice-university-19620912
Kouzes, J. M., & Posner, B. Z. (2017). *The leadership challenge* (6th ed.). Wiley.
Liker, J. K. (2004). *The Toyota way: 14 management principles from the world's greatest manufacturer*. McGraw-Hill.
Moin, S. M. A. (2025). *Storytelling in marketing and brand communications*. Routledge.
Nadella, S., Shaw, G., & Nichols, J. (2017). *Hit refresh: The quest to rediscover Microsoft's soul and imagine a better future for everyone*. HarperBusiness.
Polman, P., & Winston, A. (2021). *Net positive: How courageous companies thrive by giving more than they take*. Harvard Business Review Press.
Schein, E. H. (2010). *Organizational culture and leadership* (4th ed.). Jossey-Bass.
Simmons, A. (2006). *The story factor: Inspiration, influence, and persuasion through the art of storytelling* (2nd ed.). Basic Books.
Smith, P. (2019). *10 stories great leaders tell*. AMACOM.
Snyder, C. R. (2002). Hope theory: Rainbows in the mind. *Psychological Inquiry, 13*(4), 249–275.
Stephens, G. J., Silbert, L. J., & Hasson, U. (2010). Speaker–listener neural coupling underlies successful communication. *Proceedings of the National Academy of Sciences, 107*(32), 14425–14430. https://doi.org/10.1073/pnas.1008662107
Taleb, N. N. (2012). *Antifragile: Things that gain from disorder*. Random House.
United States Department of Justice. (2022). *Theranos founder Elizabeth Holmes convicted of fraud*.

Vance, A. (2015). *Elon Musk: Tesla, SpaceX, and the quest for a fantastic future*. HarperCollins.

Weick, K. E. (1995). *Sensemaking in organizations*. Sage.

Yunus, M. (2007). *Creating a world without poverty: Social business and the future of capitalism*. PublicAffairs.

Zak, P. J. (2014). Why inspiring stories make us react: The neuroscience of narrative. *Cerebrum, 2014*, Article 2. www.ncbi.nlm.nih.gov/pmc/articles/PMC4445577/

Chapter 7

The Moral Gyroscope

Maintaining Stability through Ethics, Values, and Character

Introduction

Leadership in the twenty-first century demands more than simply choosing between right and wrong. The contemporary landscape is characterised by a VUCA environment – Volatile, Uncertain, Complex, and Ambiguous (Kouzes & Posner, 2012; Mumford et al., 2002) – and is accelerating into what is known as the Imagination Age (Moin, 2022). In this era, leaders are expected not only to adapt but to innovate ethically in the face of unprecedented complexity. Traditional moral guidance systems, often analogised as a *moral compass* pointing north, prove insufficient when the magnetic field of the organisational environment is constantly shifting (Johnson, 2008). What leaders require is a mechanism for dynamic equilibrium and consistent orientation – a framework that ensures stability and integrity regardless of the environmental turbulence.

This chapter introduces the Moral Gyroscope, a novel framework designed to conceptualise the internal mechanisms that provide leaders with balance, orientation, and integrity under pressure. A gyroscope maintains its equilibrium and orientation through the interplay of its spinning axes, resisting external forces that would otherwise cause it to topple. This model provides a robust lens through which leaders can navigate the extreme possibilities and daunting challenges.

The Imagination Age amplifies the need for this stabilising force. This epoch, driven by connectivity and creativity, places an immense premium on novelty, vision, and the ability to conceptualise new realities (Mumford et al., 2002). Leaders are encouraged to challenge the status quo, which inherently creates ethical ambiguities. While innovation is vital for survival, unchecked creativity without a grounding moral structure can lead to significant ethical failures, as seen in various technology and data privacy scandals. The *possibilities* of the Imagination Age such as limitless connectivity, AI-driven solutions, and global reach are balanced by the *challenges* of rapid disruption, lack of regulation, and pervasive uncertainty.

In a VUCA world, decision-making speed is critical, and leaders frequently act with incomplete or evolving information (Cameron & Quinn, 2011). Under such conditions, reliance on external rules or formal controls alone is insufficient.

DOI: 10.4324/9781003766414-7

Leaders require an internalised mechanism for rapid ethical self-correction. The Moral Gyroscope proposes that effective decisions emerge from the simultaneous integration of its three axes – ethics, values, and character – further stabilised by emotional intelligence. Together, these elements enable leaders to remain relevant, trustworthy, and morally coherent amid uncertainty.

This chapter delves into each of these axes in detail, illustrating their unique functions and their collective necessity. The Moral Gyroscope moves beyond static notions of morality to offer a dynamic, integrated framework for ethical orientation in a rapidly changing world. By developing all three axes and emotional intelligence, leaders can build the resilience and trustworthiness required to harness the exciting possibilities of the Imagination Age while successfully navigating the inherent volatility of the modern environment.

Ancient Wisdom, Global Paradigms, and Contemporary Models of Ethical Leadership

The Moral Gyroscope framework – anchored in ethics, values, and character – rests on a long intellectual tradition concerned with virtuous living, just governance, and responsible power. Across cultures and centuries, scholars have converged on a core insight: effective leadership is sustained not merely by external rules or competencies, but by internal moral mechanisms that stabilise judgement and action. From ancient philosophy to contemporary leadership research, this continuity forms the theoretical bedrock of the Moral Gyroscope.

Ancient Philosophical Foundations: Character as the Core

Ancient philosophical thought places character at the heart of leadership. Plato's *Republic* presents the ideal of the philosopher-king: leaders governed not by appetite or ambition, but by wisdom and justice (Plato, trans. 2004). Plato warned that leaders driven by wealth, status, or power inevitably corrupt governance. His model emphasised the cultivation of the soul – reason, spirit, and desire – in harmony, orienting leadership toward an objective conception of the "good." This insistence on inner moral orientation directly informs the Moral Gyroscope's premise that leadership stability depends on alignment with higher ethical principles rather than situational advantage.

Aristotle advanced this foundation through virtue ethics, shifting focus from abstract ideals to lived moral practice. In the *Nicomachean Ethics*, he argued that virtues are acquired through habituation, not inherited traits (Aristotle, trans. 1999). Ethical leadership, in this view, emerges from repeated, intentional practice guided by *phronesis* – practical wisdom that enables discernment of the "mean" between excess and deficiency (Johnson, 2008). Aristotle's framework offers the most direct precursor to the character axis of the Moral Gyroscope, underscoring that trustworthiness and credibility are the cumulative result of consistent moral conduct.

Western Ethical Paradigms: Principles and Consequences

Modern Western ethics diversified into deontological and consequentialist traditions, each contributing critical but partial insights. Kantian deontology emphasises duty and universal moral law, asserting that ethical actions must be guided by principle rather than expedience (Johnson, 2008). This perspective reinforces the ethics axis by highlighting non-negotiable standards that constrain leadership behaviour.

Utilitarianism, articulated by Bentham and Mill, evaluates morality through outcomes – seeking the greatest good for the greatest number – and offers a consequentialist lens that helps leaders consider systemic impact and stakeholder effects in complex environments (Bentham, 1789/2007; Mill, 1863/1998). However, as critics have noted, rules and outcomes alone cannot ensure moral consistency when values conflict or pressures intensify (Shaub et al., 1993). The Moral Gyroscope integrates both paradigms within the ethics-axis while recognising their insufficiency without internal anchoring through values and character. Together, they clarify what leaders should evaluate, but not who leaders must become.

Eastern Ethical Paradigms: Relational and Values-Based Leadership

Eastern philosophies, particularly Confucianism, enrich the Moral Gyroscope by foregrounding relational ethics and moral self-cultivation. Confucius emphasised *ren* (benevolence) and *yi* (righteousness) as foundational leadership virtues, arguing that leaders govern most effectively through moral example rather than coercion (Confucius, trans. 1998). The ideal leader (*junzi*) embodies *lian* (integrity) and cultivates harmony through the disciplined observance of *li* (ritual propriety), thereby reinforcing social trust and cohesion (Low & Ang, 2013).

This relational perspective strongly supports the values and character axes of the Moral Gyroscope. Leadership legitimacy arises not from authority alone, but from consistent alignment between inner values and outward behaviour. Stability is achieved through self-regulation, humility, and continuous moral refinement. These are essential qualities for sustaining trust in both organisations and societies.

Contemporary Leadership Models: Reintegrating the Inner Life

Contemporary leadership research has increasingly returned to these ancient insights, recognising that technical competence alone cannot sustain leadership effectiveness in volatile and ethically ambiguous contexts.

Ethical leadership theory defines leadership as the modelling and reinforcement of normatively appropriate conduct through behaviour, communication, and decision-making (Brown et al., 2005). Rooted in social learning theory, this model affirms that leaders shape ethical climates by example, echoing Aristotelian habituation.

Authentic leadership theory further emphasises self-awareness, clarity, and behavioural consistency as foundations of trust (Avolio & Gardner, 2005). Integrity – the alignment between espoused values and enacted behaviour – emerges as a central stabilising force, particularly under pressure (Simons, 2002). These insights map directly onto the values and character axes of the Moral Gyroscope.

Servant leadership extends this integration by reframing leadership as moral responsibility rather than positional power. Greenleaf (1977) argued that the primary test of leadership is whether it serves the growth and wellbeing of others. This service orientation reinforces the ethics axis, anchoring leadership purpose beyond self-interest.

Emerging perspectives in systems leadership and moral identity further support the gyroscope model, highlighting that leaders operate within interconnected social, technological, and ecological systems. Moral stability increasingly requires leaders to integrate ethical judgement, emotional regulation, and long-term responsibility – capacities aligned with the dynamic calibration of the Moral Gyroscope.

The Moral Gyroscope as Leadership's Stabiliser

Leadership in a VUCA world demands more than strategic direction. Without moral stability and emotional awareness, even well-intended leadership can drift into inconsistency, ethical compromise, or relational harm – affecting both leaders and the organisations they serve. While the Leadership Compass offers orientation by clarifying purpose, people, performance, possibility, and storytelling, direction alone does not guarantee balance. Orientation without stability increases the risk of ethical lapses, value misalignment, erosion of trust, and impaired judgement under pressure.

What leaders require alongside direction is an internal stabilising mechanism that maintains coherence amid competing demands and sustained uncertainty. This mechanism is the Moral Gyroscope (Figure 7.1).

The Moral Gyroscope synthesises ancient wisdom, global ethical paradigms, and contemporary leadership research into a coherent framework for moral stability. Rather than privileging rules, outcomes, or character in isolation, it argues that leadership resilience emerges from the integration of ethics (principled judgement), values (internal alignment), and character (consistent moral action). Like a physical gyroscope maintaining balance amid turbulence, leaders grounded across these three axes remain oriented toward the common good, resistant to ethical drift, and credible under pressure. In the Imagination Age, the Moral Gyroscope offers a timeless yet adaptive foundation for responsible leadership. It strengthens judgement under pressure, sustains integrity in action, and reflects a leader's moral orientation through consistent decision-making.

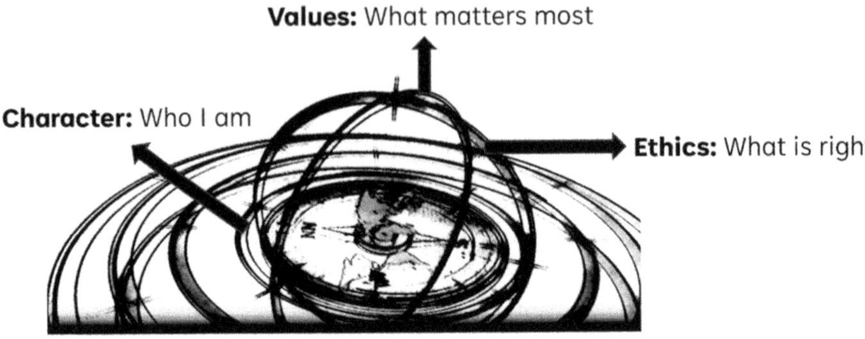

Figure 7.1 The Moral Gyroscope.

Source: Developed by the author through synthesis of leadership and organisational literature.

The Moral Gyroscope rests on three interconnected axes:

Ethics (Axis X): Principles that guide judgement and define right action.
Values (Axis Y): The internal compass that aligns behaviour with purpose and priorities over time.
Character (Axis Z): The integration of ethics and values into consistent, trustworthy action, sustaining credibility, resilience, and moral courage.

Ethics (Axis X): Guiding Right Action

Ethical decision-making is no longer abstract or episodic; it is a daily operational necessity. In the Imagination Age, where complexity multiplies and consequences scale rapidly, ethics provides the first stabilising anchor. Ethics represents the leader's moral literacy – commitment to principles of justice, fairness, rights, and responsibility (Ciulla, 2003). It forms the objective plane of the gyroscope, constraining action within moral boundaries and preventing drift into purely expedient or self-serving choices. Rather than relying on a single ethical doctrine, effective leaders integrate three enduring ethical perspectives.

Consequentialism: Evaluating Outcomes

Consequentialism, associated with Bentham (1789/2007) and Mill (1863/1998), evaluates actions based on their outcomes. In leadership contexts, this lens encourages consideration of stakeholder impact, systemic effects, and long-term consequences. Research shows that leaders who account for stakeholder welfare build greater trust and organisational legitimacy (Brown et al., 2005; Resick et al., 2013). However, in complex systems – especially those involving AI, automation, or social algorithms – predicting consequences is increasingly difficult. Ethical leadership therefore requires anticipatory judgement and humility regarding unintended effects.

Deontology: Upholding Moral Principles

Deontological ethics, rooted in Kant's moral philosophy, emphasises duty and respect for human dignity irrespective of outcomes (Kant, 1785/1993). For leaders, this framework reinforces non-negotiable standards such as honesty, fairness, and consent. Organisational research links deontological leadership with trust, predictability, and ethical climates grounded in rule consistency (Mayer et al., 2009). Deontology serves as a critical stabiliser when outcome-based reasoning tempts leaders to justify harmful means for desirable ends.

Virtue Ethics: Cultivating Moral Character

Virtue ethics shifts focus from decisions to the decision-maker. Originating with Aristotle (c. 350 BCE/2004), it asks not "What should I do?" but "Who should I be?" Character traits such as courage, integrity, empathy, and humility shape how leaders interpret and respond to ethical dilemmas. Studies consistently show that leaders' virtues influence organisational culture and ethical behaviour (Ciulla, 1998; Brown et al., 2005). Together, consequentialism, deontology, and virtue ethics form a *triangulated ethical approach*, enabling leaders to evaluate outcomes, honour principles, and act with integrity – an approach well suited to morally ambiguous environments (Resick et al., 2013).

Values (Axis Y): Anchoring the Inner Compass

Reflect on the leadership decisions you have made as a leader over the past year. While ethics may have helped you distinguish right from wrong, another force consistently shaped your choices: values. Unlike ethics, which prescribe universal duties, values function as an inner compass to shape behaviour, priorities, and leadership identity (Schwartz, 2012; Schein, 2010). They are the lenses through which leaders interpret complexity, assign meaning, and decide what truly matters. In the Imagination Age – marked by accelerating change and persistent uncertainty – values act as stabilising anchors, enabling leaders to act with consistency even when external pressures shift or data points conflict. Without clearly articulated values, even ethically sound decisions risk becoming fragmented or misaligned with purpose.

As the second axis of the Moral Gyroscope, values represent a leader's core convictions and enduring priorities (Rokeach, 1973). This vertical axis provides authenticity and intrinsic motivation, sustaining engagement and commitment over time. Leaders with well-defined values can explain why they prioritise certain actions over others, articulate a compelling vision, and inspire trust among followers. Values help leaders remain grounded in their identity and purpose amid environmental turbulence.

Values are enduring beliefs about what is important in life and work. In organisational contexts, they serve several critical functions (Schwartz, 2012; Schein, 2010):

Guiding Behaviour: Values inform daily decisions, helping leaders navigate trade-offs and set priorities.
Shaping Culture: Leaders' values influence organisational norms and collective behaviour.
Motivating Purpose: Values provide meaning, fostering engagement, resilience, and long-term commitment.

Leaders such as Ratan Tata, Abdul Kalam, and Jack Ma exemplify how deeply held values translate into consistent action and broad societal impact. In the Imagination Age, effective leadership requires both personal clarity and collective alignment – the leader's inner compass must resonate with organisational mission and social purpose. Several foundational frameworks illuminate the role of values in leadership.

Schwartz's Theory of Basic Human Values

Schwartz (1992/2012) identifies value dimensions, such as openness to change, self-transcendence, self-enhancement, and conservation. Leaders who are high in self-transcendence – prioritising the welfare of others and societal good – are particularly effective in guiding organisations through complexity and uncertainty.

Transformational Leadership and Values

Transformational leaders inspire followers by aligning organisational vision with shared values (Bass & Steidlmeier, 1999). When leaders consistently model and communicate their values, they foster trust, loyalty, and creativity.

Value Congruence

Empirical research shows that alignment between leaders' personal values and organisational values enhances job satisfaction, ethical behaviour, and organisational commitment (Edwards & Cable, 2009). Value congruence requires leaders to continually assess whether strategic decisions remain aligned with their core beliefs.

Values are not abstract ideals; they are actionable guides, and they have practical implications. Leaders can strengthen Axis Y through deliberate practices such as:

Self-Reflection: Regular journaling or reflection to clarify and recalibrate core beliefs.
Values-based Decision Checks: Assessing choices against personal and organisational values.
Explicit Communication: Modelling values in action and explaining the rationale behind decisions.
Cultural Embedding: Reinforcing values through policies, rituals, and recognition systems.

These practices ensure that leadership choices remain coherent, purposeful, and aligned with ethics and character.

Values in the Imagination Age

The Imagination Age intensifies the importance of values by expanding both choice and ethical ambiguity (Harari, 2018; Schwab, 2016). Technology can amplify impact at unprecedented speed, but without values as anchors, leaders risk prioritising efficiency, innovation, or growth at the expense of human dignity and societal wellbeing. Axis Y – the leader's inner compass – is therefore essential to ensure that leadership is not only effective, but also responsible, humane, and meaningful.

Character (Axis Z): The Leader Within

Pause for a moment and observe how rapidly the world is changing. The Imagination Age confronts leaders with unprecedented decisions – choices carrying far-reaching technological, societal, and ethical consequences. Many leaders we admire for their innovation and vision have achieved extraordinary success, yet history also records how some have faltered, leaving legacies of unintended harm. The following lines, drawn from Munroe's stark observation, paint a vivid picture of the character deficit in leadership and reveal why character is indispensable:

> In the dynamic drama of contemporary leadership playing on the world stage today, there are many characters who lack character. Moreover, the trail of history is littered with would-be great men and women who harnessed the reins of power in various fields – political, social, economic, corporate, athletic, spiritual and more. They wielded great influence and/or control over lives of others; many felt the weight of material wealth and fame – only to have it all disintegrate and blow away like dust in the wind because of their tragic deficiencies of character.
>
> (Munroe, 2014, p. 1)

Without a strong Axis Z, the Moral Gyroscope cannot function. Ethics may guide judgment and values may anchor priorities, but character determines whether leadership endures, inspires trust, and leaves a positive legacy. Character is the axis of rotation that translates ethical principles and values into consistent, credible action (Badaracco, 2001; Kouzes & Posner, 2012). Knowing what is right is insufficient; leaders must repeatedly do what is right, demonstrating behavioural integrity under pressure (Simons, 2002). In volatile, uncertain, complex, and ambiguous environments, character provides the dynamic stability required to resist compromise. And so we arrive at the essential question – what does character mean in the life of a leader?

Defining Character in Leadership

Character is the sustained integration of ethics and values into behaviour across situations and over time (Crossan et al., 2015; Seijts et al., 2015). It is not charisma or reputation, but the moral backbone of leadership. Leaders with character act with integrity, responsibility, and concern for others even when unobserved.

Peterson and Seligman (2004) identify six core virtues that underpin character:

Wisdom: sound judgment and perspective.
Courage: moral bravery under risk.
Humanity: empathy and compassion.
Justice: fairness and civic responsibility.
Temperance: humility and self-regulation.
Transcendence: higher purpose and meaning.

These virtues align with Crossan et al.'s (2015) emphasis on actionable leadership traits such as judgment, drive, collaboration, integrity, accountability, and humility. In practice, leaders operationalise character by embedding these traits into everyday routines. For instance, before approving high-stakes predictive analytics or algorithmic decision systems, effective leaders convene diverse perspectives to test assumptions, anticipate unintended consequences, and assess fairness – demonstrating both wisdom and justice in action.

Character in the Imagination Age

History shows that leaders who gain extraordinary power or visibility without corresponding character often collapse under ethical lapses, arrogance, or unchecked ambition (Kellerman, 2004; Munroe, 2014). In today's hyperconnected world, leadership impact – and risk – is magnified. A single misjudgement can cascade across organisations, markets, and societies. The Imagination Age intensifies these stakes (Moin, 2022). Artificial intelligence, big data, and biotechnology offer unprecedented capacity to shape the future, but without moral anchoring, even well-intentioned innovation can cause harm. Character therefore functions as a preventative mechanism, ensuring that intelligence, ambition, and vision are exercised with restraint and responsibility.

Table 7.1 Dimensions of Character and Their Application in the Imagination Age

Dimension	*Definition*	*Application in the Imagination Age*
Wisdom	Insight and sound judgment	Evaluating AI-driven decisions and anticipating societal consequences
Courage	Moral bravery and resolve	Challenging unethical norms and making unpopular but necessary choices
Humanity	Empathy and care	Designing inclusive technologies and considering stakeholder welfare
Justice	Fairness and equity	Ensuring equitable access to innovation and preventing discrimination
Temperance	Self-regulation and humility	Resisting hubris and balancing ambition with ethical restraint
Transcendence	Higher purpose and meaning	Inspiring collective action and embedding meaning in organisational missions

Source: Developed by author from existing literature.

The virtues of character translate directly into contemporary leadership challenges (see Table 7.1). For example, wisdom guides AI governance decisions, courage enables resistance to unethical norms, and justice ensures equitable access to innovation. Effective leaders operationalise these virtues through everyday practices – such as convening diverse perspectives before approving high-stakes algorithmic systems – to anticipate unintended consequences and uphold fairness.

Cultivating Character as a Leadership Discipline

Character is not fixed; it is developed through deliberate practice, reflection, and relational learning (Gardner, 2006; Seijts et al., 2015). Leaders who sustain ethical effectiveness adopt disciplined routines, including:

- Reflective journalling to align actions with values.
- Mentorship and candid feedback.
- Ethical scenario rehearsal under pressure.
- Public accountability mechanisms that reinforce integrity.

These practices strengthen the Moral Gyroscope, enabling leaders to remain grounded amid turbulence, temptation, and uncertainty. In the Imagination Age, character is the stabilising force that keeps leadership oriented toward long-term value, ethical responsibility, and true north – even as the pace of change accelerates.

From Integration to Practice: Implications and Challenges of the Moral Gyroscope

The integration of ethics, values, and character produces tangible organisational outcomes – but only when leaders possess the emotional intelligence required to access these capacities under pressure. A well-aligned moral gyroscope, stabilised by emotional self-awareness, self-regulation, and empathy, enables leaders to build trust, sustain performance, and navigate uncertainty with credibility. Conversely, weak moral integration – often compounded by low emotional intelligence – exposes organisations to ethical failure, reputational damage, and long-term decline.

Organisational Implications of Moral Integration

Empirical research demonstrates that morally grounded leadership enhances stakeholder trust, employee engagement, and organisational legitimacy (Brown et al., 2005). When ethical reasoning, values alignment, and character consistency are supported by emotional intelligence, leaders are better able to manage stress, regulate impulses, and remain open to feedback – capabilities essential for sustained ethical action (Goleman, 1998 a & b; Boyatzis, 2018).

Decisions that are ethically reasoned, values-aligned, and character-driven support long-term performance, adaptability, and strategic foresight. During crises, emotionally intelligent leaders are more likely to respond decisively without becoming defensive or reactive, preserving integrity while maintaining trust. Values-driven leadership exemplified by the Tata Group illustrates how emotional restraint, moral clarity, and empathy reinforce organisational resilience.

By contrast, failures of moral integration – such as Theranos and the Wells Fargo scandal – have resulted in fraud, regulatory penalties, financial collapse, and enduring reputational harm (Crossan et al., 2015; Seijts et al., 2015). These cases highlight that ethical breakdowns are rarely caused by ignorance of right and wrong; rather, they stem from emotionally driven rationalisation, fear, overconfidence, or conformity. Ethical weakness is therefore not only a moral concern but a material business risk.

Ethical Stability in the Imagination Age

In the Imagination Age – defined by technological acceleration, global visibility, and ethical ambiguity – moral stability requires more than ethical clarity. Leaders must also possess the emotional intelligence to manage fear, ambition, and social pressure. Leadership failure rarely occurs through sudden collapse; it more often emerges through gradual moral drift, fuelled by emotional fatigue, rationalisation, and unexamined stress (Bennis, 2009). Continuous recalibration of ethics, values, and character – supported by emotional awareness and regulation – is therefore essential.

Forces That Distort the Moral Gyroscope

Multiple systemic, psychological, and emotional forces destabilise ethical judgement:

- Performance pressure narrows moral reasoning and triggers survival thinking, reducing attention to long-term consequences (Bagley, 2003). Emotional overload intensifies this effect, as seen in scandals at Wells Fargo, Volkswagen, and Enron.
- Normalisation of deviance allows small violations to become culturally acceptable when consequences are delayed, gradually eroding values (Vaughan, 1996).
- Obedience to authority and conformity override personal ethics, especially when fear of exclusion or reprisal is high (Milgram, 1974; Asch, 1955). Emotional intelligence – particularly courage and self-regulation – is critical to resisting these pressures.

Internal cognitive distortions further compound risk. Moral disengagement enables leaders to rationalise unethical behaviour while preserving a positive self-image (Bandura, 1999). Overconfidence bias reduces perceived ethical vulnerability (Tenbrunsel & Messick, 2004), while ethical blind spots obscure harm to stakeholders (Bazerman & Tenbrunsel, 2011).

Organisational systems often amplify these distortions. Culture shapes behaviour more powerfully than formal codes (Schein, 2010). Toxic cultures, misaligned incentives, and accelerated decision cycles – intensified by digital overload – erode ethical reflection and emotional regulation (Turkle, 2015).

When the Gyroscope Fails and When It Holds

Cases such as Theranos, the Boeing 737 Max crisis, and Uber's early organisational culture illustrate how ethical failure is accelerated by emotional defensiveness, fear-driven decision-making, and unchecked ego. In contrast, leaders such as Ratan Tata, Jacinda Ardern, and Satya Nadella demonstrate how emotional intelligence strengthens ethical resilience, enabling calm judgement, empathy in crisis, and values-consistent action. These leaders show that emotional intelligence does not soften leadership – it stabilises it.

Strengthening the Moral Gyroscope

Strengthening the Moral Gyroscope requires discipline rather than intention alone. Ethical foresight – the capacity to anticipate consequences before acting – is central to ethical leadership and depends on emotional regulation and reflective distance (Kahneman, 2011).

Values alignment requires translating espoused values into consistent behaviour, particularly under stress (Argyris & Schön, 1978; Schwartz, 2012). Character development, grounded in universal virtues such as wisdom, courage, humanity, justice, temperance, and transcendence, is cultivated through deliberate practice rather than assumed as innate (Peterson & Seligman, 2004; Crossan et al., 2017). Emotional intelligence enables these virtues to be expressed reliably rather than episodically.

Relational accountability further stabilises the system. Leaders who cultivate mentors, peers, and truth-tellers demonstrate greater emotional balance, ethical consistency, and judgement (Kouzes & Posner, 2017). At the institutional level, ethical leadership is reinforced through transparent decision processes, aligned incentives, whistleblowing protections, and psychological safety (Schein, 2010). Ultimately, leadership in the Imagination Age is defined not merely by knowing what is right, but by sustaining the emotional and moral capacity to act rightly when doing so is difficult, costly, or inconvenient. The Moral Gyroscope remains effective only through continual recalibration – ethical, emotional, and intentional.

Conclusion

The Moral Gyroscope offers a dynamic and integrative response to the ethical and leadership challenges of the Imagination Age. In environments defined by volatility, ambiguity, and accelerating technological power, leadership can no longer rely on static moral rules or isolated competencies. Instead, it requires an internal system capable of maintaining balance, orientation, and integrity amid constant motion. The three axes of the Moral Gyroscope – ethics, values, and character – provide this foundational stability, each contributing a distinct yet interdependent function to moral judgement and leadership behaviour. When these elements are aligned, leaders are better equipped to navigate uncertainty, build trust, and make decisions that are not only effective but humane.

The chapter demonstrates that leadership failure in the Imagination Age is rarely the result of a lack of intelligence or innovation; more often, it stems from misalignment within the leader's moral architecture. The Moral Gyroscope provides both a diagnostic and developmental framework, allowing leaders to identify imbalance, recalibrate their orientation, and strengthen their moral capacity over time. Ultimately, leadership in this age is not about control or certainty, but about coherence and stewardship. By cultivating ethics, values, character, and emotional intelligence as an integrated system, leaders can sustain moral clarity, act responsibly in moments of ambiguity, and contribute to organisations and societies that flourish amid change rather than fracture under it.

Reflective Questions

1. When facing pressure, uncertainty, or conflicting incentives, how do your ethics, values, and character guide your judgement and actions as a leader?
2. In what ways do you consciously cultivate moral awareness and self-reflection to ensure that your leadership remains aligned with your principles rather than drifting with circumstances?
3. How can leaders sustain integrity and trust in environments where technological power, organisational pressures, and rapid change often test moral courage?

References

Argyris, C., & Schön, D. A. (1978). *Organizational learning: A theory of action perspective*. Addison-Wesley.

Aristotle. (1999). *Nicomachean ethics* (T. Irwin, Trans.). Hackett Publishing Company. (Original work ca. 350 BCE).

Aristotle. (2004). *Nicomachean ethics* (T. Irwin, Trans.). Hackett Publishing. (Original work ca. 350 BCE).

Asch, S. E. (1955). Opinions and social pressure. *Scientific American, 193*(5), 31–35.

Avolio, B. J., & Gardner, W. L. (2005). Authentic leadership development: Getting to the root of positive forms of leadership. *The Leadership Quarterly, 16*(3), 315–338. https://doi.org/10.1016/j.leaqua.2005.03.001

Badaracco, J. L., Jr. (2001). *Defining moments: When managers must choose between right and right*. Harvard Business School Press.

Bagley, C. E. (2003). The ethical leader's decision tree. *Harvard Business Review, 81*(2), 18–19.

Bandura, A. (1999). Moral disengagement in the perpetration of inhumanities. *Personality and Social Psychology Review, 3*(3), 193–209. https://doi.org/10.1207/s15327957pspr0303_3

Bass, B. M., & Steidlmeier, P. (1999). Ethics, character, and authentic transformational leadership behavior. *The Leadership Quarterly, 10*(2), 181–217. https://doi.org/10.1016/S1048-9843(99)00016-8

Bazerman, M. H., & Tenbrunsel, A. E. (2011). *Blind spots: Why we fail to do what's right and what to do about it*. Princeton University Press.

Bennis, W. (2009). *On becoming a leader*. Basic Books.

Bentham, J. (2007). *An introduction to the principles of morals and legislation*. Dover Publications. (Original work published 1789).

Boyatzis, R. E. (2018). The behavioral level of emotional intelligence and its measurement. *Frontiers in Psychology, 9*, Article 1438. https://doi.org/10.3389/fpsyg.2018.01438

Brown, M. E., Treviño, L. K., & Harrison, D. A. (2005). Ethical leadership: A social learning perspective for construct development and testing. *Organizational Behavior and Human Decision Processes, 97*(2), 117–134. https://doi.org/10.1016/j.obhdp.2005.03.002

Cameron, K. S., & Quinn, R. E. (2011). *Diagnosing and changing organizational culture: Based on the competing values framework* (3rd ed.). Jossey-Bass.

Ciulla, J. B. (1998). *Ethics, the heart of leadership*. Praeger.

Ciulla, J. B. (2003). *The ethics of leadership* (2nd ed.). Wadsworth.

Confucius. (1998). *The Analects* (S. Leys, Trans.). W. W. Norton & Company. (Original work ca. 500 BCE).

Crossan, M., Byrne, A., Seijts, G., Reno, M., Monzani, L., & Gandz, J. (2017).Toward a framework of leader character in organizations. *Journal of Management Studies, 54*(7), 986–1018. https://doi.org/10.1111/joms.12254

Crossan, M., Seijts, G., Gavin, M., Good, J., Ehrlich, S. B., & Lehnert, K. (2015). Developing leadership character in the C-suite. *Organizational Dynamics, 44*(3), 183–193. https://doi.org/10.1016/j.orgdyn.2015.05.007

Edwards, J. R., & Cable, D. M. (2009). The value of value congruence. *Journal of Applied Psychology, 94*(3), 654–677. https://doi.org/10.1037/a0014891

Gardner, H. (2006). *Five minds for the future*. Harvard Business School Press.

Goleman, D. (1998a). What makes a leader? *Harvard Business Review, 76*(6), 93–102.
Goleman, D. (1998b). *Working with emotional intelligence*. Bantam Books.
Greenleaf, R. K. (1977). *Servant leadership: A journey into the nature of legitimate power and greatness*. Paulist Press.
Harari, Y. N. (2018). *21 lessons for the 21st century*. Spiegel & Grau.
Johnson, C. E. (2008). *Meeting the ethical challenges of leadership* (3rd ed.). Sage.
Kahneman, D. (2011). *Thinking, fast and slow*. Farrar, Straus and Giroux.
Kant, I. (1993). *Groundwork of the metaphysics of morals* (A. W. Wood, Trans.). Yale University Press. (Original work published 1785).
Kellerman, B. (2004). *Bad leadership*. Harvard Business School Press.
Kouzes, J. M., & Posner, B. Z. (2012). *The leadership challenge: How to make extraordinary things happen in organizations* (5th ed.). Jossey-Bass.
Kouzes, J. M., & Posner, B. Z. (2017). *The leadership challenge* (6th ed.). Wiley.
Low, K. C. P., & Ang, S. L. (2013). Confucian ethics, governance and corporate social responsibility. *International Journal of Business and Management, 8*(4), 30–43. https://doi.org/10.5539/ijbm.v8n4p30. Also see: file:///C:/Users/bsw924/Downloads/20722-80840-1-PB.pdf
Mayer, D. M., Kuenzi, M., Greenbaum, R., Bardes, M., & Salvador, R. (2009). How low does ethical leadership flow? Test of a trickle-down model. *Organizational Behavior and Human Decision Processes, 108*(1), 1–13. https://doi.org/10.1016/j.obhdp.2008.04.002; Science Direct link: www.sciencedirect.com/science/article/abs/pii/S0749597808000551?via%3Dihub
Milgram, S. (1974). *Obedience to authority: An experimental view*. Harper & Row.
Mill, J. S. (1998). *Utilitarianism*. Hackett Publishing. (Original work published 1863).
Moin, S. M. A. (2022). *Creativity in the imagination age: Theories, practice and application*. Palgrave Macmillan.
Mumford, M. D., Zaccaro, S. J., Harding, F. D., Jacobs, T. O., & Fleishman, E. A. (2002). Leadership skills for a changing world: Solving complex social problems. *Leadership Quarterly, 13*(4), 393–416.
Munroe, M. (2014). *Character matters: Leadership lessons from the world stage*. Thomas Nelson.
Peterson, C., & Seligman, M. E. P. (2004). *Character strengths and virtues*. Oxford University Press.
Plato. (2004). *The Republic* (G. M. A. Grube, Trans.; revised by C. D. C. Reeve). Hackett Publishing Company, Inc.
Resick, C. J., Hargis, M. B., Shao, P., & Dust, S. B. (2013). Ethical leadership, moral equity judgments, and discretionary workplace behavior. *Human Relations, 66*(7), 951–972. https://doi.org/10.1177/0018726713481633
Rokeach, M. (1973). *The nature of human values*. Free Press.
Schein, E. H. (2010). *Organizational culture and leadership* (4th ed.). Jossey-Bass.
Schwab, K. (2016). *The fourth industrial revolution*. World Economic Forum.
Schwartz, S. H. (1992). Universals in the content and structure of values. *Advances in Experimental Social Psychology, 25*, 1–65.
Schwartz, S. H. (2012). An overview of the Schwartz theory of basic values. *Online Readings in Psychology and Culture, 2*(1). https://doi.org/10.9707/2307-0919.1116
Seijts, G. H., Crossan, M., Reno, M., & Gandz, J. (2015). Developing character in leaders. *Journal of Management Education, 39*(6), 819–850.

Shaub, M. K., Finn, D. W., & Munter, P. (1993). The effects of auditors' ethical orientation on commitment and ethical sensitivity. *Behavioral Research in Accounting, 5*, 145–169.
Simons, T. (2002). Behavioral integrity. *Academy of Management Journal, 45*(1), 18–35.
Tenbrunsel, A. E., & Messick, D. M. (2004). Ethical fading: The role of self-deception in unethical behavior. *Social Justice Research, 17*(2), 223–236. https://doi.org/10.1023/B:SORE.0000027411.35832.53
Turkle, S. (2015). *Reclaiming conversation: The power of talk in a digital age*. Penguin Press.
Vaughan, D. (1996). *The Challenger launch decision*. University of Chicago Press.

Chapter 8

The Leadership Manifesto

Reclaiming Freedom, Presence, and Power in the Imagination Age

Introduction

Anna woke up before sunrise. The lab was quiet, still bearing marks of unfinished work. On the bench sat a half-built prototype – full of promise, yet paused. She felt two things at once: excitement about what they were creating, and deep tiredness. Her days had filled with meetings, deadlines, and urgent requests. For months, her calendar had been running her life.

She realised she was no longer making choices based on what truly mattered. She was reacting to emails, meetings, and "urgent" tasks. She was busy, but drifting. Moving fast, but going nowhere. It was action without direction. Speed without meaning.

As she held her cold coffee, Anna thought about the leaders she admired. They moved quickly, yet stayed grounded. They were ambitious, yet deeply human. She wondered how they did it. How they resisted constant pressure. How they escaped the trap of urgency and led with clarity and freedom.

Then it became clear. Leadership in the Imagination Age is not just about new technologies or clever ideas. It is about a new way of being. It requires discipline, intention, and courage. It needs a manifesto – a set of commitments and daily habits that anchor leaders in purpose, ethics, and imagination, even under pressure.

Anna's moment of clarity marks the beginning of this chapter. What follows is a practical and ethically grounded manifesto for leaders who want not just to act, but to act wisely. It is written for those who want to regain control in a world that never slows down – choosing presence over autopilot, integrity over convenience, and creation over constant reaction.

Drawing on contemporary leadership thinking and grounded in the Leadership Compass and Moral Gyroscope introduced earlier, this chapter offers clear, step-by-step practices. Through declarations, rituals, and a 90-day plan, it shows how leaders can build a form of leadership that is imaginative, ethical, and sustainable.

DOI: 10.4324/9781003766414-8

Why a Manifesto and Why Now? The Case for Reclaiming Freedom

The Imagination Age brings powerful enabling forces: algorithmic automation, distributed creativity, and networked collaboration. Yet these forces also accelerate attention fragmentation and amplify ethical complexity. Leaders face a dual challenge: move fast while maintaining moral clarity (Schwab, 2016; Uhl-Bien & Arena, 2018). The urgency of opportunities often collides with long-term commitments and human costs. In this context, a manifesto functions as a means of personal and collective recalibration – a public yes to values and practices that keep a leader anchored.

Psychological and leadership literature emphasise the role of intentionality in wellbeing and effective action. Self-determination theory argues that autonomy, competence, and relatedness are essential for motivation (Ryan & Deci, 2000). Attention research shows that deliberate attention management enhances both creativity and ethical reflection (Kabat-Zinn, 2005). Organisational studies indicate that leaders who articulate clear, value-based commitments promote trust and sustained performance (Brown & Treviño, 2006; Avolio & Gardner, 2005).

A manifesto is not mere rhetoric. It is a practice: a repeated recommitment that reorients habitual cognition and behaviour. For Anna – who represents readers and is already a leader or an aspiring leader eager to make a positive impact – writing a manifesto would be an act of reclaiming agency. It is a way to make explicit the internal bearings (Gyroscope) and external directions (Compass) she intended to follow.

The Three Freedoms of the Imagination Age Leader

Anna sat in her car for a long time after the meeting, the echoes of the morning still ringing in her mind. It had been a routine leadership huddle – updates, timelines, budget notes. Yet she had felt strangely absent, as if she were performing her role rather than inhabiting it. The meeting had ended with her team waiting for her vision, but she found herself offering only direction – not inspiration, not clarity, not presence. Just direction.

It was then she realised that modern leadership had become something of a paradox: leaders were expected to chart direction for others while quietly drifting away from themselves. They were expected to inspire imagination in organisations, yet rarely had space to breathe or imagine anything at all. The velocity of the Imagination Age – AI acceleration, constant data, relentless demands – had forced leaders to outrun their own interior worlds (Scharmer, 2016).

And so, sitting silently behind the steering wheel, Anna understood something essential. The first task of a leader is to reclaim inner freedom. That realisation serves as the foundation for the next layer of this chapter. Drawing on inspiration from Brendon Burchard's reflections on "personal freedom" as the gateway to agency and power (Burchard, 2014), the Imagination Age reframes freedom not as escape but as alignment. Leaders must reclaim three freedoms to show up with authenticity, courage, and clarity at a time when noise threatens to overwhelm the signal. These three freedoms – Freedom of Intention, Freedom of Integrity, and Freedom of Imagination – form the psychological and moral core of transformative leadership.

Freedom of Intention: Reclaiming the Inner North Star

In most organisations, days are structured around urgency. Emails are viewed as priorities. Calendars dictate movement. Notifications pull attention in different directions at once. Leaders, even experienced ones, often discover that their day has been shaped more by reaction than by design (Newport, 2016).

Yet intention is the quiet power behind all great leadership. When leaders move with intention, they are not simply performing tasks. They are aligning their actions with their purpose – their True North. They are acting from who they are, not from external noise.

This is what Burchard calls *freedom from distraction and drift* – the liberation that comes when one chooses what truly matters instead of being consumed by what merely demands attention (Burchard, 2014). In the language of Leadership Compass, this is the Northern orientation: a deliberate return to meaning, mission, and the "why" that guides the journey.

Freedom of Intention means:

- Choosing to shape your day, rather than letting your day shape you.
- Prioritising work that aligns with values and purpose.
- Protecting time for thinking, reflecting, and imagining.
- Acting with clarity, not simply with speed.

It is an antidote to autopilot leadership. But it is also a practice, one strengthened through:

- Morning intention-setting
- Boundary-making
- Purpose mapping
- Deep work rituals
- Reflective pauses

Each of these acts reinforces agency, allowing leaders to operate from consciousness rather than compulsion. Research in leadership psychology suggests that leaders who practice intention-setting demonstrate better emotional regulation, higher ethical sensitivity, and greater clarity in decision-making (Kiel, 2015).

Intention returns the leader to themselves. This is essential because only grounded leaders can guide others.

Freedom of Integrity: The Courage to Be Whole

If intention orients the leader, integrity stabilises them. It is the internal gyroscopic force that prevents collapse under pressure. Yet integrity in the Imagination Age is not simply adherence to rules or compliance frameworks. It is the alignment of the leader's Ethics, Values, and Character – the three axes of the Moral Gyroscope that we have discussed previously. Integrity, in this model, is not perfection. It is coherence.

It is the ability to say:

- "This is who I am."
- "This is what I stand for."
- "This is how I will act – even when no one is watching."

The modern world places immense pressure on leaders to compromise, to bend, to rationalise, or to over-justify. Scholars have described this as moral fatigue of contemporary leadership (Ciulla, 2020). The velocity of change, paired with the ambiguity of emergent technologies, makes ethical clarity even harder to maintain. This is why *Freedom of Integrity* is essential. Burchard's view is that personal power comes from choosing our own identity rather than inheriting one unconsciously from culture (Burchard, 2014). In leadership, this means reclaiming the right to stand in one's own moral centre – to lead from values rather than anxieties.

Integrity liberates leaders in several ways:

- It frees them from the fear of external judgment.
- It protects them from drift into unethical territory.
- It creates trust within teams.
- It enhances psychological safety by modelling honesty.
- It anchors decision-making in principles rather than convenience.

Research continually affirms that integrity is the single most important predictor of leadership trustworthiness and long-term impact (Palanski & Yammarino, 2009). A leader's ethical consistency becomes the invisible architecture of organisational culture. When leaders live in alignment with their Ethics, Values, and Character, they do not simply behave ethically – they become ethical forces, shaping space through presence. This is the heart of the Moral Gyroscope. Before leaders attempt to change the world, they must first decide what world they stand for.

Freedom of Imagination: The Horizon of the West

The third freedom is the most expansive and perhaps the most urgent today: the freedom to imagine possibilities not yet visible, not yet certain, and not yet safe. Industrial Age leadership rewarded conformity. Information Age leadership rewarded efficiency. But Imagination Age leadership rewards the courage to envision and create new worlds (Amabile, & Kramer, 2011; Florida, 2002; Moin, 2022).

Yet imagination is often the first casualty of overwhelm. When leaders are exhausted, pressured, or overextended, they lose the ability to dream. Their thinking collapses around constraints. Vision narrows. Creativity shrinks. Teams feel the contraction. Cultures stagnate. This is why freedom of imagination must be reclaimed – not as indulgence, but as necessity.

Imagination allows leaders to:

- See beyond current structures.
- Envision alternative futures.
- Explore what-ifs without fear.
- Stimulate innovation.
- Spark collective creativity.
- Move teams out of the gravity of "the way things are."

Burchard (2014) emphasises that personal freedom rests on the ability to dream freely and boldly without internal censorship. In leadership, this translates into creating intellectual spaciousness, cultivating possibility mindsets, and refusing to let fear dictate the horizon line. In your Leadership Compass, this is the West – the realm of possibility, vision, and sunset wisdom. Leaders at the West do not merely forecast. They imagine. And imagination is not passive. It is active world-building. Neuroscience research confirms that imagination activates brain networks essential for planning, empathy, and moral reasoning (Immordino-Yang, 2015). This means that imagination is not escapism – it is leadership capability.

To nurture imagination, leaders must:

- Slow down.
- Enter reflective and creative states.
- Give space for divergent thinking.
- Encourage unconventional ideas.
- Engage with art, metaphor, and story.
- Think from the future backward.

It is here that storytelling, possibility, and purpose converge – forming the luminous outer rim of the Compass. Freedom of imagination allows leaders to lead futures, not just organisations.

Bringing the Three Freedoms Together

When leaders reclaim intention, integrity, and imagination, something profound happens – they become capable of guiding others not by force, but by presence.

These freedoms transform leadership from external performance to internal alignment.

- Freedom of Intention honours purpose.
- Freedom of Integrity honours moral grounding.
- Freedom of Imagination honours possibility.

Together, they form the soil from which courage grows. They create the inner spaciousness needed to navigate complexity. They awaken the human capacity to lead not reactively, but consciously.

As Anna drove home that evening – sunlight softening across the horizon – she felt that inner spaciousness forming. For the first time in months, she was not thinking about deadlines or metrics. She was thinking about what leadership could be. And she understood that the journey ahead was not merely organisational. It was personal. It was moral. It was imaginative. It was free.

Nine Declarations for Leaders of the Imagination Age

Anna woke the next morning before her alarm, the sky still blue-black and waiting. Something inside her felt different – subtle but undeniable. The day before, she had glimpsed what it meant to reclaim freedom: the freedom to act with intention rather than impulse, to stand in integrity rather than convenience, and to imagine futures bold enough to inspire movement. Now, as she poured her first cup of tea and stepped into the quiet of dawn, she sensed the next step was not reflection but declaration.

Declarations are not wishes. Declarations are commitments. Declarations are the vows leaders make to themselves about who they choose to be. In *The Motivation Manifesto*, Burchard (2014) argues that declarations create the psychological and moral architecture that supports meaningful action. Leaders in the Imagination Age need such architecture more than ever: the velocity of change, the rise of AI, and the fluidity of organisations demand a leadership foundation rooted in clarity, courage, and consciousness (Scharmer, 2016; Ciulla, 2020).

Drawing on the insights of Burchard's (2014), *The Motivation Manifesto,* the following nine declarations are offered as a manifesto for leaders who seek to live with purpose (North), elevate people (East), cultivate excellence (South), imagine boldly (West), and navigate ethically through the Gyroscopic forces of Ethics, Values, and Character. These are not instructions. These are invitations.

Declaration 1: We Shall Lead with Purpose – Returning to Our True North

Leaders in the Imagination Age must resist being swept into tasks that feel urgent but lack meaning. Purpose is not merely a statement; it is the central gravitational force that prevents drift. Research shows that leaders with a clearly articulated sense of purpose demonstrate higher resilience, better decision-making, and stronger moral grounding (George, 2007). Purpose protects the leader from the erosion of vision.

To declare purpose is to say:

I will not be ruled by noise.
I will orient myself toward what matters.

Anna wrote a single sentence in her journal that morning: "My leadership must serve something larger than momentum." It was her first act of reclamation.

Declaration 2: We Shall Reclaim Our Agenda – Choosing Creation Over Reaction

The world will always attempt to claim a leader's time. Emails, crises, meetings, and requests create a gravitational pull away from intention. But creation – not reaction – is the work of leadership (Newport, 2016). To reclaim one's agenda is an act of courage. It means protecting time for thinking, designing, imagining, and cultivating. It means refusing to live at the mercy of notifications. Burchard (2014) argues that personal freedom begins with deciding what deserves one's attention; this insight applies equally to leadership. The declaration states:

I am the author of my story.

Anna began by blocking the first hour of each morning for strategy and reflection. The shift was small but transformative. Her team soon noticed that she spoke from a deeper place, not from a place of haste.

Declaration 3: We Shall Expand Human Potential – Illuminating the East

Every human being carries a rising sun within them. Leaders in this new era are not task managers; they are potential expanders. They create environments where people can grow, thrive, and imagine who they might become.

Psychological safety, autonomy, and belonging – each supported by decades of research – are essential conditions for expanding human potential (Edmondson, 2019; Ryan & Deci, 2017). These conditions do not occur by chance but are deliberately cultivated. This declaration says:

I will see the brilliance in others before they see it in themselves.

Anna adopted a practice of closing each week by writing a short message of encouragement or recognition to at least one team member. Over time, these small messages became catalytic moments – sparking courage, creativity, and trust.

Declaration 4: We Shall Practice Disciplined Excellence – Standing at the Southern Meridian

Performance is not a by-product; it is a practice. It requires discipline, reflection, and a commitment to continuous improvement. But in the Imagination Age, excellence cannot be pursued as perfectionism or productivity obsession. It must be grounded in moral clarity and human sustainability (Dutton & Spreitzer, 2014).

This declaration frames performance as acts inspired by a culture of excellence:

"I will pursue excellence that elevates rather than exhausts."

The South of the Compass symbolises the zenith – the bright clarity of noon – where discipline meets integrity. Leaders who embrace disciplined excellence build cultures of mastery, not burnout.

Anna began reassessing team goals with one question: "Do these push us toward excellence or simply toward exhaustion?" It immediately changed the tone of conversations.

Declaration 5: We Shall Imagine Boldly – Visioning at the Western Edge

Innovation is not institutional; it is imaginative. Leaders who cannot imagine cannot innovate. The future belongs to those who refuse to be confined by current structures or past paradigms (Florida, 2002). This declaration rejects the tyranny of the probable and embraces the possibility of the possible.

It states:

I will give myself permission to dream beyond what exists.

Anna created a monthly "What If" session for her team – one hour where all constraints were suspended. Ideas emerged that would become central to their next strategic cycle. Imagination, she realised, was not a luxury; it was a catalyst for leadership.

Declaration 6: We Shall Tell the Stories That Transform – Guiding the Needle

Storytelling is not decoration; it is direction. It aligns meaning, shapes culture, and drives collective action. Humans do not follow data – they follow narratives that speak to identity and aspiration (Denning, 2011).

This declaration affirms narrative responsibility:

I will speak stories that elevate, unite, and illuminate.

Great leaders tell stories that clarify purpose, honour people, and invite courage. They narrate futures that others can see, feel, and begin to inhabit.

Anna discovered that her team responded not to her directives but to her stories – moments when she articulated *why* their work mattered. Storytelling became her compass needle, pointing collective energy toward shared meaning.

Declaration 7: We Shall Anchor Ourselves in Ethics – Stabilising the Gyroscope

The Moral Gyroscope is built on three axes: ethics, values, and character. Ethics guide action; values guide priorities; character guides consistency. When leaders lose this inner alignment, they drift into moral fog – a phenomenon that has destabilised many organisations today (Ciulla, 2020).

This declaration affirms:

"I will remain morally awake, even when the world grows dim."

Anchoring in ethics requires continuous reflection, humility, and moral imagination. It also demands courage: ethical decisions rarely feel convenient. Leaders must often choose integrity over approval.

Anna began holding monthly ethical reflections with her leadership team – discussing dilemmas, not directives. The conversations deepened trust and sharpened clarity.

Declaration 8: We Shall Lead as Interdependent Beings – Embracing Quantum Connectedness

Quantum leadership acknowledges that individuals and systems are deeply interconnected. Influence is not linear; it is relational, emergent, and systemic (Zohar, 2020). In the Imagination Age, no leader stands alone. We shape, and are shaped by, the organisations, ecosystems, and cultures around us.

This declaration states:

"I will lead with the awareness that my presence affects the whole."

Quantum leadership invites humility: leaders must see themselves as nodes in a vast web of influence rather than isolated authorities. It also invites generosity: leadership becomes an act of contribution rather than control.

Anna began approaching decisions not as isolated choices but as vibrations within a system. This shift changed how she listened, collaborated, and imagined outcomes.

Declaration 9: We Shall Walk with Courage – Choosing What Is Right, Even When It Is Hard

Every leadership act is, at its core, an act of courage for what is right. Courage to speak honestly. Courage to imagine boldly. Courage to act ethically. Courage to make positive change. Courage to walk into uncertainty for creating something of value when there is no map. Burchard (2014) notes that courage is the ultimate expression of personal freedom. Leadership research supports this: courageous leadership is among the strongest predictors of trust, innovation, and organisational resilience (Sinek, 2011; Hannah et al., 2011).

This declaration becomes the final vow:

I will step forward even when the path is unclear.

Anna realised that courage was not the absence of fear but the presence of commitment. She understood that the future belongs to those willing to walk toward it with steady conviction.

Closing Reflection: Living the Declarations

When Anna finished writing her nine declarations that morning, she felt a quiet and powerful clarity settle over her. She did not feel perfect. She did not feel invincible. She felt aligned. The nine declarations are not promises of certainty. They are commitments to consciousness. They are invitations to lead with depth, imagination, and moral clarity. Leaders of the Imagination Age are not defined by title or authority.

They are defined by what they choose to declare.

A Recalibration Practice for Leaders

Anna stood by the window after her morning journalling, watching sunlight break across the rooftops. The nine declarations she had written were still open on her desk, the ink not yet faded. But even as she reread them, she realised something essential: declarations do not transform us by being written. They transform us by being lived.

And living them required practice. In the same way a gyroscope stabilises through continuous motion, and a gyrocompass must settle to true north and be periodically checked to maintain alignment with true north – while a magnetic compass requires correction for variation and deviation – leaders must build rhythms of recalibration: rituals that return them to purpose, integrity, imagination, and presence. Leadership in the Imagination Age is not a static state; it is a dynamic process of return. Returning to purpose. Returning to values. Returning to people. Returning to what matters.

Without practice, even the most inspiring declarations fade into aspiration. With practice, they become oriented. Drawing on insights from leadership psychology (Boyatzis & McKee, 2005), mindfulness science (Kabat-Zinn, 2013), ethical decision-making research (Rest, 1986), and high-performance scholarship (Burchard, 2014), here we offer a practical recalibration system for leaders who seek not just to think differently but to be differently.

These practices are divided into daily, weekly, and monthly rhythms. Each rhythm deepens different aspects of the Leadership Compass and Moral Gyroscope.

Daily Recalibration: The Micro-Practices of Alignment

Daily practices are small, simple, and powerful. They anchor intention, sharpen ethical attention, and keep leaders tethered to meaning during busyness. Research shows that micro-reflections significantly enhance emotional regulation, moral sensitivity, and leadership effectiveness (Reitz et al., 2020). Below are five daily recalibration practices.

Daily Recalibration 1: Morning Intention-Setting (True North Alignment)

Before opening an email or stepping into meetings, leaders can take five minutes to ask:

- *What is my purpose today?*
- *What energy do I want to bring?*
- *Which of my nine declarations matters most right now?*

Even brief morning reflection improves clarity and reduces reactivity throughout the day (Kabat-Zinn, 2013). This practice keeps the leader oriented toward the North of the Compass – Purpose.

Daily Recalibration 2: Ethical Micro-Check (Moral Gyroscope Activation)

Inspired by Rest's (1986) model of ethical awareness, leaders can pause briefly – perhaps before a major decision – and ask:

- *Is this choice aligned with my ethics, values, and character?*
- *What might I regret if I act in haste?*

This micro-check strengthens the three gyroscopic axes: Ethics, Values, and Character. Over time, it builds moral intuition.

Daily Recalibration 3: People Atonement (Eastern Orientation)

Once a day, leaders can pause to consider:

- *Who might need support, encouragement, or recognition?*
- *Who has contributed quietly without acknowledgement?*

Research on relational leadership shows that even brief acts of attunement significantly increase trust, psychological safety, and collective motivation (Edmondson, 2019). This practice reorients the leader toward the East – People.

Daily Recalibration 4: Possibility Pulse (Western Horizon)

At any moment – perhaps mid-afternoon – leaders can ask:

- *What possibility am I not seeing?*
- *If constraints disappeared, what could this become?*

This activates the brain's imagination networks, which support innovation and future-oriented thinking (Immordino-Yang, 2015).

The question shifts attention from "*what is*" to "*what could be.*"

Daily Recalibration 5: Story of the Day (The Needle's Direction)

Before leaving work, leaders should take one minute to ask:

- *What story did I tell today – about myself, my team, or our future?*
- *Did my words elevate or diminish the possibility?*

This practice builds narrative consciousness and aligns communication with purpose (Denning, 2011). Daily practices are small, but their cumulative impact is profound. They recalibrate leadership at the level of attention, intention, and imagination.

Case Study 8.1 Systems-Based Behavioural Change and Leadership: Insights from Atomic Habits

Introduction

James Clear's *Atomic Habits* (2018) explains how small, consistent behaviours can lead to meaningful personal and professional growth. Although written for a general audience, its ideas apply directly to leadership. This case study explores how systems-based habits strengthen leadership behaviour, shape team culture, and support long-term effectiveness.

Background

Clear (2018) explains that habits are driven by the systems people build – the routines and structures that shape everyday behaviour. He emphasises that success depends less on ambitious goals and more on the quality of the systems supporting daily actions. This perspective redirects attention from outcomes to the small, consistent behaviours that create them.

Problem Statement

Leaders often struggle to:

- Maintain consistent leadership behaviours.
- Turn strategic intentions into everyday actions.
- Build cultures that reinforce positive habits.
- Replace unhelpful or entrenched routines.

Clear (2018) suggests that these challenges arise when leaders focus on goals rather than the systems that support them.

Intervention: Applying the Atomic Habits Framework

Systems Over Goals

Clear (2018) emphasises that sustainable results come from improving the processes that generate behaviour. Leaders who refine their daily systems – rather than relying on motivation or targets – create more reliable and lasting change.

Identity-Based Habits

Clear (2018) argues that habits reflect identity: each action is a "vote" for the kind of person one wants to become. For leaders, this means embedding identity-driven statements ("I am a leader who listens," "I am a leader who develops others") into daily routines to reinforce authentic leadership behaviour.

The Four Laws of Behaviour Change

Clear's (2018) model can be directly applied to leadership practice:

- **Make it obvious** – Use cues that prompt leadership actions (e.g., reminders for check-ins).
- **Make it attractive** – Link leadership tasks to meaningful rewards.
- **Make it easy** – Reduce friction so positive behaviours are simple to perform.
- **Make it satisfying** – Reinforce actions with immediate acknowledgement or reflection.

Outcomes and Leadership Implications

When leaders apply these principles:

- **Consistency increases** as small actions compound over time.
- **Team culture strengthens** because systems reinforce shared values.
- **Leadership identity deepens,** making behaviour more authentic.
- **Organisational routines improve**, making positive habits easier for everyone.

Discussion

Clear's (2018) approach aligns with research showing that small, repeated improvements create significant long-term gains. Leaders who design supportive systems reduce reliance on willpower, create positive feedback loops, and make effective behaviour the default rather than the exception.

Conclusion

Atomic Habits (Clear, 2018) demonstrates that meaningful change comes from intentional, consistent systems rather than occasional effort. For leaders, habit-based approaches strengthen identity, improve culture, and support sustained performance. Leadership excellence grows through small, repeated actions – one habit at a time.

Weekly Recalibration: Building Rhythms of Reflection and Refinement

Weekly practices deepen alignment beyond the surface of daily action. They allow leaders to step back, assess patterns, and adjust course. Research suggests that weekly structured reflection increases performance, reduces burnout, and strengthens moral reasoning (Sonnentag & Fritz, 2015). Below are five weekly recalibration rituals.

Weekly Recalibration 1. Performance Reflection (Southern Discipline)
Once a week – often Friday afternoon – leaders should ask:

- *What moved us closer to excellence?*
- *What drained energy or clarity?*
- *What should we discontinue next week?*

This practice aligns with the South of the Compass: Performance, discipline, and excellence.

Weekly Recalibration 2: Values Check (Gyroscopic Return)
Leaders reflect on:

- *Which of my values felt lived this week?*
- *Where did I act out of alignment?*

Research shows that values reflection increases leadership authenticity and moral courage (Avolio & Gardner, 2005).

Weekly Recalibration 3: Storytelling Review (Narrative Awareness)
Leaders should ask:

- *What narratives shaped my team this week?*
- *Do we need to reframe a story that is limiting us?*

Cultural psychology suggests that collective stories shape organisational identity more than metrics or mandates (Weick, 1995).

Weekly Recalibration 4: Human Connection Mapping (Eastern Care and Inclusion)
Once a week, leaders should reflect on key relationships:

- *Who did I connect with meaningfully?*
- *Who might be drifting to the margins?*
- *Who needs support next week?*

This strengthens belonging – an essential driver of performance and wellbeing (Ryan & Deci, 2017).

Weekly Recalibration 5: Future Thinking Session (Western Possibility)
Leaders can spend 20–30 minutes imagining:

- *Emerging opportunities*
- *Potential innovations*
- *Long-range impacts of decisions*
- *Changes in the ecosystem*

Future-thinking practices increase adaptability and resilience (Scharmer, 2016). These weekly rhythms sharpen perspective and maintain alignment between action and aspiration.

Monthly Recalibration: Depth Work for Leadership Renewal

Monthly recalibration rituals are deeper, more spacious, and more transformative. They are the equivalent of adjusting the internal compass and recalibrating the entire gyroscopic system. These practices draw from developmental psychology, systems thinking, and moral philosophy.

Monthly Recalibration 1: Character Audit (Gyroscopic Coherence)
Leaders can ask:

- *Where did my actions reflect the leader I want to be?*
- *Where did fear, ego, or exhaustion distort my choices?*
- *What must I strengthen this month?*

Character audits cultivate humility, self-awareness, and grounded decision-making (Kiel, 2015).

Monthly Recalibration 2: Ethical Foresight Session (Anticipatory Integrity)
Leaders need to engage with emerging dilemmas:

- AI and privacy
- Equity and inclusion
- Power and responsibility
- Long-term societal impact

Ethical foresight increases moral imagination and reduces unintentional harm (Ciulla, 2020).

Monthly Recalibration 3: Westward Imagination Retreat (Vision Expansion)
Once a month, leaders need to create space – one or two hours – to imagine without constraint:

- Possible futures
- New models
- Alternative scenarios

This practice strengthens creative cognition and visionary thinking (Lee et al., 2018).

Monthly Recalibration 4: People and Purpose Alignment (Compass Synchronisation)
Leaders need to revisit:

- Team strengths
- Team tensions
- Purpose evolution
- Cultural alignment

This promotes coherence between the Compass elements – Purpose, People, Performance, and Possibility.

Monthly Recalibration 5: System-Level Reflection (Quantum Leadership)
Leaders need to examine:

- Patterns in the organisation
- Unintended consequences
- Interdependencies
- Ecosystem relationships

Systemic awareness is crucial for leaders to be effective in complex environments (Zohar, 2020). Monthly recalibrations build depth, vision, and moral grounding – qualities difficult to cultivate in the rush of daily leadership. Table 8.1 presents recalibration practices at a glance.

At the end of the first month of practising these rhythms, Anna noticed something subtle but transformative. She was no longer reacting her way through the week. She was *shaping* it. She was thinking more clearly, speaking more intentionally, listening more deeply, and imagining more boldly.

Table 8.1 Summary of Daily, Weekly, and Monthly Recalibration Practices

Rhythm	*Practice*	*Compass/gyroscope alignment*	*Purpose*
Daily	Morning Intention	North (Purpose)	Orient the day toward meaning
	Ethical Micro-Check	Ethics–Values–Character	Strengthen moral awareness
	People Attunement	East (People)	Enhance empathy and connection
	Possibility Pulse	West (Possibility)	Stimulate imagination
	Story of the Day	Storytelling Needle	Build narrative consciousness
Weekly	Performance Reflection	South (Performance)	Promote disciplined excellence
	Values Check	Gyroscope	Maintain integrity
	Storytelling Review	Needle	Align narratives with purpose
	Connection Mapping	East	Support inclusion and belonging
	Future Thinking	West	Expand horizons
Monthly	Character Audit	Gyroscope	Deepen self-awareness
	Ethical Foresight	Ethics	Anticipate dilemmas
	Imagination Retreat	West	Vision expansion
	People–Purpose Alignment	Compass	Strengthen coherence
	System Reflection	Quantum Leadership	Reveal interdependencies

The recalibration practices did not eliminate complexity. They gave her the internal posture to meet it. Leadership in the Imagination Age does not demand perfection. It demands presence. And presence comes from practice. Leaders who recalibrate regularly become steady, attentive, courageous, and imaginative – qualities the future will not simply reward but require.

Conclusion

Leadership in the Imagination Age requires more than clever strategy or technological mastery. It requires leaders who are present, principled, and imaginative – who can hold complex futures and human dignity at once. A manifesto is neither a panacea nor a polished brand; it is a practice of renewed agency. It is a vow to show up – to act with intention, to test decisions through ethics, and to imagine boldly.

Anna's morning in the lab became the hinge of a new way of leading. The manifesto she crafted was not a rigid set of rules; it was a living set of commitments that shaped how she started each day, how she said yes and no, and how she co-created futures with her team. You can write your manifesto today. The act of declaring is itself transformational: it changes the field of possibility.

Reflective Questions

1. What personal practices or habits help you remain present, reflective, and ethically grounded while navigating the speed and complexity of the Imagination Age?
2. How might adopting intentional disciplines – such as the Nine Declarations or a structured recalibration process – reshape the way you lead yourself, others, and your organisation?
3. In balancing immediate performance pressures with long-term ethical responsibility, how do you cultivate the courage and imagination required to lead toward a more meaningful and sustainable future?

References

Amabile, T. M., & Kramer, S. J. (2011). *The progress principle: Using small wins to ignite joy, engagement, and creativity at work.* Harvard Business Review Press.

Avolio, B. J., & Gardner, W. L. (2005). Authentic leadership development: Getting to the root of positive forms of leadership. *The Leadership Quarterly, 16*(3), 315–338. https://doi.org/10.1016/j.leaqua.2005.03.001

Boyatzis, R., & McKee, A. (2005). *Resonant leadership: Renewing yourself and connecting with others through mindfulness, hope, and compassion.* Harvard Business School Press.

Brown, M. E., & Treviño, L. K. (2006). Ethical leadership: A review and future directions. *The Leadership Quarterly, 17*(6), 595–616. https://doi.org/10.1016/j.leaqua.2006.10.004

Burchard, B. (2014). *The motivation manifesto: 9 declarations to claim your personal power.* Hay House.

Ciulla, J. B. (2020). *Ethics, the heart of leadership* (4th ed.). ABC-CLIO.
Clear, J. (2018). *Atomic habits: An easy & proven way to build good habits & break bad ones*. Avery.
Denning, S. (2011). *The leader's guide to storytelling: Mastering the art and discipline of business narrative*. Jossey-Bass.
Dutton, J. E., & Spreitzer, G. M. (2014). *How to be a positive leader: Small actions, big impact*. Berrett-Koehler Publishers.
Edmondson, A. C. (2019). *The fearless organization: Creating psychological safety in the workplace for learning, innovation, and growth*. Wiley.
Florida, R. (2002). *The rise of the creative class: And how it's transforming work, leisure, community, and everyday life*. Basic Books.
George, B. (2007). *True north: Discover your authentic leadership*. Jossey-Bass.
Hannah, S. T., Sweeney, P. J., & Lester, P. B. (2011). Toward a courageous mindset: The role of courage in leadership development. *Consulting Psychology Journal: Practice and Research, 63*(3), 154–172. https://doi.org/10.1037/a0024986
Immordino-Yang, M. H. (2015). *Emotions, learning, and the brain: Exploring the educational implications of affective neuroscience*. W. W. Norton & Company.
Kabat-Zinn, J. (2005). *Coming to our senses: Healing ourselves and the world through mindfulness*. Hyperion.
Kabat-Zinn, J. (2013). *Full catastrophe living: Using the wisdom of your body and mind to face stress, pain, and illness*. Bantam Books.
Kiel, D. (2015). *Return on character: The real reason leaders and their companies succeed.* Harvard Business Review Press.
Lee, S., Olson, B., & Trimi, S. (2018). Co-innovation: How to build innovation ecosystems. *Business Horizons, 61*(4), 567–575. https://doi.org/10.1016/j.bushor.2018.03.007
Moin, S. M. A. (2022). *Creativity in the imagination age: Theories, practice and application.* Palgrave Macmillan.
Newport, C. (2016). *Deep work: Rules for focused success in a distracted world.* Grand Central Publishing.
Palanski, M. E., & Yammarino, F. J. (2009). Integrity and leadership: Clearing the conceptual confusion. *European Management Journal, 27*(3), 171–184. https://doi.org/10.1016/j.emj.2009.01.001
Reitz, M., Ashkanasy, N., & Jordan, P. (2020). Micro-practices for ethical leadership: Daily interventions to improve ethical awareness and behavior. *Journal of Business Ethics, 162*, 345–361. https://doi.org/10.1007/s10551-018-3966-3
Rest, J. R. (1986). *Moral development: Advances in research and theory*. Praeger.
Ryan, R. M., & Deci, E. L. (2000). Intrinsic and extrinsic motivations: Classic definitions and new directions. *Contemporary Educational Psychology, 25*(1), 54–67. https://doi.org/10.1006/ceps.1999.1020
Ryan, R. M., & Deci, E. L. (2017). *Self-determination theory: Basic psychological needs in motivation, development, and wellness*. Guilford Press.
Scharmer, O. C. (2016). *Theory U: Leading from the future as it emerges* (2nd ed.). Berrett-Koehler.
Schwab, K. (2016). *The fourth industrial revolution*. World Economic Forum.
Sinek, S. (2011). *Start with why: How great leaders inspire everyone to take action*. Portfolio.
Sonnentag, S., & Fritz, C. (2015). Recovery from job stress: The stressor-detachment model as an integrative framework. *Journal of Organizational Behavior, 36*(S1), S72–S103. https://doi.org/10.1002/job.1924

Uhl-Bien, M., & Arena, M. (2018). Leadership for organizational adaptability: A theoretical synthesis and integrative framework. *The Leadership Quarterly, 29*(1), 89–104. https://doi.org/10.1016/j.leaqua.2017.12.009

Weick, K. E. (1995). *Sensemaking in organizations*. Sage.

Zohar, D. (2020). *Quantum leadership: Advancing innovation, transforming health care*. Jossey-Bass.

Chapter 9

Cosmic Leadership

Synchronising with the Rhythm of the Universe

Introduction

For much of modern history, leadership has been framed as optimising organisations, maximising efficiency, outperforming competitors, and scaling growth within clearly bounded institutional systems. This organisation-centric worldview has delivered remarkable economic progress. Yet in the Imagination Age – shaped by climate instability, technological acceleration, social fragmentation, and global interdependence – its limitations are increasingly evident. Models that once produced success now falter when confronted with challenges that extend far beyond organisational walls.

Today's most pressing crises do not appear as discrete managerial problems. Climate change, biodiversity loss, pandemics, digital surveillance, and widening inequality unfold across interconnected social, ecological, and technological systems. When leadership remains confined to short-term metrics and institutional silos, responsibility fragments and harm is routinely externalised – strategically rational and legally defensible, yet morally and ecologically unsustainable (Peter Senge et al., 2008). Leaders may succeed locally while contributing to systemic failure globally.

This tension exposes a deeper flaw in organisation-centric leadership: the assumption that responsibility ends at the organisational boundary. Decisions are evaluated through profitability, productivity, or market share, while long-term and cumulative consequences remain obscured. Planetary systems, however, do not recognise corporate charters, national borders, or quarterly reporting cycles. They respond only to aggregate action – and inaction. Climate instability and ecological breakdown are not organisational problems but planetary ones that transcend sectors, jurisdictions, and generations (Johan Rockström et al., 2009).

As complexity intensifies, scholars argue that leadership must evolve beyond optimisation toward stewardship, and beyond control toward participation in living systems (Donella Meadows, 2008). Organisations are not autonomous entities; they are nested within social and ecological systems whose health determines their own viability. Leadership, therefore, is not merely managerial – it is relational, ethical, and existential.

DOI: 10.4324/9781003766414-9

This chapter introduces Cosmic Leadership as a practical necessity for the Imagination Age. It situates leadership within wider patterns of interdependence, inviting leaders to move from ownership to stewardship, from dominance to coherence. Leadership becomes less about imposing will and more about aligning inner values with the deeper rhythms that sustain human and planetary flourishing.

Conceptualising the Cosmos: Divine Order, Human Responsibility, and Leadership

Cosmic Leadership begins with how the cosmos itself is understood. Across science, philosophy, art, and scripture, the universe is not portrayed as random or morally neutral, but as an ordered creation – governed by harmony, intelligibility, and purpose. These traditions converge on a central insight: the cosmos is the creation of God, sustained by balance and relational order, and human beings are entrusted participants within it, not owners over it. Leadership, when viewed through this lens, becomes a moral and spiritual responsibility rather than a purely organisational function.

The Cosmos Through the Lens of Science: Order as Divine Intelligibility

Classical and modern science have consistently revealed the universe as governed by laws that point to coherence rather than chaos. Isaac Newton, whose scientific work was inseparable from theological conviction, described the universe as a manifestation of divine order: "This most beautiful system of the sun, planets, and comets could only proceed from the counsel and dominion of an intelligent and powerful Being" (Newton, 1687/1999, p. 544). For Newton, scientific discovery was not a negation of God, but a means of discerning divine design. The cosmos was intelligible precisely because it was created with purpose.

Albert Einstein, though cautious about doctrinal religion, repeatedly affirmed the spiritual dimension of cosmic order: "The most incomprehensible thing about the universe is that it is comprehensible" (Einstein, 1936/2013, p. 292). Elsewhere, Einstein described his sense of reverence toward the universe:

> Try and penetrate with our limited means the secrets of nature and you will find that, behind all the discernible concatenations, there remains something subtle, intangible and inexplicable. Veneration for this force beyond anything that we can comprehend is my religion. To that extent I am, in point of fact, religious.
>
> (Einstein, 1927)

In contemporary physics, Michio Kaku articulates the universe in explicitly harmonic terms: "The universe is a symphony. And the 'mind of God,' which Einstein wrote about, is cosmic music resonating through eleven-dimensional hyperspace" (Kaku, 2011, p. 336). Scientific inquiry thus reveals not randomness, but law, harmony, and intelligibility, reinforcing the theological claim that the cosmos is created and sustained by divine wisdom. Leadership, in such a universe, cannot be grounded in domination but must be aligned with coherence.

The Cosmos Through the Lens of Philosophy: Moral Order and Self-Knowledge

Philosophy approached the cosmos not merely as a physical structure, but as a moral order. Socrates' injunction – *know thyself* – was an ethical orientation rather than psychological introspection. As recorded by Plato, Socrates argued that ignorance of the self leads inevitably to injustice (Plato, trans. 2004). Plato envisioned leadership as guardianship of cosmic and moral order: "Until philosophers rule as kings… cities will have no rest from evils" (Plato, *Republic*, trans. 2004, 473c). Aristotle further grounded leadership in alignment with natural and moral purpose: "The good for man is an activity of the soul in accordance with virtue" (Aristotle, *Nicomachean Ethics*, trans. 1999, 1098a). For Aristotle, leadership excellence required harmony between character, action, and the telos (purpose) embedded in creation. This philosophical tradition positions leadership as moral participation in a divinely ordered cosmos rather than unchecked power.

The Cosmos Through the Lens of Art and Literature: Role, Meaning, and Humility

Poets and writers grasped cosmic truths through metaphor and moral imagination. With his "All the world's a stage, … all the men and women merely players" (*As You Like It*, Act II, Scene VII), William Shakespeare captured humanity's role within a larger order. This metaphor affirms agency while denying ownership. Meaning lies not in commanding the stage, but in playing one's role faithfully. Rabindranath Tagore warned against human arrogance divorced from reverence: "The highest education is that which does not merely give us information but makes our life in harmony with all existence" (Tagore, 1917, p. 142). Leo Tolstoy echoed this moral restraint, asserting that the meaning of life is found in serving others (Tolstoy, 1886/2005). Through art, leadership is framed as service, humility, and moral responsibility within a sacred order.

The Cosmos Through the Lens of Scripture: Creation, Signs, and Trust

Sacred texts make explicit what science, philosophy, and art imply. The Qur'an repeatedly affirms that the universe is created in balance (*mīzān*): "He raised the heaven and established the balance – so that you may not transgress the balance" (Qur'an 55:7–8). It further declares: "We will show them Our signs in the horizons and within themselves until it becomes clear to them that it is the Truth" (Qur'an 41:53). Similarly, the Bible presents creation as a trust rather than a possession: The Lord God took the man and put him in the Garden of Eden to till it and keep it (Genesis 2:15, The Holy Bible: New Revised Standard Version, 1989). Both scriptures locate leadership within accountability to God, creation, and future generations.

Humanity as Khalīfah: *Leadership as Vicegerency*

The Qur'anic concept of *khalīfah* provides the clearest articulation of Cosmic Leadership: "Indeed, I will place upon the earth a vicegerent" (Qur'an 2:30). *Khalīfah* signifies delegated authority – not ownership. Humans are entrusted with protecting balance, ensuring justice, and sustaining life. When leaders exploit ecosystems, destroy biodiversity, or prioritise domination over stewardship, they violate this trust and fall out of synchronicity with the cosmos.

Integrative Insight: One Creation, One Moral Calling

Across science, philosophy, art, and scripture, a unified truth emerges:

> The cosmos is the creation of God – ordered, intelligible, and morally charged – and leadership must align with this reality. Cosmic Leadership is therefore not a metaphorical aspiration but a return to humanity's entrusted role: to lead with humility, coherence, justice, and stewardship – so that human ambition serves, rather than disrupts, the divine balance sustaining life itself.

Synchronicity with the Cosmos: Harmony, Balance, and Justice

Synchronicity with the cosmos refers to a leadership orientation grounded in harmony, balance, and justice – an understanding that human systems are inseparable from the wider ecological, moral, and planetary order. Across systems science, economics, and ethics, sustainable order is not achieved through domination or unlimited growth, but through dynamic equilibrium (Meadows, 2008). Living systems flourish when feedback loops are respected, limits are acknowledged, and relationships remain mutually sustaining.

From a planetary perspective, humanity exists within clearly defined ecological boundaries. Rockström et al. (2009) demonstrate that transgressing planetary limits destabilises Earth's life-support systems, creating risks that cascade across climate, biodiversity, food, and social systems. Leadership aligned with cosmic synchronicity recognises limits not as constraints on ambition, but as moral boundaries that protect collective flourishing.

Justice emerges naturally from balance. Raworth's (2017) Doughnut Economics framework reframes prosperity as the space where social foundations are met without overshooting ecological ceilings. Leadership within this "safe and just space" integrates economic vitality with human dignity and planetary health.

Justice, in this sense, is not merely distributive; it is systemic – ensuring that benefits and burdens are shared fairly across communities, species, and generations.

Systems thinking reinforces this perspective by highlighting interdependence rather than linear causality (Meadows, 2008; Senge, 2006). Decisions taken in one domain inevitably reverberate elsewhere. Leaders acting in synchronicity therefore ask not only whether an action benefits their organisation, but whether it preserves balance within the wider system.

In this framing, leadership becomes an act of attunement. To lead in harmony with the cosmos is to align human intention with natural rhythms, ethical responsibility, and relational justice. Progress is no longer measured solely by growth or efficiency, but by whether leadership sustains life, dignity, and long-term coherence within an interconnected world.

When Leadership Falls Out of Alignment

When leadership falls out of alignment with cosmic and ecological order, imbalance follows. History repeatedly shows that systems collapse not from scarcity alone, but from excess, hubris, and the refusal to respect limits (Meadows, 2008). Leadership driven by extraction, short-term optimisation, and ownership mentalities destabilises the very systems on which prosperity depends.

An ownership mindset treats nature, labour, and even future generations as resources to be consumed rather than relationships to be stewarded. This logic underpins many contemporary crises: deforestation, climate instability, biodiversity loss, and widening inequality (Rockström et al., 2009). Holling (2001) warns that such exploitative dynamics reduce resilience, making systems increasingly fragile and prone to sudden collapse.

Economically, growth-at-any-cost models distort value by privileging output over wellbeing. Stiglitz et al. (2010) argue that conventional metrics such as GDP systematically ignore social and ecological degradation, enabling leaders to make decisions that appear successful while causing long-term harm. When leaders pursue performance without justice or balance, progress becomes illusory.

Ethically, misalignment erodes trust. Leaders who externalise costs – onto ecosystems, marginalised communities, or future generations – violate principles of fairness and intergenerational justice (Rawls, 1999). What appears efficient in the short term often proves unjust and unsustainable over time.

Systems theory makes clear that force-based intervention in complex systems amplifies instability rather than restoring order (Meadows, 2008). Leadership that seeks to control rather than coordinate, dominate rather than participate, ultimately generates resistance and breakdown.

Falling out of alignment is therefore not merely an environmental failure; it is a moral one. It reflects a refusal to recognise humanity's embeddedness within living systems. Cosmic Leadership emerges precisely as a corrective – calling leaders to replace ownership with stewardship, extraction with regeneration, and short-term gain with responsibility for the whole.

The Shift in Mindset for Cosmic Leadership

Cosmic Leadership requires a profound shift in mindset. As humanity's influence on planetary systems intensifies, leaders are increasingly called to move beyond models rooted in control, extraction, and limitless growth. The emerging paradigm of planetary and cosmic leadership reframes leadership as an act of alignment – one that recognises humanity as an integral part of a larger, living system rather than its master.

From Control to Coexistence

Traditional leadership models have been shaped by assumptions of control: controlling markets, resources, people, and outcomes. While control may offer short-term efficiency, it proves fragile in complex, interconnected systems. Ecological crises, social fragmentation, and systemic risk reveal the limits of command-and-control thinking (Meadows, 2008). Coexistence, by contrast, acknowledges interdependence. It recognises that organisations, economies, and societies exist within social and ecological systems that cannot be dominated without consequence. Leadership grounded in coexistence seeks harmony rather than supremacy. Decisions are made with awareness of second- and third-order effects – on communities, ecosystems, and future generations. This mindset aligns with systems thinking, which emphasises relationship, feedback, and balance over linear prediction and control (Senge, 2006). Coexistence does not imply passivity; it demands humility, attentiveness, and ethical restraint.

From Extraction to Regeneration

The extractive paradigm views nature, labour, and even human attention as resources to be consumed. Under this logic, success is measured by what can be taken and converted into growth. Yet extraction without renewal inevitably leads to depletion of soils, oceans, trust, and social cohesion (Rockström et al., 2009). Regenerative leadership reverses this logic. It asks not only how value is created, but whether systems are left stronger than they were found. Regeneration emphasises restoration, renewal, and reciprocity. In organisational terms, this means building cultures that replenish human energy, economies that restore ecosystems, and innovations that serve long-term resilience rather than short-term profit (Raworth, 2017). Regenerative leaders recognise that true prosperity emerges when economic, social, and ecological systems are mutually reinforcing.

From Growth-at-Any-Cost to Flourishing-for-All

For decades, leadership success has been equated with continuous expansion – higher output, larger markets, and accelerated consumption. However, growth-at-any-cost has revealed its ethical and ecological limits. It concentrates wealth, externalises harm, and destabilises planetary boundaries (Stiglitz et al., 2010). Flourishing-for-all represents a more mature aspiration. It reframes progress in terms of wellbeing, justice, dignity, and sustainability. Flourishing acknowledges that systems thrive not when a few maximise gain, but when many have the conditions to reach their full potential. Leadership aligned with flourishing prioritises inclusion, intergenerational equity, and the protection of life-supporting systems. It asks not "How much more can we grow?" but "How well can we live together?"

Intellectual Adda | Leadership, Cosmos, and Stewardship at Sea: A Conversation with Rear Admiral Khandakar Akhter Hossain

Before we begin this Intellectual Adda, let me introduce Rear Admiral Khandakar Akhter Hossain. His leadership was forged not in abstraction, but in steel, tides, and responsibility. An engineer and naval architect by training, he spent decades at the heart of maritime capability – leading four major shipyards and working hands-on with both U.S. and Chinese shipbuilding ecosystems. As Chief Engineer Officer and Project Chief Naval Architect of a modern Corvette, he played a direct role in advancing Bangladesh's maritime self-reliance and technological sovereignty. Yet his leadership was not confined to docks and design tables. Through United Nations peacekeeping missions, he encountered leadership where command must coexist with restraint, empathy, and moral judgment under pressure. A scholar as much as a practitioner, Rear Admiral Hossain holds two doctoral degrees from prestigious universities in Bangladesh and the United States, respectively. With many journal publications and several books, and as an avid reader of Albert Einstein and Michio Kaku, he brings a cosmological sensibility to leadership that sees beyond silos to systems, beyond tasks to patterns, and beyond authority to responsibility. In May 2025, he assumed office as the 5th Vice Chancellor of Bangladesh Maritime University (BMU), carrying a vision both ambitious and grounded: to elevate BMU to international standards while anchoring it firmly in Bangladesh's maritime destiny and human future. Since taking office, he has actively engaged global partners – from the World Maritime University to Japanese maritime researchers and national regulators. At the core of his leadership lies a deep commitment to the blue economy, human capital development, and the ethical stewardship of the oceans that sustain livelihoods, nations, and life itself.

This conversation, therefore, is not merely with a Vice Chancellor or a naval Admiral. It is a dialogue with a thinker – a leader navigating leadership at a cosmic scale where engineering meets ethics, oceans meet imagination, and power gives way to stewardship. In this Intellectual Adda, we explore how leadership, when viewed through the lens of the cosmos, invites us to rethink authority, responsibility, and our role in the grand theatre of existence – where every leader, like every sailor, must learn not only how to command a vessel, but how to read the stars.

Author: *You have led organisations, institutions, and complex systems. How has your study of thinkers like Einstein and Michio Kaku shaped the way you understand leadership – not merely as command, but as alignment with larger natural and systemic orders?*

Rear Admiral Hossain: The study of Einstein taught me that reality is relational – nothing exists in isolation. Kaku extends this by revealing the universe as an elegant, lawful symphony rather than a chaotic one. These ideas reframed leadership for me: command alone is insufficient in complex systems. True leadership is alignment: with physical laws, human systems, and ethical order. In naval operations, forcing outcomes against systemic realities leads to failure; alignment with conditions produces effectiveness. Leadership, therefore, is less about control and more about coherence – understanding patterns, respecting limits, and acting in harmony with larger forces. When leaders align themselves with these deeper orders, influence becomes sustainable and purposeful.

Author: *In this chapter, we argue that leaders are participants in the cosmic theatre, not its owners. From your naval and maritime perspective, how do you interpret humanity's obligation to the oceans and the cosmos – as stewards rather than exploiters?*

Rear Admiral Hossain: From a naval and maritime perspective, the ocean teaches humility very quickly. No matter how advanced our ships or technologies become, the sea always reminds us that we operate within forces far greater than ourselves. This naturally leads to a stewardship mindset. The oceans are not commodities to be owned; they are living systems that sustain life, climate, trade, and culture. When leaders behave as owners, exploitation follows – overfishing, pollution, and ecological collapse. But when we see ourselves as stewards, responsibility replaces entitlement. Stewardship means restraint, foresight, and respect for balance. In the cosmic sense, humanity is a custodian placed within a larger order. Our obligation is to preserve harmony so that the oceans continue to serve not only us, but generations yet to come.

Author: *Maritime systems are deeply interconnected – technology, ecology, geopolitics, and human skill. What lessons from naval engineering and shipbuilding best illustrate why leaders today must think systemically rather than linearly?*

Rear Admiral Hossain: Naval engineering is, by nature, systems thinking in action. A ship is not simply steel and machinery; it is an integration of propulsion, electronics, human skill, logistics, and environmental conditions. A minor failure in one subsystem can compromise the entire mission. During ship design and operations, we learn that optimisation in isolation often creates vulnerability elsewhere. This lesson applies directly to leadership. Linear thinking assumes cause and effect are simple, but maritime systems teach us that outcomes emerge from interactions. Leaders who ignore ecology, human factors, or geopolitical context may succeed briefly but fail systemically. The sea rewards leaders who understand interdependence and penalises those who pursue narrow efficiency at the expense of resilience.

Author: *In quantum theory, entanglement shows that seemingly separate entities remain deeply connected. How can this idea help leaders reimagine responsibility, ethics, and decision-making in a world where actions in one domain – technology, environment, or policy – have far-reaching and often unseen consequences?*

Rear Admiral Hossain: Quantum physics is the golden child of modern science. It is the basis of our understanding of atoms, radiation, and so much else, from elementary particles and basic forces to the behaviour of materials. But for a century, it has also been the problem child of science as it has been overwhelmed by intense disagreements between its inventors, strange paradoxes, and implications that seem like the stuff of fantasy. To understand the universe, quantum physics explores the behaviour of the smallest particles in existence, such as quarks, electrons, and photons, revealing a world that defies our everyday experiences and expectations. Quantum entanglement reminds us that separation is often an illusion. In leadership, this insight reframes responsibility: decisions made in technology, policy, or the environment are never isolated acts, but are entangled with social trust, ecological balance, and future generations. When leaders recognise this deep interconnection, ethics shifts from short-term compliance to long-term consciousness. Responsibility expands beyond immediate outcomes to unseen ripple effects across systems. Entangled leadership requires humility, systems thinking, and moral foresight – acting with the awareness that harm or care in one domain inevitably resonates elsewhere. In an entangled world, ethical leadership is the art of choosing with the whole in mind.

Author: *Standing at the edge of the sea often invites reflection beyond the immediate mission. When you think about the future of the oceans and humanity, what kind of leadership do you believe the cosmos itself is calling us to embody?*

Rear Admiral Hossain: The sea covers most of our planet and sustains millions of livelihoods, economies, and ecosystems. When we damage it, we damage ourselves. The leadership the future demands is one of preservation before expansion, balance before exploitation. The cosmos teaches us order, rhythm, and limits – nothing grows endlessly without consequence. Leaders must therefore embody restraint, long-term thinking, and reverence for life. This is not weak leadership; it is mature leadership. The oceans are central to climate stability, food security, and global trade. Protecting them is not optional – it is existential. The leadership the cosmos calls for is stewardship-driven, ethically grounded, and system-aware – leaders who act not as conquerors of nature, but as guardians of Earth's most vital commons.

Cosmic Leadership Model

The Cosmic Leadership Model (Figure 9.1) presents leadership not as a position or privilege, but as a *relational responsibility embedded within a living, interconnected universe*. It invites every individual to recognise themselves as a conscious participant in the cosmic theatre – entrusted with influence, moral agency, and the responsibility to contribute to harmony rather than disorder. In this sense, leadership is universal: every human being is a *khalīfah* (vicegerent) on Earth, entrusted with stewardship over creation (Qur'an 2:30).

At the centre of the model lies *Inner Coherence and Consciousness*. This core represents the leader's inner world and self-awareness, moral clarity, emotional regulation, and spiritual grounding. Leadership influence begins here, not with action but with awareness. Neuroscience and emotional intelligence research consistently show that leaders' internal states shape judgement, behaviour, and organisational climate (Damasio, 1999; Goleman & Boyatzis, 2008). When inner coherence is fragmented by ego, fear, or misalignment, the effects ripple outward as confusion, mistrust, and instability. When coherence is cultivated, it becomes a stabilising force within complex systems.

Surrounding this centre is *Harmonic Integration*, which visually divides the inner domain into intellectual, emotional, moral, and spiritual dimensions. This reflects the idea that effective leadership arises when these dimensions are aligned

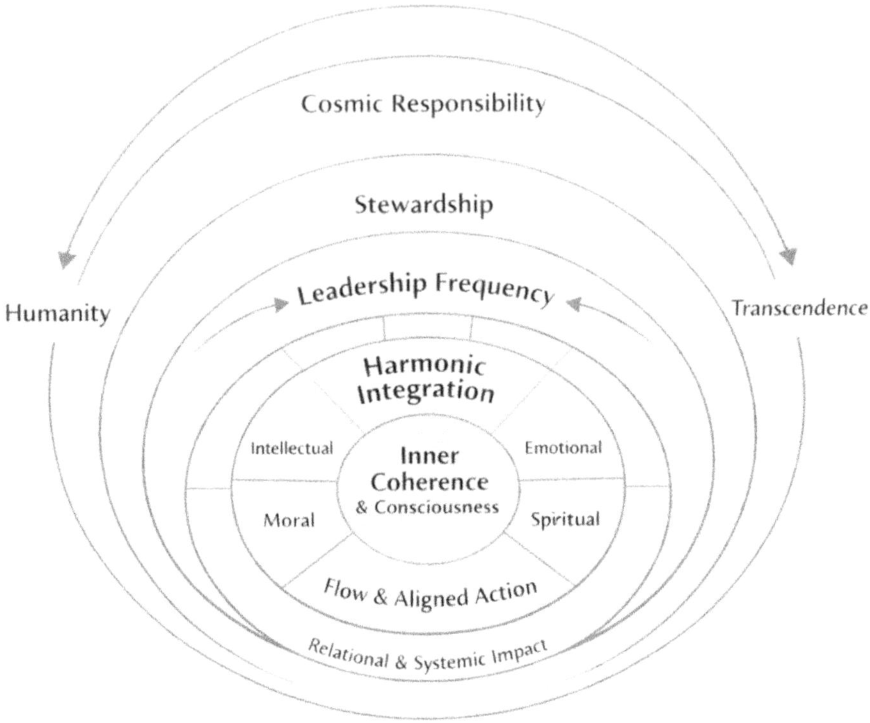

Figure 9.1 The Cosmic Leadership Model.

Source: Developed by the author through synthesis of interdisciplinary literature.

rather than operating in isolation. Systems thinking reminds us that wholes cannot be understood by analysing parts separately; it is the quality of relationships among parts that determines system behaviour (Meadows, 2008). Harmonic integration ensures that reason is guided by ethics, emotion by empathy, ambition by humility, and spirituality by responsibility.

Radiating outward is *Leadership Frequency*, representing the emotional and moral signal a leader transmits into the system. Leaders continuously broadcast tone, intention, and presence, shaping collective mood and behaviour long before strategy or structure takes effect (Fredrickson, 2013; Goleman & Boyatzis, 2008). High-frequency states – such as compassion, courage, gratitude, and integrity – create psychological safety and trust, while fear-based or ego-driven states generate instability. In systemic terms, leadership frequency acts as an attractor, subtly influencing patterns of interaction across the organisation or community.

The next is *Flow and Aligned Action*, which reflects leadership in rhythm with context. Flow emerges when inner coherence meets situational awareness, enabling action that is timely, proportionate, and non-forced (Csikszentmihalyi, 1990). Rather than imposing control, leaders work *with* the system's dynamics.

This resonates with systems thinking and complexity leadership, which emphasise adaptation, feedback loops, and emergence rather than linear cause-and-effect control (Uhl-Bien et al., 2007). Flow-based leadership recognises that sustainable change arises from alignment, not acceleration.

At the bottom of the model, the layer labelled *Relational & Systemic Impact* highlights an essential systems insight: leadership effects do not stop at the individual or organisational boundary. Decisions propagate through networks – affecting teams, cultures, supply chains, communities, ecosystems, and future generations. Meadows (2008) reminds us that systems are interconnected and delayed effects often mask responsibility. This visual grounding reinforces that leadership is always systemic, whether acknowledged or not.

Encircling these inner dynamics is Stewardship, which reframes power as trust rather than ownership. Leaders do not own people, resources, or the planet; they hold them in trust temporarily. This aligns strongly with the Qur'anic concept of vicegerency, where humanity is entrusted with care, balance, and justice on Earth (Qur'an 2:30). Stewardship-oriented leadership prioritises long-term resilience over short-term optimisation and recognises ecological and social limits as moral boundaries (Jonas, 1984; Raworth, 2017).

The outermost ring, *Cosmic Responsibility*, expands leadership beyond organisational or national interests to planetary and intergenerational horizons. As awareness expands, so does ethical obligation. Climate change, biodiversity loss, technological power, and social inequality are systemic challenges that demand leaders capable of moral imagination and long-term thinking (Rockström et al., 2009). Systems thinking is critical here: actions taken in one domain inevitably affect others, often in non-linear ways.

Finally, the arrows pointing toward *Humanity* on one side and *Transcendence* on the other symbolise the dual orientation of Cosmic Leadership. Leaders are grounded in human responsibility – care for people, dignity, and justice – while simultaneously oriented toward transcendence: higher purpose, meaning, and alignment with divine and cosmic order. This echoes the Qur'anic insight that signs are revealed both "within themselves and on the horizons" (Qur'an 41:53), linking inner awareness with outer responsibility.

In essence, the *Cosmic Leadership Model* teaches that to lead is to participate consciously in the cosmic theatre. Each person, as a vicegerent, is called to discover their unique role, cultivate their talents, and deploy them for the betterment of all creation. Leadership becomes an act of synchronisation – aligning inner coherence with systemic impact, human responsibility with cosmic order. When leaders play their roles with humility, stewardship, and awareness, they contribute not only to organisational success, but to harmony within the wider universe itself.

Leader's Role in the Cosmic Theatre

In the cosmic theatre, leaders are no longer the central protagonists seeking dominance, control, or fleeting applause. They are participants within a far larger, interconnected drama – one that unfolds across generations, ecosystems, cultures, and planetary boundaries. In this expanded horizon, leadership responsibility transcends organisational success and short-term performance. It becomes an ethical calling: stewardship of life-supporting systems, guardianship of shared futures, and conscious participation in a universe governed by balance, rhythm, and relation. Leadership, seen this way, is not about owning the stage, but about honouring one's place within it.

Self as a Node in the Cosmos

At the heart of Cosmic Leadership lies an ancient and enduring insight: to know the world, one must first know oneself. Socrates' injunction – *know thyself* – was never an invitation to narcissism or self-absorption. It was a call to orientation: to understand one's limits, responsibilities, and place within a larger moral and cosmic order. As mentioned before, Shakespeare echoes this truth in *As You Like It*, Act II, Scene VII. To be a "player" is not to diminish agency, but to recognise that each life is entrusted with a role. Meaning arises not from dominating the stage, but from inhabiting one's role with integrity, humility, and care.

Self-knowledge, in this sense, becomes the foundation of responsibility. A leader who understands their own finitude, power, and influence is better positioned to act in ways that preserve balance rather than disrupt it. To know oneself is to recognise that leadership is relational, provisional, and accountable – to people, to the planet, and to time itself.

Yet knowing thyself reaches even deeper. It is not only psychological or ethical awareness; it is also cosmic awareness. It is the capacity to contemplate the vastness of existence and one's place within it – to encounter the majesty of the Divine architecture that sustains all things. The Qur'an speaks to this depth of awareness through the concept of *Ulul Albab* – those who reflect deeply on creation: "Indeed, in the creation of the heavens and the earth and the alternation of the night and the day are signs for those of understanding… who reflect on the creation of the heavens and the earth" (Qur'an 3:190–191).

This awareness situates the human being not as a detached observer of the universe, but as a node within it – embedded, relational, and dynamically connected. Leadership influence, from this perspective, does not arise primarily from position or authority, but from the quality of inner alignment and presence that a leader brings into the relational field.

Modern science increasingly affirms this insight. Human beings function as complex, energetic, and relational systems. The heart, brain, and nervous system operate through oscillatory and electromagnetic processes that shape internal states and influence interpersonal dynamics. Emotion, attention, and intention generate patterns of resonance that ripple through social systems, subtly shaping trust, coherence, and collective behaviour. Leadership, therefore, is not merely about directing external events; it is also about modulating coherence within oneself, because inner fragmentation inevitably produces outer instability.

This inner-outer unity is echoed powerfully by modern physics. Michio Kaku offers a striking metaphor for the structure of reality itself:

> If we had a microscope powerful enough, we could see that electrons, quarks, neutrinos, etc. are nothing but vibrations on minuscule loops resembling rubber bands. If we pluck the rubber band enough times and in different ways, we eventually create all the known subatomic particles in the universe. This means that all the laws of physics can be reduced to the harmonies of these strings. Chemistry is the melodies one can play on them. The universe is a symphony. And in the mind of God, which Einstein eloquently wrote about, is cosmic music resonating throughout space time.
>
> (Kaku, 2011, p. 3)

Here, science does not strip the universe of meaning – it deepens it. The cosmos is revealed not as mechanical chaos, but as harmony, vibration, and music. Leadership, then, is not external to this symphony; it is one note within it. The quality of that note – whether coherent or dissonant – depends on the leader's inner state. To lead without awareness of this harmony is to risk creating dissonance that reverberates across organisations, communities, and ecosystems.

Rumi captures the same truth through poetic wisdom: "You are not a drop in the ocean. You are the entire ocean, in a drop." The Qur'an affirms this unity once more by declaring that divine signs are revealed both "in the horizons and within themselves" (Qur'an 41:53). Inner awareness and outer reality are not separate realms; they mirror and inform one another. Leadership emerges precisely at this intersection – where inner coherence meets outer responsibility.

Cosmic Leadership, therefore, begins not with control, but with consciousness. The leader who knows themselves as a *dot in the cosmos* understands both their smallness and their significance. Such leaders act not from ego, but from alignment; not from domination, but from participation. They recognise that every thought, emotion, and decision carries energetic and relational consequences. In this way, leadership becomes a conscious act of harmonising the self with the wider rhythms of existence – an ethical, relational, and deeply human responsibility within the cosmic whole.

Leadership as Conscious Participation

Cosmic Leadership is not about control, domination, or self-aggrandisement. It is about discernment – recognising one's role within the unfolding drama of existence and acting in alignment with ethical clarity, relational harmony, and the rhythms of the whole. Leaders are neither owners of the cosmos nor masters of nature; they are conscious participants entrusted with influence for a finite moment.

To lead in the cosmic theatre is to choose humility over hubris, stewardship over extraction, and presence over performance. It is to understand that every decision reverberates beyond immediate outcomes, shaping ecosystems, communities, and generations yet unborn. Leadership thus becomes a moral and, in many traditions, sacred responsibility: to play one's part well so that the larger symphony remains in balance. True leadership is measured not by how loudly one commands the stage, but by how faithfully one serves the harmony of the whole.

Leaders as Stewards

At the heart of Cosmic Leadership lies stewardship. Stewardship rests on a simple but profound recognition: authority is temporary, while responsibility endures. Leaders do not own organisations, resources, or institutions; they hold them in trust for the benefit of the wider system (Block, 2013). This mindset reframes leadership away from extraction and control toward care, continuity, and balance.

Steward leaders prioritise long-term resilience over short-term optimisation. They evaluate decisions not only through financial metrics but also through their social, ecological, and cultural consequences. Research on responsible leadership shows that stewardship-oriented leaders cultivate greater trust, legitimacy, and sustainable performance because their actions are perceived as serving collective wellbeing rather than narrow self-interest (Maak & Pless, 2006). Within the cosmic theatre, stewardship aligns leadership with a foundational principle of nature itself: sustaining balance rather than destabilising the systems on which life depends.

Leaders as Trustees of Future Generations

Cosmic Leadership also extends responsibility across time. Many of today's most consequential leadership decisions – concerning climate change, artificial intelligence, biodiversity, and resource use – produce immediate benefits while transferring risks to future generations. This temporal asymmetry creates a moral obligation to represent those who cannot yet speak for themselves (Rawls, 1971).

Acting as trustees of future generations requires leaders to cultivate intergenerational moral imagination: the capacity to anticipate long-term consequences and act with foresight rather than immediacy (Hannah et al., 2011; Jonas, 1984). Such a stance challenges dominant short-term incentives and performance pressures. Leaders who embrace trusteeship are more likely to support sustainable innovation, precautionary approaches to emerging technologies, and policies that preserve ecological and social capital. In doing so, they align leadership with justice not only across societies, but across time itself.

Leaders as Guardians of Balance

In the cosmic theatre, leaders also serve as guardians of balance. Complex systems –ecological, social, and organisational – do not thrive through perpetual expansion, but through dynamic equilibrium. When growth is pursued without regard for limits, systems become brittle and vulnerable to collapse (Meadows, 2008). Guarding the balance, therefore, becomes a central leadership responsibility.

This role demands heightened awareness, ethical judgement, and emotional intelligence. Leaders must sense early signals of imbalance – burnout, inequality, environmental degradation, or ethical drift – and intervene before harm becomes systemic. Emotional intelligence is critical here, enabling leaders to regulate ego, manage competing pressures, and respond with empathy and restraint rather than reactivity (Goleman, 1998). In this context, restraint is not weakness but wisdom.

Guardianship also requires humility in the face of uncertainty. Rather than positioning themselves as masters of complex systems, leaders work with feedback, learning, and adaptation. They cultivate cultures where dissent is welcomed, truth is spoken, and corrective action is possible – conditions essential for maintaining equilibrium in volatile environments (Schein, 2010).

Leadership Beyond the Self

Taken together, these roles – steward, trustee, and guardian – define leadership as a moral practice embedded within a living cosmos. Cosmic Leadership calls leaders to move beyond organisational self-interest toward responsibility for the wider web of life. It reframes success not as dominance or accumulation, but as a contribution to harmony, justice, and flourishing for all. In the cosmic theatre, leaders do not stand above nature or society; they stand within it. Their task is not to conquer complexity, but to remain in synchronicity with it – aligning human ambition with planetary limits, ethical responsibility, and the enduring rhythms of the universe.

Practical Embodiment of Cosmic Leadership

Cosmic Leadership is not realised through insight alone; it must be embodied in daily life. Without lived practice, the model risks remaining conceptual rather than transformational. Leadership coherence is not something leaders activate occasionally – it is something they cultivate continuously. This section demonstrates how Cosmic Leadership becomes tangible through simple, disciplined practices that stabilise inner coherence, deepen relational presence, and sustain rhythmic alignment. These practices are not add-ons to leadership; they are the means through which leadership becomes trustworthy, humane, and effective.

Stillness: Creating Inner Space for Coherence

Stillness is the foundation of embodied leadership. In environments saturated with urgency, information overload, and constant reaction, leaders easily lose clarity. Intentional stillness – through silence, reflection, or contemplative pause – creates the inner space necessary for discernment and ethical judgement.

Neuroscience shows that moments of stillness activate neural networks associated with insight, empathy, and self-regulation (Goleman & Davidson, 2017).

Across wisdom traditions, stillness has long been understood as a gateway to wisdom. Far from reducing effectiveness, stillness prepares the ground for wise, proportionate action.

Breath: Regulating Inner Rhythm

Breath is the most immediate and reliable instrument of alignment. Conscious breathing stabilises the nervous system, synchronises heart–brain rhythms, and enhances decision-making under pressure (McCraty, 2017; Porges, 2017).

Within Cosmic Leadership, breath functions as an internal metronome, regulating pace, presence, and response. Leaders who attend to breath cultivate calm authority rather than reactive urgency, allowing coherence to precede action.

Attunement: Listening Beyond Analysis

Attunement extends listening beyond cognition into embodied and relational awareness. Leaders learn to notice subtle cues – bodily sensations, emotional shifts, and intuitive signals – that inform judgement.

Psychology refers to these signals as *somatic markers* guiding ethical and adaptive decision-making (Damasio, 1999). Spiritual traditions describe similar insight as *ilhām* – gentle inner knowing. Attunement transforms leadership from problem-solving alone into relational perception, integrating mind, body, and conscience.

Ethical Reflection: Sustaining Moral Direction

Cosmic Leadership requires ongoing ethical grounding. Power without reflection produces fragmentation rather than coherence. Regular ethical reflection – through journalling, dialogue, or contemplative inquiry – strengthens moral clarity and responsibility.

Research shows that ethical leadership is transmitted primarily through modelling and presence, not rules alone (Brown & Treviño, 2006). In this model, ethics is not compliance-based but coherence-based – alignment between intention, action, and consequence.

Gratitude: Expanding Perception

Gratitude recalibrates leadership perception from scarcity to sufficiency. Empirical studies demonstrate that gratitude enhances emotional resilience, creativity, and relational trust (Emmons & McCullough, 2003).

As a daily discipline, gratitude shifts attention toward connection and meaning, strengthening the leader's relational field. In Cosmic Leadership, gratitude functions as a stabilising frequency that amplifies coherence.

Presence: The Leader's Primary Instrument

Presence is the most influential resource a leader brings into any interaction. Social neuroscience confirms that emotional states propagate rapidly within groups, particularly from those in leadership roles (Goleman & Boyatzis, 2008).

Undivided attention – free from distraction – creates psychological safety, depth, and trust. Presence is not performative; it is the natural outcome of inner alignment.

Rhythm-Based Practices: Living in Flow

Cosmic Leadership is sustained through rhythm rather than acceleration. Flow emerges when inner coherence meets external demand without force (Csikszentmihalyi, 1990).

Simple practices – pausing between tasks, mindful transitions, reflective journalling – help leaders honour cycles of action and rest. Leadership becomes sustainable not through speed, but through alignment with natural rhythm.

Taken together, these disciplines cultivate coherence, presence, and ethical clarity. Leadership, in this sense, is not performed – it is inhabited.

Implications for Leadership in the Imagination Age

The Imagination Age is defined by rapid technological advancement, artificial intelligence, systemic complexity, and profound uncertainty. Leadership models rooted in linear planning, hierarchical control, and predictive certainty are increasingly inadequate for this terrain. Cosmic Leadership matters now because it offers a framework suited to nonlinear, interconnected, and ethically charged realities.

AI, Complexity, and the Limits of Linear Leadership

Artificial intelligence has transformed decision-making, productivity, and organisational design. While machines outperform humans in speed and optimisation, they lack moral discernment, contextual wisdom, and ethical imagination (Floridi, 2019).

Complexity science demonstrates that outcomes in dynamic systems cannot be fully predicted or controlled; they emerge from interaction and relationships (Uhl-Bien et al., 2007). Force-based leadership often amplifies instability rather than resolving it. Cosmic Leadership responds by shifting from control to coherence, recognising that influence operates through alignment and presence.

Case Story 9.1 The Observatory Classroom: A Doctrine for Leading in the Age of AI

When the university senate approved the pilot module *AI and the Future of Learning*, few anticipated how deeply it would unsettle long-held assumptions. Co-led by Professor Amara Rahman, a philosopher of systems, and Dr Leo Chen, an AI scientist known for his quiet optimism, the classroom – nicknamed *the Observatory* – resembled a studio more than a lecture hall: open, experimental, and designed for thinking rather than transmission.

On the first day, a student named Maya voiced the fear many carried:

> "Will AI replace us?"
>
> "It will replace repetition," Dr Chen replied, "not responsibility."

As the semester unfolded, AI proved astonishingly efficient – drafting essays, summarising theories, solving routine problems. Yet its limits soon became clear. AI could produce answers, but it could not judge which questions mattered, nor grasp ethics, context, or consequence without human guidance. The faster the tools became, the more essential human judgement felt.

Professor Rahman cautioned against the prevailing myths – that AI would eliminate jobs, make learning effortless, or fix education itself. "Technology amplifies systems," she reminded them. "It doesn't redeem them." As AI absorbed repetitive tasks, some students advanced rapidly – not because they knew more, but because they learned *how to learn*. They experimented, failed, reflected, and adapted. The most curious and optimistic learned the fastest.

The institution itself began to change. Assessments were redesigned, rules rewritten, and small experiments replaced grand plans. Education shifted from content mastery toward cultivating agility, robustness, and ethical imagination.

By the final session, Maya reflected aloud: "AI didn't fix education. It showed us what education is really for." Professor Rahman nodded. "Teaching is no longer about answers. It is about helping humans remain adaptable, responsible, and awake."

This story – although fictional – explains why leadership in the Age of AI cannot be governed by plans alone. The speed, scale, and unpredictability of change render even the most sophisticated strategies fragile. When maps fail, what endures is *doctrine* – a set of guiding principles that orient judgement when certainty dissolves.

Cosmic Leadership begins with recognising AI as a systemic force that amplifies both human potential and human risk. Like a pandemic, it disrupts routines, exposes fragilities, and demands adaptation. AI will take over much of what is repetitive, but it cannot replace moral judgement, responsibility, or meaning-making. These remain irreducibly human.

At its heart, Cosmic Leadership rests on three commitments: human judgement over machine optimisation; learning systems over linear control; and stewardship over dominance. It asks leaders not to predict the future, but to orient themselves within it – guided by moral compass, stabilised by ethical gyroscope, and animated by disciplined imagination.

Leadership, in this sense, is no longer about winning the future.

It is about making the future worth inhabiting.

Imagination as a Leadership Capability

In the Imagination Age, leadership is less about optimisation and more about meaning-making and possibility creation. Imagination enables leaders to envision futures not yet formed, integrate diverse perspectives, and respond creatively to unprecedented challenges (Bennett & Lemoine, 2014). Within Cosmic Leadership, imagination is disciplined rather than fanciful – grounded in ethical responsibility and systemic awareness. As Einstein observed, imagination becomes indispensable when knowledge reaches its limits.

Ethics and Coherence in a Technological World

As technological power expands, moral responsibility deepens. Decisions related to AI governance, data ethics, environmental sustainability, and human dignity demand leaders who integrate technical understanding with moral clarity (Jonas, 1984; Floridi, 2019). Cosmic Leadership frames ethics not as constraint but as coherence – alignment between intention, action, and consequences across time and systems. Without ethical grounding, innovation accelerates harm; with coherence, innovation becomes stewardship.

Leaders as Stabilising Forces in Volatile Systems

In volatile systems, the most valuable leaders are not those who dominate, but those who stabilise. Research in social neuroscience shows that leaders' emotional and moral states strongly influence collective behaviour, particularly under stress (Goleman & Boyatzis, 2008). Cosmic Leaders function as nodes of coherence – reducing anxiety, fostering trust, and enabling adaptive response. They do not provide all the answers; they create the conditions in which wise action can emerge.

Why This Model Matters Now

Cosmic Leadership matters because the challenges humanity faces are no longer isolated or technical – they are systemic, moral, and existential. Climate instability, technological acceleration, and social fragmentation demand leaders who can synchronise inner clarity with outer complexity. In the Imagination Age, leadership is not about commanding the future, but about participating responsibly in its emergence. Cosmic Leadership offers a model fit for this moment – integrating imagination, ethics, coherence, and stewardship to support flourishing in an interconnected world.

Case Study 9.2 Leaders as Philosophers in the Cosmic Theatre

Two leaders were appointed to guide organisations facing uncertainty and rapid change. Both had authority, intelligence, and ambition. Yet their legacies unfolded in profoundly different ways – not because of technical skill alone, but because of how they *understood leadership, purpose, and time.*

Leader A: The Philosopher-Leader

Leader A approached leadership as a form of contemplation. Before making major decisions, they paused to reflect – not only on profits or targets, but on *meaning*. They often asked quiet but powerful questions: *Why are we here? Who will be affected by our decisions? What responsibility do we carry beyond today?*

Inspired by philosophy, faith, and a sense of cosmic order, Leader A saw leadership as a trust, not an entitlement. They believed their role was temporary, but its consequences were lasting. Decisions were made with humility, recognising that the organisation was part of a wider human, social, and ecological system.

This leader encouraged their team to think long-term, to value ethics over speed, and to see work as service. Curiosity was welcomed. Reflection was normalised. Success was measured not only by outcomes, but by the integrity, impact, and growth of people. Over time, the organisation became resilient, trusted, and purpose-driven. Employees felt they were contributing not just to a company, but to something meaningful – on Earth, and beyond it.

Leader B: The Short-Sighted Leader

Leader B, by contrast, lived in the urgency of the present. Decisions were driven by quick wins, visibility, and personal recognition. There was little time for reflection; speed was prized over wisdom. Questions of ethics, long-term impact, or deeper purpose were dismissed as distractions.

This leader sought power, status, and immediate results. Pressure replaced trust. Fear replaced curiosity. While early successes created excitement, cracks soon appeared. Teams became exhausted, values eroded, and short-term gains led to long-term damage. People felt used rather than valued.

Without philosophical depth or moral reflection, Leader B's organisation lost coherence. What remained was instability, disillusionment, and a legacy defined more by loss than by contribution.

Reflection

This case reveals a simple truth at the heart of Cosmic Leadership:

> Leaders are not just decision-makers; they are meaning-makers.
>
> Philosopher-leaders recognise their small but sacred place in the vast cosmic theatre. They lead with humility, purpose, and responsibility – seeking success not only in this world, but in the moral and spiritual account of their actions. In doing so, they build legacies that endure, inspire, and uplift – guiding others not only toward achievement, but toward a deeper understanding of life itself.

Conclusion

Leadership, at its deepest level, is not defined by position, authority, or technical competence, but by *becoming*. Cosmic Leadership frames leadership as an ongoing process of inner alignment, ethical refinement, and relational resonance. Leaders are called to cultivate consciousness, regulate their inner states, and synchronise with the broader rhythms of life, recognising themselves as nodes within interconnected human, ecological, and planetary systems (Bohm, 1980; McCraty, 2017).

Within this framework, influence flows less from control or instruction and more from presence, coherence, and moral clarity (Goleman & Boyatzis, 2008). The leader's inner journey – through awareness, alignment, and integrity – shapes how decisions are made, how relationships are held, and how power is exercised. Ethical character and emotional regulation are therefore not peripheral attributes, but foundational conditions for responsible leadership.

Inner coherence naturally extends into outer responsibility. Leaders who cultivate clarity, integrity, and resonance act with a heightened awareness of impact, contributing to the stability and flourishing of organisations, societies, and ecosystems

(Jonas, 1984; Peterson & Seligman, 2004). Their decisions are guided not by ego or short-term gain, but by stewardship, foresight, and moral imagination. In this sense, leadership becomes a bridge between personal development and systemic responsibility.

Cosmic Leadership also invites attentiveness – to the signs within and beyond. As the Qur'an reminds us, "We will show them Our signs in the horizons and within themselves" (Qur'an 41:53). Insight emerges through reflective awareness, ethical sensitivity, and the ability to perceive patterns across scales. Leaders attuned in this way respond to complexity with humility and adaptability rather than domination or force.

Ultimately, Cosmic Leadership reframes power as participation. Leaders become carriers of resonance, cultivating trust, creativity, and ethical alignment through their presence and actions. Service becomes the outward expression of inner coherence, and stewardship the moral commitment to life, future generations, and the shared planetary home (White, 1987; Ciulla, 2020). Leadership is thus revealed not merely as something one *does*, but as a way of *being* – aligned, responsible, and in harmony with the larger whole.

Reflective Questions

1. How does recognising your role as a participant in a larger "cosmic theatre" reshape your understanding of leadership – from control and authority toward stewardship, responsibility, and service?
2. In what ways can aligning your inner world – your values, intentions, and consciousness – with the wider systems of society, technology, and nature help you lead with greater coherence and integrity?
3. What practices might help leaders cultivate humility, wonder, and awareness of interdependence, so that leadership becomes less about domination and more about regeneration and care for future generations?

References

Aristotle. (1999). *Nicomachean ethics* (T. Irwin, Trans.). Hackett Publishing. (Original work c. 350 BCE).

Bennett, N., & Lemoine, G. J. (2014). What VUCA really means for you. *Harvard Business Review*. https://hbr.org/2014/01/what-vuca-really-means-for-you

Block, P. (2013). *Stewardship: Choosing service over self-interest* (2nd ed.). Berrett-Koehler.

Bohm, D. (1980). *Wholeness and the implicate order*. Routledge.

Brown, M. E., & Treviño, L. K. (2006). Ethical leadership: A review and future directions. *The Leadership Quarterly, 17*(6), 595–616. https://doi.org/10.1016/j.leaqua.2006.10.004

Ciulla, J. B. (2020). *Ethics, the heart of leadership* (4th ed.). ABC-CLIO.

Csikszentmihalyi, M. (1990). *Flow: The psychology of optimal experience*. Harper & Row.

Damasio, A. R. (1999). *The feeling of what happens: Body and emotion in the making of consciousness*. Harcourt Brace.

Einstein, A. (1927). *Letter to Alfred Kerr*. Unpublished manuscript.
Einstein, A. (2013). *The world as I see it* (A. Harris, Trans.). Snowball Publishing. (Original work published 1936).
Emmons, R. A., & McCullough, M. E. (2003). Counting blessings versus burdens. *Journal of Personality and Social Psychology, 84*(2), 377–389.
Floridi, L. (2019). *The ethics of information*. Oxford University Press.
Fredrickson, B. L. (2013). Positive emotions broaden and build. *Advances in Experimental Social Psychology, 47*, 1–53. https://doi.org/10.1016/B978-0-12-407236-7.00001-2
Goleman, D. (1998). *Working with emotional intelligence*. Bantam Books.
Goleman, D., & Boyatzis, R. (2008). Social intelligence and the biology of leadership. *Harvard Business Review, 86*(9), 74–81.
Goleman, D., & Davidson, R. J. (2017). *Altered traits*. Avery.
Hannah, S. T., Avolio, B. J., & May, D. R. (2011). Moral maturation and moral conation: A capacity approach to explaining moral thought and action. *Academy of Management Review, 36*(4), 663–685. https://doi.org/10.5465/amr.2010.0128
Holling, C. S. (2001). Understanding the complexity of economic, ecological, and social systems. *Ecosystems, 4*(5), 390–405.
Jonas, H. (1984). *The imperative of responsibility: In search of an ethics for the technological age*. University of Chicago Press.
Kaku, M. (2011). *Physics of the future*. Doubleday.
Maak, T., & Pless, N. M. (2006). Responsible leadership in a stakeholder society: A relational perspective. *Journal of Business Ethics, 66*(1), 99–115. https://doi.org/10.1007/s10551-006-9047-z
McCraty, R. (2017). *Heart intelligence*. HeartMath Institute.
Meadows, D. H. (2008). *Thinking in systems: A primer*. Chelsea Green Publishing.
Newton, I. (1999). *The principia* (I. B. Cohen & A. Whitman, Trans.). University of California Press. (Original work published 1687).
Peterson, C., & Seligman, M. E. P. (2004). *Character strengths and virtues: A handbook and classification*. Oxford University Press.
Plato. (2004). *The republic* (C. D. C. Reeve, Trans.). Hackett Publishing. (Original work c. 375 BCE).
Porges, S. W. (2017). *The pocket guide to the polyvagal theory: The transformative power of feeling safe*. W. W. Norton & Company.
Rawls, J. (1971). *A theory of justice*. Harvard University Press.
Rawls, J. (1999). *A theory of justice* (Rev. ed.). Harvard University Press.
Raworth, K. (2017). *Doughnut economics: Seven ways to think like a 21st-century economist*. Chelsea Green Publishing.
Rockström, J., Steffen, W., Noone, K., Persson, Å., Chapin, F. S., & Lambin, E. F. (2009). A safe operating space for humanity. *Nature, 461*(7263), 472–475. https://doi.org/10.1038/461472a
Sahih International. (1997). *The Qur'an: Arabic text with corresponding English meanings*. Abul-Qasim Publishing House. https://quran.com
Schein, E. H. (2010). *Organizational culture and leadership* (4th ed.). Jossey-Bass.
Senge, P. M. (2006). *The fifth discipline: The art and practice of the learning organization* (Rev. ed.). Doubleday.
Senge, P. M., Smith, B., Kruschwitz, N., Laur, J., & Schley, S. (2008). *The necessary revolution: How individuals and organizations are working together to create a sustainable world*. Doubleday.

Shakespeare, W. (2007). *As you like it*. Arden Shakespeare. (Original work c. 1599).

Stiglitz, J. E., Sen, A., & Fitoussi, J.-P. (2010). *Mismeasuring our lives: Why GDP doesn't add up*. The New Press.

Tagore, R. (1917). *Nationalism*. Macmillan.

The Holy Bible: New Revised Standard Version National Council of Churches of Christ in the United States of America. (1989). *The Holy Bible: New Revised Standard Version.*

Tolstoy, L. (2005). *What then must we do?* (A. Maude, Trans.). Oxford University Press. (Original work published 1886).

Uhl-Bien, M., Marion, R., & McKelvey, B. (2007). Complexity leadership theory. *The Leadership Quarterly, 18*(4), 298–318.

White, F. (1987). *The overview effect*. Houghton Mifflin.

Yusuf Ali, A. (2004). *The meaning of the Holy Qur'an*. Amana Publications. https://quran.com

Chapter 10

Humanity at the Helm

When Leadership Becomes a Symphony for All

Introduction

As the world enters the Imagination Age, humanity stands at a profound crossroads. Never before have we possessed such powerful means to reshape reality – technologically, socially, and ecologically – yet never have the risks of fragmentation, exclusion, and deepening inequality been more acute. The very forces that amplify creativity and innovation also magnify disparities, challenging leaders to decide not only *what* can be done, but *for whom* and *at what cost*.

Living in the Imagination Age, humanity is, in many ways, playing the game of life. At one end of the spectrum, life resembles a vast dreamscape, where possibilities seem limitless, and desires appear within reach. At the other end, starkly different realities persist: millions of people across the world continue to live without adequate food, shelter, or security. The Fourth Industrial Revolution has brought humanity to a decisive threshold, ushering in unprecedented disruption and transformation. How the next chapter of human history will be written remains uncertain: will the future become a shared home where all can flourish, or will widening inequalities leave many struggling for the most basic necessities of life? (Moin, 2022).

This moment represents a collective choice – a defining moment for humanity. The central question is no longer simply how to lead *effectively*, but how to lead *humanely*. What kind of world are we composing through our leadership choices? Who is heard, who is included, and who is left behind?

This chapter brings leadership back to the helm, where imagination, responsibility, and compassion converge. Therefore, "Humanity at the Helm: When Leadership Becomes a Symphony for All" is an invitation to envision leadership as a collective composition rather than a solitary performance. It calls for a world that works for everyone, where leadership harmonises diverse voices, talents, and perspectives, and where progress is measured not by the success of a few, but by the wellbeing of all. To embark on this path, leaders must first recognise inclusion as a foundational moral imperative that demands conscious intention, ethical courage, and a commitment to shaping a future in which every human being can live with dignity, creativity, and purpose.

DOI: 10.4324/9781003766414-10

Listening Before We Lead

Every era calls forth its own music of leadership. In the age of hunting and gathering, the melody of leadership was shaped by survival, courage, and collective protection – leaders guided through instinct, trust, and shared vigilance. In the agrarian age, the melody shifted toward stewardship and stability, as leadership centred on land, seasons, and the coordination of community life. With the industrial age came a louder, more mechanistic rhythm – leadership driven by efficiency, hierarchy, scale, and control, orchestrated to maximise production and order. In the information age, the melody evolved again, becoming faster and more complex, as leadership created symphonies with data, knowledge, networks, and speed, often privileging optimisation and innovation over reflection.

In the Imagination Age, however, music is no longer a solo performance driven by authority, velocity, or command. It is a symphony shaped by listening, coordination, and shared purpose – the product of collective imagination and responsible creativity. Humanity now stands at the helm of unprecedented creative and technological power, capable of composing futures that either deepen fragmentation or cultivate collective flourishing. This final chapter offers ten leadership notes – distinct yet interdependent – that together form a symphony for all. Each note invites leaders to listen more deeply to humanity, to align imagination with moral responsibility, and to conduct systems, technologies, and institutions toward dignity, inclusion, and shared wellbeing. What follows is not a prescription, but a composition – an invitation to lead in harmony with the full human story.

Leadership Note I: Setting the Overture – A Vision for an Inclusive World in the Imagination Age

The Imagination Age – shaped by artificial intelligence, biotechnology, automation, and pervasive connectivity – holds a paradoxical promise. These forces can either deepen existing inequalities or open pathways toward shared and universal flourishing. As Schwab and Davis (2018) observe, the Fourth Industrial Revolution has already unleashed unprecedented innovation, yet its benefits remain unevenly distributed, often amplifying structural disparities rather than dissolving them. Harari (2020) similarly cautions that without deliberate ethical intent, technologies such as artificial intelligence may concentrate wealth and power in the hands of a few, while marginalising many.

Within this symphony of change, leadership determines whether technology becomes discord or harmony. From a human-centric perspective, technology is neither inherently liberating nor oppressive. Its moral character is shaped by who designs it, how it is governed, and whose lives it ultimately serves. Leaders who place humanity at the helm understand technology as an instrument – one capable of amplifying dignity, expanding opportunity, and weaving inclusion into the fabric of society. This chapter explores how leadership, attuned to imagination and moral responsibility, can rise to the ethical challenge of composing an inclusive world – one in which science, policy, governance, and culture are guided not by narrow interests, but by a shared commitment to human flourishing.

Leadership Note II: Hearing the Moral Key – Inclusion as a Moral Calling

Inclusion is often framed as a matter of organisational policy or social justice advocacy. Yet when viewed through a broader lens, inclusion reveals itself as something far more fundamental: a reflection of the interconnected nature of reality itself. Just as the universe exists as an integrated field of matter, energy, and relationships, human societies are integrated together through shared ecosystems, economies, histories, and futures. Exclusion – whether economic, social, racial, or geographic – fractures this field, creating dissonance that reverberates across generations.

Leadership attuned to the moral gravity of inclusion recognises that expanded power brings expanded responsibility. The universe does not merely offer resources to exploit; it reveals an ethical architecture that calls for stewardship, humility, and care. This moral orientation is powerfully echoed in the Qur'anic vision of human diversity and dignity:

> O humanity! Indeed, We created you from a male and a female, and made you into peoples and tribes so that you may get to know one another. Surely the most noble of you in the sight of Allah is the most righteous among you. Allah is truly All-Knowing, All-Aware.
>
> (Qur'an 49:13)

This verse reframes difference not as a hierarchy to be exploited, but as a sacred invitation to relationship, mutual recognition, and ethical responsibility. Human diversity is presented not as a problem to be managed, but as an intentional design – one that calls leaders to foster understanding, dignity, and justice rather than division. Worth is not measured by status, power, or identity, but by moral character and righteousness. The unprecedented power humanity holds through technology, policy, and global influence demands a future-oriented ethic that safeguards the vulnerable, the unborn, and the unknown consequences of present choices (Jonas, 1984). Inclusion, therefore, is not an act of benevolence or political correctness; it is a moral obligation grounded in justice and sustained by the coherence of the whole. When leadership honours diversity as a source of ethical meaning and shared destiny, it transforms difference into harmony and power into responsibility.

Leadership Note III: Imagining the Unwritten – The Role of Imagination in Inclusive Futures

Imagination lies at the heart of human creativity and collective progress. In the Imagination Age, leaders are not merely problem solvers; they are composers of possibility, envisioning futures before they take form. At the heart of Leadership

Note III is the Power of Collective Imagination. History demonstrates that transformative change begins in the realm of imagination. Martin Luther King Jr.'s "I Have a Dream" did not describe an existing reality; it articulated a moral vision that mobilised collective action toward racial justice. Similarly, Nobel Laureate Muhammad Yunus imagined a world in which poverty would exist only in museums – a vision so audacious that it inspired new economic models, social enterprises, and policy innovation (Yunus & Weber, 2007).

Leadership that becomes a symphony for all asks not only "*What is?*" but "*What could be?*" and "*What should be?*" When imagination is inclusive by design – centred on dignity, access, and opportunity – it becomes a generative force. By envisioning a world where every human being has access to food, shelter, education, and purpose, leaders activate a field of possibility that shapes emerging realities. Such imagination is not escapism; it is participatory creation and ethical authorship of the future.

Leadership Note IV: Aligning the Score – Human-Centric Goals for Collective Flourishing

While global frameworks for sustainable development already exist, leadership guided by cosmic and human-centred awareness requires more than adoption – it demands embodiment. Goals must be lived, not merely listed. "Zero Poverty, Zero Unemployment, Zero Carbon" – a future-oriented leadership symphony aligns itself with audacious yet necessary aspirations: the eradication of poverty, the elimination of involuntary unemployment, and the achievement of net-zero carbon emissions. These aims resonate deeply with the United Nations Sustainable Development Goals, which articulate a comprehensive vision for human and planetary wellbeing (United Nations, 2015).

Realising these goals requires:

- Global cooperation that transcends narrow national self-interest
- Economic systems that prioritise dignity, opportunity, and meaningful participation
- Technological innovation that uplifts rather than displaces
- Policies that safeguard both humanity and the Earth's ecosystems

When leaders orient toward these shared goals, they shift from optimising efficiency to conducting equity and sustainability – transforming isolated efforts into a coherent global composition.

Leadership Note V: Humanity at the Helm – Governing Technology with Purpose

Technological advancement carries immense promise, but also profound ethical risk. Leadership determines whether innovation becomes an instrument of inclusion or a force of exclusion. We need to remember that technology is an instrument, not the conductor. Emerging technologies such as artificial intelligence, automation, and genetic engineering are reshaping societies at an unprecedented speed. If ownership and governance of these tools remain concentrated in a few centres of power, inequality will intensify, and new forms of marginalisation will emerge. Unchecked technological centralisation can give rise to data colonialism and systemic domination (Harari, 2020).

Human-centric leadership insists that technology serve humanity, not replace it. This demands:

- Equitable access to technological tools and infrastructure.
- Ethical principles embedded into design and deployment.
- Regulatory frameworks that protect privacy, dignity, and agency.
- Global collaboration to ensure fair and inclusive technological norms.

Initiatives such as open-access digital education platforms demonstrate that when guided by inclusive values, technology can dramatically expand opportunity. When innovation amplifies learning, creativity, and participation, leadership integrates technology into harmony with human potential.

Leadership Note VI: Inspiring the Next Movement – Reforming Education for Imagination and Compassion

Education is the rehearsal space for future leadership. In the Imagination Age, it must cultivate not only knowledge, but character, creativity, and moral vision. The focus of education should be not only what we know but who we become. Therefore, there should be a shift from knowing to becoming.

As Robinson (2017) argues, education should nurture imagination and creativity – the very capacities that distinguish human contribution in an age of automation. Yet many systems remain narrowly focused on technical proficiency, neglecting empathy, ethical reasoning, and collaborative problem-solving.

A reimagined educational score would:

- Integrate sustainability and SDG literacy.
- Cultivate creativity and moral reasoning.
- Develop social intelligence and cross-cultural empathy.
- Encourage lifelong learning and reflective curiosity.

Such an education does not merely produce skilled workers; it shapes whole human beings capable of listening, collaborating, and contributing meaningfully to an inclusive world.

Case Study 10.1 Teaching Humanity First: Education as the First Movement of Ethical Leadership

Context

In conversations about leadership in the Imagination Age, attention often centres on technology, strategy, and systems. Yet the foundations of ethical leadership are laid much earlier – when children first encounter education itself. If moral values, compassion, and integrity are absent at this formative stage, technical brilliance alone can produce leaders capable of great harm.

Amid many troubling examples, there are moments of clarity that remind us of education's true purpose. One such moment was shared by Mrs C. Crossley in a Wychwood School blog, recalling her first teaching post. On her first day, she was handed a letter written by a Holocaust survivor:

> Dear Teacher: I am a survivor of a concentration camp. My eyes saw what no man should witness: Gas chambers built by learned engineers. Children poisoned by educated physicians. Infants killed by trained nurses. Women and babies shot and burned by high school and college graduates. So, I am suspicious of education. My request is: Help your students become human. Your efforts must never produce learned monsters, skilled psychopaths, educated Eichmanns. Reading, writing, arithmetic are important only if they serve to make our children more human.
>
> (Moin, 2022, p. 154)

The letter offers a sobering reminder: education that neglects morality can become a tool of destruction rather than liberation.

Leadership Insight

This testimony exposes a fundamental leadership failure – not of competence, but of character. It demonstrates that knowledge without ethics does not neutralise harm; it amplifies it. Education that prioritises achievement without humanity risks producing leaders who are efficient yet morally unanchored.

It is deeply troubling that, even as global leaders possess unprecedented power and education, the world continues to witness wars that claim countless innocent lives. The failure of moral leadership is visible in Gaza, where prolonged violence has inflicted immense human suffering, particularly on children and civilians. Many of the leaders shaping these decisions are graduates of the world's most prestigious universities, trained in strategy, governance, and technology, yet unable – or unwilling – to agree on the most basic imperative: the protection of human life.

This moment compels us to confront a difficult question: *What, ultimately, are we teaching?* If education produces technically brilliant decision-makers who lack moral courage, compassion, and a commitment to shared humanity, then it has failed its highest purpose. The urgency of our time demands more than skilled leaders; it demands deeply human ones – leaders capable of seeing beyond borders, ideologies, and power calculations, and committed to building an inclusive world grounded in peace, dignity, and collective prosperity for all.

As today's children are tomorrow's leaders, cultivating ethical awareness and a sustainable mindset from the earliest stages of life has profound implications for human development. True leadership strength, as John Hope Bryant observes, does not arise from external symbols such as power or wealth, but from internal qualities such as integrity, wisdom, compassion, confidence, and moral courage (Bryant, 2009). These qualities cannot be purchased or performed; they are formed through value-based upbringing, education, and lived experience.

Reflection

For an inclusive world to emerge, leadership must be rooted at its source. Every school and every home should become a rehearsal space for the future, cultivating empathy and responsibility. When moral character and ethical values guide leadership in the Imagination Age, humanity gains resilience. No matter how turbulent the journey ahead, leadership grounded in humanity ensures that progress serves life rather than undermines it.

Leadership Note VII: Character as the Core – Leading with Moral Vision

No symphony holds together without a steady moral centre. Leadership grounded solely in competence or authority risks becoming hollow, no matter how technically advanced it appears to be. Character should take precedence over competence. As Munroe (2014) observes, leadership without character may wield power, but it ultimately fails humanity. Enduring leadership arises from integrity, courage, humility, compassion, and wisdom – qualities that generate trust and resilience in complex systems.

Value-driven leadership:

- Anchors decisions in ethical principles.
- Prioritises collective wellbeing over short-term advantage.
- Models accountability and humility.
- Inspires participation across cultures, sectors, and communities.

Such leaders do not impose inclusion; they *embody* it. Through moral resonance rather than coercion, they invite others to join in composing a future where leadership truly becomes a symphony for all.

Case Study 10.2 Character and Competence: Four Leadership Archetypes and the Moral Gyroscope

Introduction

In times of rapid transformation and heightened ethical complexity, leadership effectiveness depends on more than technical skill or strategic insight. It depends on moral stability. As systems accelerate and decisions scale through technology, the inner orientation of leaders increasingly determines whether organisations, societies, and technologies generate harmony or dissonance. This case study draws on Clark's (2016) four leadership archetypes to examine how the interaction between character and competence shapes leadership outcomes. These archetypes reveal why moral grounding is not an optional supplement to capability, but an essential safeguard for responsible leadership in the Imagination Age.

The Great Leader (High Character, High Competence)

Great leaders combine strong moral character with high levels of competence. They act with integrity, exercise sound judgement, and possess the skills required to deliver results. Their decisions are anchored in ethical principles, guided by clear values, and reinforced by consistent character. As a result, they generate trust, sustain performance, and develop future leaders. These leaders exemplify a fully aligned Moral Gyroscope: ethics guide what is right, values clarify what matters, and character ensures follow-through under pressure. Organisations led by such individuals tend to demonstrate long-term resilience and legitimacy.

The Failed Leader (Low Character, Low Competence)

Failed leaders lack both the moral grounding and the capability required for leadership. Poor judgment, ethical inconsistency, and insufficient skill combine to create organisational instability. Decisions are often reactive, self-serving, or incoherent, eroding trust and performance simultaneously.

The Ineffective Leader (High Character, Low Competence)

Ineffective leaders possess integrity, good intentions, and strong values but lack the skills or experience needed to lead effectively. While they rarely cause ethical harm, their inability to execute can limit organisational progress. Importantly, this archetype represents potential rather than peril. With deliberate development, mentoring, and learning, competence can be strengthened while character remains intact.

The Dangerous Leader (Low Character, High Competence)

The most hazardous archetype is the leader who is highly competent but ethically unanchored. These individuals often appear successful, persuasive, and results-driven, yet their lack of character introduces significant long-term risk. They may manipulate systems, rationalise unethical behaviour, and prioritise personal gain or short-term outcomes over collective well-being. Because competence masks moral deficiency, such leaders can evade scrutiny until damage is extensive.

Implications for Leadership in the Imagination Age

This framework underscores a critical truth: competence without character is not neutral – it is hazardous. In an era shaped by artificial intelligence, data-driven decision-making, and global visibility, moral failure scales rapidly. Sustainable leadership emerges only when capability is integrated with ethics, values, and character. Leadership development efforts that focus exclusively on technical or strategic skills, while neglecting moral formation, risk producing leaders who are efficient but unstable – technically brilliant yet ethically fragile. In a symphony of leadership, such an imbalance introduces dissonance that undermines collective flourishing.

The four leadership archetypes demonstrate that leadership quality is determined not by competence alone, but by the alignment between capability and character. Integrated leaders stabilise organisations and societies because their Moral Gyroscope remains balanced under pressure. Well-intentioned leaders require development, disoriented leaders expose systemic failures, and morally unanchored leaders pose the greatest risk to trust and long-term legitimacy. In the Imagination Age, where leadership decisions reverberate widely and rapidly, character is not a soft attribute – it is a structural necessity. Only when moral orientation and competence move together can leadership truly contribute to a symphony for all.

Leadership Note VIII: Beyond Competition – Conducting a Shared Human Destiny

In an interconnected world, no nation, organisation, or community can navigate the future alone. The challenges shaping the Imagination Age – climate change, widening inequality, pandemics, and technological disruption – are planetary in scale and interdependent. Leadership that seeks control or dominance produces fragmentation; leadership that seeks harmony enables collective survival and shared flourishing.

When leadership becomes a symphony for all, competition is no longer about winning at the expense of others. It is reframed as collaboration in the service of a shared destiny. Each nation, culture, and institution brings its own instruments, histories, and strengths, contributing to a global composition that none could perform alone.

A Symphony of Shared Purpose is a compelling call for global cooperation in the Imagination Age. It calls for leaders who are willing to listen across borders and act beyond narrow self-interest. This symphonic approach requires:

- Mutual respect for sovereignty, cultural diversity, and human dignity.
- Shared ethical frameworks for the governance of emerging technologies.
- Joint investment in human wellbeing, education, and health across nations.
- A collective commitment to environmental stewardship and planetary care.

Only through such cooperation can humanity address challenges that no single actor can solve. Leaders who conduct for the whole, rather than perform for themselves, help transform global complexity into coordinated possibility.

Leadership Note IX: Passing the Baton – An Invitation to Every Leader

This chapter is not merely an intellectual conclusion; it is an invitation to personal and collective leadership. A symphony exists only when individuals choose to participate – to listen, to play their part, and to align with a shared purpose.

You are invited to:

- Imagine inclusively, conceiving futures in which dignity and opportunity are foundational, not conditional.
- Align intentionally, tuning your inner compass toward values of justice, compassion, and responsibility.
- Act coherently, making decisions that uplift others rather than serve narrow self-interest.
- Collaborate generously, engaging across communities, organisations, and nations.
- Steward courageously, guiding technology, policy, education, and culture toward equitable and humane outcomes.

Leadership in the Imagination Age is not reserved for those with formal authority. It begins within – through awareness, intention, and ethical clarity – and then radiates outward through relationships, institutions, and systems. Each leader, in every context, contributes a vital note to the collective symphony.

Leadership Note X: The Final Movement – A Collective Call to Action

The future will not arrive fully formed; it will be composed through the choices humanity makes today – in boardrooms and classrooms, laboratories and legislatures, homes and communities. Every decision adds either harmony or dissonance to the unfolding human story.

When humanity is placed at the helm, leadership moves beyond short-term gain toward long-term flourishing. Inclusion ceases to be an afterthought and becomes the foundation upon which societies, economies, and cultures are built. In the Imagination Age, humanity holds both the creative power and the moral responsibility to ensure that the fruits of innovation, imagination, and connection are shared by all.

When leaders align their inner purpose with the larger rhythms of life, they help bring forth a world in which every human being can flourish with dignity, purpose, and belonging. The symphony is unfinished, and its future depends on who chooses to lead – and how.

The invitation remains:

Imagine inclusively.
Act compassionately.
Lead responsibly.
Compose a world where everyone thrives.

Intellectual Adda | Leadership in the Twenty-First Century: A Conversation with Brigadier General Mohammad Khalil ur Rahman

Brigadier General Mohammad Khalil ur Rahman (Retd.) has lived leadership where decisions truly mattered – not in theory, but in real life. He has led in times of peace and conflict, served under the blue helmet of the United Nations in some of the world's most fragile and dangerous regions, and later helped shape Bangladesh's digital future in the age of imagination as a senior executive. From the battlefield to peacekeeping missions, from classrooms to policy-making tables, he has commanded soldiers, mentored young leaders, built trust across cultures, and worked to ensure that technology serves humanity rather than controls it. A soldier, peacekeeper, educator, policymaker, and lifelong learner, he has led with courage, wisdom, and service.

Author: *Brigadier Khalil, let us begin our intellectual adda where leadership truly begins – not with titles or ranks, but with lived experience and life stories. Looking back on your journey, what does leadership truly mean to you today?*

Brigadier Khalil: Leadership is a voluntary moral function – an inner calling rooted in compassion for all creation. Its concern extends beyond a single organisation to the wider ecosystem it influences. True leadership transcends physical and digital boundaries and is sustained not by external rewards but by intrinsic purpose and values. Leadership truly begins when one goes beyond the call of duty, acting selflessly in service of a shared ethical mission. It is not a solitary function of authority, but an active, collaborative endeavour built through teamwork and collective responsibility. The most essential attributes of a leader include character (integrity and morality), courage (the will to lead in difficult situations), competence (the ability to contribute meaningfully), compassion (empathy and care), critical thinking and creativity (vision), and strong communication skills (the ability to express ideas and understand others). Together, these qualities build trust between leaders and followers, the true currency of leadership. Ultimately, leadership is a continuous journey of growth and learning, not a destination.

Author: *You have led in war, in peacekeeping missions, in civilian roles, and in classrooms with students. Is leadership in the 21st century the same as it was before? What has changed, and what new qualities do today's leaders need?*

Brigadier Khalil: Leadership is the function of three interdependent elements: the leader, the followers, and the environment or situation. Since followers and situations are constantly changing, leadership itself must also continuously evolve. This makes leadership a dynamic process that requires thoughtful planning, effective execution, and ongoing alignment of goals based on feedback and learning. The 21st Century is marked by exponential change, driven by disruptive and continuously evolving technologies. Globalisation, robotics, the Internet of Things, big data, cloud computing, and biotechnology have blurred physical boundaries and fundamentally transformed work, organisations, and societies. In this digitally connected world, effective leadership will heavily depend on real-time, data-driven decision-support systems. Leading across physical and virtual spaces and across cross-cultural and disciplinary contexts demands an agile, adaptive mindset, supported by continuous unlearning and relearning. Digital literacy and change management skills are no longer optional; they are indispensable for contemporary leadership.

Author: *We often describe our times as volatile, uncertain, complex, and ambiguous. From your experience, how can leaders navigate disruption and uncertainty without losing clarity and direction?*

Brigadier Khalil: From experience in high-risk, fast-changing environments, several enduring leadership principles emerge. First, leaders must anchor themselves in purpose rather than plans. In volatile conditions, plans quickly become obsolete, but a clear sense of purpose provides continuity and direction. Second, leaders should replace predictive control with adaptive control. In VUCA world settings, forecasting accuracy declines while the speed and quality of response become decisive, especially as AI, automation, and data analytics enable real-time sensing and rapid adjustment. Third, decentralise decision-making while centralising values. Uncertainty requires empowered teams, with authority placed as close as possible to the point of action, guided by shared principles. Fourth, build cognitive and emotional resilience. Disruption tests not only strategy, but human endurance; learning agility is critical, and unlearning is as important as learning. Finally, lead with moral and ethical clarity. In ambiguity, ethics become the true north. In essence, leaders navigate disruption not by controlling chaos, but by providing meaning, values, and adaptive capacity. Clarity comes from purpose over prediction, values over control, and trust over micromanagement.

Author: *Leadership today is increasingly shaped by AI, data analytics, robotics, and immersive technologies such as AR, VR, and XR. What does it mean to lead in this cyber-physical world, and how do you see technology reshaping the future of leadership?*

Brigadier Khalil: Leading in a cyber-physical world – where digital systems, intelligent machines, and human judgment constantly interact – demands a shift from controlling processes to orchestrating capabilities. Effective leadership now requires strong digital literacy, awareness of digital sovereignty and rights, ethical in cyberspace, and a sound understanding of AI systems, AI governance, and collaborative digital ecosystems.

In this environment, leaders must continuously sense change through data, from the physical and cyber world and respond adaptively. Leadership will extend to guiding integrated teams of humans and machines, people, AI agents, robots, digital twins, and immersive platforms. Leaders must consciously decide what machines should automate, what must remain human, and where a human-in-the-loop is essential. Leadership thus becomes the art of balancing automation with accountability. Crucially, leaders must question AI outputs critically and avoid bias. Leadership presence must also be digital, projecting trust, empathy, and influence through enhanced communication and emotional intelligence skills.

Author: *As technology grows more powerful, ethical questions become more urgent. How important is a moral compass for leaders today, and how can leaders remain grounded in values in the era of the Fourth Industrial Revolution?*

Brigadier Khalil: In the Fourth Industrial Revolution (4IR), leadership decisions are amplified by technology: AI, data analytics, automation, and digital platforms. These systems are inherently vulnerable to bias arising from algorithms, training data, and both intentional and unintended exclusions. Moreover, laws and regulations consistently lag behind technological advancements. As a result, leaders are often compelled to operate in ethical grey zones, where moral judgment rather than policy alone must guide action.

Therefore, leadership in the 4IR must be firmly anchored in timeless values drawn from universal human principles, religion, cultural traditions, and local constitutional norms. Beyond personal morality, ethics must be institutionalised through AI and data ethics committees, robust governance and accountability frameworks, and human-in-the-loop decision-making. Ethical leaders must ensure that 4IR technologies do not widen inequality, marginalise vulnerable groups, or displace humans without meaningful reskilling and social protection.

In this conversation, we have explored how leaders in the Imagination Age can navigate a VUCA world with conviction, courage, and conscience.

Coda: Holding the Future in Common

As this symphony of leadership draws to a close, one truth remains unmistakable: the future of humanity will be shaped not by technology alone, nor by markets, policies, or institutions in isolation, but by the quality of leadership that guides them. In the Imagination Age, leadership is no longer defined by control over resources or command over others. It is defined by the capacity to listen, to harmonise differences, and to hold the future in common.

The ten leadership notes offered in this chapter do not prescribe a single path forward. Rather, they invite a way of being – one that places humanity at the helm and recognises inclusion as the foundation of sustainable progress. When leaders attune their inner compass to dignity, justice, and compassion, their decisions begin to generate coherence across systems that once seemed fragmented. Technology becomes an instrument of empowerment rather than exclusion. Education becomes a space for becoming rather than mere training. Cooperation replaces domination, and imagination becomes a moral force shaping collective possibility.

Yet a symphony exists only when it is played. The music of inclusive leadership requires participation – across cultures, sectors, generations, and geographies. Each leader, regardless of role or title, contributes a vital note to the unfolding composition of human history. Silence, too, is a choice; disengagement carries its own consequences. The question before us is not whether change will come, but whether it will arrive as discord or as harmony.

To place humanity at the helm is to accept both creative power and ethical responsibility. It is to lead with the awareness that every decision echoes beyond the present moment, shaping lives seen and unseen, now and in generations to come. If leadership in the Imagination Age is to become a symphony for all, it must be conducted with courage, humility, and care. We need leaders with real strengths – things that are not for sale, as echoed in the words of John Hope Bryant in *Love Leadership*:

> Most people find strength in things that are outside them: money, power, titles, wardrobes, cars, But most of the things that make a leader are on the inside: integrity, wisdom, confidence, vulnerability, joy, passion, compassion, intuition, These things come from life experience, from life's trials, from the deepest part of person's soul. You can't fake them, and you can't buy them what's not for sale.
>
> (Bryant, 2009, p.30)

The music is beginning. The score is unfinished. The future waits for those willing to listen – and to lead – so that every human voice may be heard, and every life may find its place in the shared rhythm of a flourishing world.

Reflective Questions

1. How can leaders ensure that technological progress, organisational success, and innovation ultimately serve human dignity, wellbeing, and collective flourishing?
2. In what ways can your leadership actively create space for diverse voices, perspectives, and experiences so that the "symphony" of leadership truly includes everyone?
3. What responsibility do today's leaders carry in shaping institutions, education, and technologies that empower future generations to live with dignity, opportunity, and purpose?

References

Bryant, J. H. (2009). *Love leadership: The new way to lead in a fear-based world.* Jossey-Bass.

Clark, T. R. (2016). *Leading with character and competence.* Berrett-Koehler Publishers.

Harari, Y. N. (2020). *Read Yuval Harari's blistering warning to Davos in full.* World Economic Forum. www.weforum.org/stories/2020/01/yuval-hararis-warning-davos-speech-future-predications/

Jonas, H. (1984). *The imperative of responsibility: In search of an ethics for the technological age*. University of Chicago Press.

Qur'an 49:13. https://quran.com/al-hujurat/13

Moin, S. M. A. (2022). *Creativity in the imagination age: Theories, practice and application.* Palgrave Macmillan.

Munroe, M. (2014). *The power of character in leadership: How values, morals, ethics, and principles affect leaders*. Whitaker House.

Robinson, K. (2017). *Out of our minds: The power of being creative* (3rd ed.). Wiley.

Schwab, K., & Davis, N. (2018). *Shaping the future of the fourth industrial revolution: A guide to building a better world.* Portfolio Penguin.

United Nations. (2015). *Transforming our world: The 2030 agenda for sustainable development.* https://sdgs.un.org/2030agenda

Yunus, M., & Weber, K. (2007). *Creating a world without poverty: Social business and the future of capitalism*. PublicAffairs.

Wychwood School. (2019, September 9). *We do not learn for school but for life*. https://wa.wychwoodschool.org/blogs/we-do-not-learn-for-school-but-for-life/ (Authenticity of this exact URL unverified.).

Epilogue

Holding the Future Steady

The Imagination Age is not simply a technological era. It is a moral threshold.

Artificial intelligence accelerates decision-making. Systems grow more complex. Influence becomes invisible yet pervasive. Humanity stands at a crossroads where imagination can either widen possibility or deepen inequality, where innovation can either dignify life or diminish it.

Leadership, therefore, is no longer about managing change. It is about stewarding possibility.

In Chapter One, we entered the Imagination Age by recognising that disciplined imagination – not mere efficiency – defines leadership for our time. Imagination without responsibility becomes recklessness. Responsibility without imagination becomes stagnation. The task is integration.

The Leadership Compass offered that integration.

Purpose remains the True North, the quiet force that orients leaders when incentives distort judgement and speed threatens reflection. People form the living heart of leadership rather than resources to extract from, human beings to illuminate, empower, and protect. Performance transforms aspiration into disciplined progress – not through pressure alone, but through coherence, system thinking, and integrity. Possibility stretches toward the horizon not as fantasy, but as foresight anchored in ethical action.

And threading through them all is Storytelling, the needle that translates direction into shared meaning. Stories awaken imagination. Stories transmit values. Stories mobilise courage. In an age of synthetic media and algorithmic persuasion, authentic storytelling remains one of leadership's most human and indispensable practices.

Yet orientation and communication are not enough.

The Moral Gyroscope reminds us that leadership ultimately depends on inner stability. Ethics define what is permissible. Values define what is desirable. Character defines who we become when no one is watching. In a world of amplified consequences, moral drift is no longer a private failure; it becomes systemic harm. Stability must be cultivated, recalibrated, and protected.

The Leadership Manifesto translated these principles into lived commitment. The Nine Declarations and the 90-Day Recalibration Plan remind us that leadership is not abstract philosophy but daily discipline, reclaiming presence, freedom, and responsible power amid noise and distraction. A manifesto declares what we stand for. It gives voice to intention.

But declaration alone is insufficient.

Leadership in the Imagination Age demands covenantal responsibility, a binding commitment to humanity itself. Power must be legitimised by accountability. Influence must be governed by stewardship. Every decision carries weight beyond immediate outcomes.

This is where Cosmic Leadership expands the frame.

To lead cosmically is to recognise that we are not architects standing outside reality, but participants within a larger rhythm of intelligibility and interdependence. The universe unfolds as a dynamic order, which is structured yet evolving, relational yet mysterious. In this cosmic theatre, leaders are entrusted with roles to discern and enact with humility.

The question shifts from "How much can I control?" to "What is my rightful role within the unfolding whole?"

Cosmic Leadership calls for a shift:

from control to participation,
from extraction to regeneration,
from domination to service.

Enduring influence arises not from positional authority, but from coherence – the alignment between one's inner universe of conscience and the wider moral and relational patterns that sustain life. Leadership becomes resonance rather than rule, stewardship rather than possession.

And finally, the journey culminates where it must: humanity at the helm.

Leadership is not a solo performance. It is a symphony for all. Inclusion is not compliance; it is moral clarity. Technology is not destiny; it is a tool. Progress is not measured solely in growth, but in dignity expanded, opportunity widened, and voices heard.

The future will not be shaped by intelligence alone, but by conscience.

We cannot inherit the future passively. We are constructing it through algorithms, institutions, narratives, and everyday decisions. Neutrality is an illusion. Every system encodes values. Every innovation reflects a vision of the human person.

To hold the future steady is to ensure that as our tools grow more powerful, our humanity grows deeper;

that as our systems expand, our empathy expands with them;
that as we imagine new worlds, we do not lose sight of the shared world that sustains us.

The Imagination Age does not need louder leaders.
It needs wiser ones.

Leaders who are oriented.
Leaders who are stable.
Leaders who are disciplined.
Leaders who are resonant.
Leaders who place humanity at the helm.
The future is already unfolding.

Leadership begins when we choose how we will participate in it.

S M A Moin
Author

Index

For Product Safety Concerns and Information please contact our EU
representative GPSR@taylorandfrancis.com
Taylor & Francis Verlag GmbH, Kaufingerstraße 24, 80331 München, Germany

www.ingramcontent.com/pod-product-compliance
Ingram Content Group UK Ltd.
Pitfield, Milton Keynes, MK11 3LW, UK
UKHW020006200926
475702UK00015B/2504
* 9 7 8 1 0 4 1 2 8 7 6 3 6 *